That Lonely Section of Hell

THE BOTCHED

INVESTIGATION OF A

SERIAL KILLER WHO

ALMOST GOT AWAY

THAT LONELY
SECTION OF HELL

Lori Shenher

GREYSTONE BOOKS

Vancouver/Berkeley

Greystone Books Ltd.
www.greystonebooks.com

Cataloguing data available from Library and Archives Canada
ISBN 978-1-77164-093-0 (cloth)
ISBN 978-1-77164-094-7 (epub)

Editing by Nancy Flight
Copy editing by Shirarose Wilensky
Proofreading by Stefania Alexandru
Jacket and text design by Peter Cocking
Jacket photograph © Colin Knowles   ·
Typesetting by Nayeli Jimenez
Printed and bound in Canada by Friesens
Distributed in the U.S. by Publishers Group West

Canadä

We gratefully acknowledge the financial support of the Canada Council for the Arts, the British Columbia Arts Council, the Province of British Columbia through the Book Publishing Tax Credit, and the Government of Canada through the Canada Book Fund for our publishing activities.

Greystone Books is committed to reducing the consumption of old-growth forests in the books it publishes. This book is one step toward that goal.

TO MY PARTNER, Jennifer; our three children; and our nutty dog. Thank you all for your unwavering love and support, joyful distraction, and constant reminder of why I remain. None of you fully understands the difference you've all made to my life.

To Cindy, Jay, Cheryl, Sean, Monica, and Farshid, who lost your battles with mental illness. I miss you all and wish your circumstances could have been different and your pain far less. Be at peace.

"You gotta kick at the darkness 'til it bleeds daylight."
BRUCE COCKBURN, "LOVERS IN A DANGEROUS TIME"

Contents

● ● ●

Pincher Creek, Alberta
Summer 1990

THE WHITE ECONOLINE *rumbles along Highway 507 in the early morning sunlight. I squint, vowing to find my sunglasses when I stop to gas up for my trip to Calgary to deliver the negatives for the next edition of the* Pincher Creek Echo. *I enjoy the weekly adventure: while the Calgary printer churns out the papers, I spend eight or ten hours with my friends, playing basketball and catching up, before heading back south to Pincher Creek in the late evening, loaded down with papers filled with stories I have written for distribution the following day.*

As I drive east, a flock of sparrows—there must be more than a hundred—takes flight from a ditch on my right toward the road in front of me, angling to cross the front of my van. For one hopeful moment, I reassure myself that they will easily clear the van. The next instant, I realize with horror that they will not.

Ba, ba, ba, ba, ba, ba, ba, ba! Bird after tiny bird pelts the windshield, grill, and front bumper as I fight to maintain control of the wheel, resisting the instinct to veer into the oncoming traffic in an effort to save them.

My hands are shaking. I pull off the highway at the town's last gas station. Small impossibly perfect bodies litter the windshield.

Why? You could have so easily saved yourselves, just a little more altitude, a little more speed, and you were good. Why?

I imagine them lying in a nest as eggs, working hard to hatch, learning to fly under the watchful eye of their parents, only to end up like this—one minute soaring in flight, the next dead, stuck fast to my van. Bile rises in my throat.

I pick the first still body off the windshield and gently hold it in my palm. It is still warm. I marvel at the total absence of blood or visible injury and say a silent prayer of thanks, though I no longer have religion. In no time, I hold a small stack of four tiny birds in my hand and look around for something to put them in. The bell on the station door startles me and I turn to see a petite middle-aged woman walk out toward me. Her efficiency both comforts and alarms me, as though she encounters such events often.

"Oh, goodness. Let's get the poor things off of here," she says as she begins gently plucking one flawless body after another from the grill. Dumb with grief, I shake my head. She glances into my eyes and continues her grim harvest.

"I thought they would make it," I offer. "I thought they'd clear the van. They just..." My throat constricts with emotion. "They just flew straight into the van."

She straightens up from the grill and faces me. "I do taxidermy. I can keep them in my little fridge for the day and take them home, if you like," she suggests. It feels strange to think of myself as their guardian, the next of kin to these little creatures I've only known in the briefest seconds of life and the finality of sudden death.

"Um, sure. That would be great," I answer. "But, I mean, I don't think I need to get them back from you after." I worry she has mistaken me for someone who would want a reminder of this day. Someone who mounts dead birds on her wall.

"I understand, dear," she assures me, patting my arm with the hand not full of birds. "I'm happy to keep them."

"Thank you for helping me with this."

"It's my pleasure." I believe then that it truly is.

She takes the birds into her office and I fill the van's tank. I stare at my face in the mirror as I wash my hands in the station's filthy washroom sink. How can it be that I detect no outward evidence of the utter helplessness and despair I feel? How will I wear this irrational cloak of failure?

Preface

● ● ●

"Writing a book is a horrible, exhausting struggle, like
a long bout with some painful illness. One would never
undertake such a thing if one were not driven on by some
demon whom one can neither resist nor understand."
GEORGE ORWELL, "WHY I WRITE"

THIS IS THE story of my work as the first police detective
assigned to find the missing women of Vancouver's Downtown Eastside and the effect of that experience, spanning
more than fourteen years, on my life. I have tried to recall
these events accurately; this story arises from my memory
and reflects my interpretation of these events as I experienced
them. Others may have different memories or interpretations
of these events.

I began my assignment in the Vancouver Police Department's (VPD) Missing Persons Unit in July 1998, and in the
first week, I received an anonymous Crime Stoppers tip that
implored me to look at a man named Willie Pickton, who lived
on a farm in Port Coquitlam, a community about eighteen

miles outside of Vancouver. The tipster said Pickton bragged to his friends about his ability to dispose of bodies on his property and he offered them the use of his grinder. The tipster believed Pickton could be responsible for the deaths of the missing women. Thus began my repeated futile attempts to convince the police of that jurisdiction—the Royal Canadian Mounted Police (RCMP)—to investigate Pickton, while I continued my own search for the women.

This is the story of the many obstacles to the Pickton investigation and of the women who died as a result of our inability to work together in those three and a half years before we finally searched Pickton's farm and discovered the victims' remains. It chronicles the investigation and the physical and emotional toll this took on me as a police officer and as a human being.

There are places in this book where my words may seem irreverent. Please know that I have only survived by maintaining a sense of humor, and it is not my intention to disrespect the victims or their families in any way. I apologize in advance to anyone I may offend.

My goal has only ever been to help the families understand the factors at play behind the scenes so that they might better appreciate or gain insight into the investigation. There is no information contained in this book about the victims or their families that has not already been in the public domain through the trial of Robert Pickton or the Missing Women Commission of Inquiry. As I stated in my testimony at the Missing Women Commission of Inquiry, the struggles I have endured through my association with this file are nothing in comparison to those of the victims and their families.

I have used many people's real names, but where I have used a pseudonym—for privacy or legal reasons—I have indicated that with an asterisk. The official report, entitled *Forsaken*:

The Report of the Missing Women Commission of Inquiry, written by Commissioner Wally Oppal, is available online at www.missingwomeninquiry.ca, and I refer to it and to VPD Deputy Chief Constable Doug LePard's report *Missing Women Investigation Review*.

I am blessed with a loving community of family, friends, and health professionals, whose care and guidance lifted me through the darkest times when I doubted that I could revisit these events and tell my story in its entirety without further jeopardizing my mental health. Without the support of these people, this book would not have been possible. I feel so fortunate they simply would not allow me to isolate myself when my depression compelled me to do so.

This is my story, but it has never been my tragedy. The tragedy is the cataclysmic demise of far too many disenfranchised women. It is for them that I tell my story and for their families and supporters that I continue to pursue the deeper truth behind the causes of this tragedy and the myriad ways the system failed to protect vulnerable people.

A May 29, 2014, piece in the *Guardian* about Maya Angelou's death quoted her as once saying, "There is no greater agony than bearing an untold story inside you." Although I have struggled with such an untold story, I believe living with poverty, addiction, violence, racism, sexism, and classism are greater agonies. I interpret Ms. Angelou's words to mean that we do not speak out because we believe that no one will care about our stories. Therein lies the terrible shame. This book is for the missing and murdered women and all of their untold stories.

Prologue

• • •

"There is only one kind of shock worse than the unexpected:
the expected for which one has refused to prepare."
MARY RENAULT, THE CHARIOTEER

O N THE NIGHT of February 5, 2002, while the rest of the city lay down to sleep, a team of police officers prepared to execute a search warrant. But this was not just another search warrant; this would be the groundbreaking moment in the largest police investigation in Canadian history. Robert Pickton would soon become infamous around the world as the killer of Vancouver's missing drug-addicted sex workers, all of them women. A floundering police investigation had suddenly and sickeningly become the hottest story in town.

Unaware of the warrant, I readied myself for bed, knowing that another restless, nightmare-filled night awaited me. Just the night before, I had dreamt that I was standing at the top of a snow-covered mountain, watching dozens of tumbling women, some far below me, others falling past me.

Their screams echoed in the crisp night air. Despite the darkness of the night, huge spotlights illuminated the entire mountain, and the trees cast giant shadows all around me. The last woman slid past me, hands outstretched, eyes imploring me to help her. As I grabbed her cold, translucent hand, dried scabs scraped against my own palms.

Suddenly, her hands were greasy and slick, impossible for me to hang onto. I shouted out to her, *Why? Why are your hands so slippery?* But no words came out. I screamed, *Hang on!* But, again, no words came out, and she slipped from my grasp and plummeted down the mountain, her screams accentuating my failure. As usual, I awoke soaked in sweat and lay in bed for another couple of hours, unable to sleep.

Variations on this nightmare had haunted my nights since 1998, when I became the first and only Vancouver Police Department (VPD) detective assigned full time to find Vancouver's missing sex workers. I had learned of Robert Pickton my first week on the file, and he had rarely left my thoughts since. The night of February 5 was no different.

VPD Detective Mark Chernoff paged me late in the afternoon of February 6, 2002, entering his badge number, my office number, and 911, which meant to call him immediately. I'd left as usual at three o'clock for a workout before heading home and calculated that I must have missed him by an hour or so. It felt strange to dial my own number.

"Hey, Mark, what's up?" I asked.

"Lor, where are you?" His tone was somber. My chest tightened with anxiety.

"At home. What's going on?"

"They're searching Pickton's place; they got on the property. Beach just called me, so I came to find you." The silence fell like a heavy fog. "They found Sereena's inhaler," he added after a few seconds.

Mark's words landed on me like an anvil. At some point, I sat down at the kitchen table, but I don't remember moving. I knew nothing; I knew everything.

Shock, elation, dread, excitement, sorrow, grief, nausea—it was all there, jumbled up together. But for several seconds I couldn't will myself to grasp what he was saying. Then, slowly, it began to sink in.

When you've been grappling with the whereabouts of some thirty or forty missing sex workers, you know the likelihood that they have met a violent end is high. Intellectually, I thought I had prepared for that long ago. I'd always suspected they'd be at Pickton's. I'd always wished we'd find them somewhere else.

"Lor?"

"I can't believe it," I croaked, my voice choked with emotion. "This is *not* happening."

"I know, I know." I could hear the anguish in his voice.

"Are you okay?" I asked.

"No. You?"

All I could do was laugh, a completely irrational response to shock.

"I am so *not* okay," I finally said. We reassured each other that we had people to keep us company that evening and made plans to meet for breakfast the following morning at the Ovaltine Cafe on Vancouver's Downtown Eastside, the nexus of these horrific crimes. My partner, Jennifer, entered the kitchen, knowing something serious had happened. I took one look at her and burst into tears, my body shaking with huge wracking sobs. She held me, and neither of us spoke for a long time.

They were my victims, and I couldn't save them, despite my best efforts. Not only had I not saved them in life; I had failed them in death. And here it was: RCMP officers were searching the property of the man I had always considered our number one suspect, and they were finding *evidence*. It was a hollow victory, and all I could do was cry. I had been right, but so much had gone wrong.

I wished that it weren't the Pickton farm that police were searching but some property belonging to some man we had never heard of, someone so clever and surreptitious in his activities that it was only pure fluke that the police had ever found him. I thought fleetingly that if I hoped, prayed, and wished it to be so, I could make it not be Pickton.

But it was. It had always been Pickton.

PART ONE

1

Becoming One of Them

• • •

"Police business is a hell of a problem. It asks for the highest type of men, and there's nothing in it to attract the highest type of men. So we have to work with what we get."
RAYMOND CHANDLER, THE LADY IN THE LAKE

IN EARLY DECEMBER 1990, when I was working in Morinville, Alberta, as a reporter for the *Morinville Gazette*, I flew to Vancouver to pick up the application materials for a job with the Vancouver Police Department (VPD). The rules stipulated you had to collect the forms and return them in person. I left on a 6:00 AM flight.

From the Vancouver airport, I took a bus to the downtown core and then started walking. As I descended into the area I would come to know as the Downtown Eastside, I stared, openmouthed, at the hollow-eyed, dirty, wet people hanging out on the sidewalks. Little did I know that every inch, every nook, and every cranny of these streets would become as familiar to me as the backyard I grew up in.

The people on the sidewalks truly gave the appearance of *hanging*—slumped over, half-bent, leaning on lampposts and slouched against doorways like rain-rumpled costumes on coat hangers. It wasn't until I later came to live and work there that I realized the almost constant mutterings of "Up? Down?" meant was I looking for coke or heroin? I wondered if this was really the career I wanted.

At the VPD recruiting office I joined several young, scrubbed, suit-wearing men in the waiting area. I stood at the large glass window until a young woman with a heavy mane of black hair looked up at me.

"Can I help you?"

"Yes, I'd like an application, please," I replied, trying to sound natural but also authoritative and polite—the way I thought a police officer should speak.

"Sure." The woman reached beneath the counter and pulled out a thick yellow envelope. Setting it on the desk just beyond my reach, she gave me a friendly but appraising look. "What level of education have you attained?"

"I have a bachelor's degree in English from the University of Calgary."

"Have you ever applied to the VPD before?"

"No, I haven't."

"Have you ever applied to any police department or the RCMP in Canada?"

"Yes," I replied. "I applied to Calgary in 1988, but I wasn't accepted because I failed the vision exam." I'd applied to the Calgary police department near the end of my last year of university at the urging of two basketball friends who were Calgary police officers.

"Corrected or uncorrected?" she asked, seemingly pleased that I was so forthcoming. I wondered if a lot of applicants lied to her. It didn't strike me as a great way to start a career in law enforcement.

"Uncorrected. My right was better than the standard, but my left was a little lower, so I failed. They're both twenty-twenty with my contacts and glasses."

"Did they have you keep your contacts and glasses off for forty-eight hours before the test?"

"No." I'd never heard of this possibility before. I'd felt disappointed not to have been accepted by Calgary but hadn't pursued it.

"Okay, well, we can deal with that after you submit your application, but you'll want to get an answer on that before we go any further." She pushed the envelope toward me across the counter, seemingly a reward for my answers. "When can you have your application in?" I was surprised at the speed with which this all seemed to be moving.

"Well, I'm living in Edmonton right now, so getting back here to submit it might take me a couple of months," I said, hoping that wouldn't be a problem. She held up a palm to me.

"Hang on a sec." She walked away from the counter and disappeared into an office. I heard low murmurs of conversation I assumed were about me. She returned in less than a minute.

"Okay, Sergeant Day has agreed you can send your application in by courier to save you the expense of traveling back." She gave me a meaningful look. "Sooner would be better."

I WAS BACK in my rented room in Morinville before eight that evening. My friend and landlord Ted turned the TV channel to COPS that night, kidding with me that I should see what police work was like before I embarked on this career. In the episode we watched, members of the Las Vegas PD dealt with a very drunk older homeless couple that was causing problems in a restaurant a few blocks off the strip. The two young policemen tried valiantly to speak respectfully and offer reasonable alternatives to the drunks, but they would have none of it. As the situation escalated into a power struggle in which the police tried to get the two to leave the Denny's and they refused, the show went to a commercial.

"You know," Ted said, "that is a job where there's just no way to look good, no matter what you're doing." I'd been thinking the same thing, and I knew he was right. "Except if maybe you're riding a motorcycle or a horse in a parade or letting kids dunk you in a dunk tank at a fair."

The remainder of the show did little to improve my view of policing, but I hoped my experience would be better.

On February 14, 1991, Ted; his wife, Louise; their huge German shepard, Max; and I left Morinville for Vancouver, along with all my worldly possessions, so that I could write the entrance exam and go through the whole application process—though I was not at all certain that I would take the position if it was offered. We drove all night and on the afternoon of February 15 rolled up to the house I would be sharing with an environmentalist couple and a doctor. I continue to observe February 15 as the date I officially started my new life. It was one of those gorgeous dry February days that I would learn to welcome as precious gifts after the gloom of November, December, and January in Vancouver, and after unpacking and meeting my new housemates, I celebrated with a long run in the gorgeous rain forest of Pacific Spirit Park. Breathing in the fragrant rain forest air, I felt as though I'd come home.

The following week I wrote the entrance exam, and a couple of days later I met with Recruiting Detective Chris Beach so that he could give me my mark.

"Lori, this is the highest mark I've seen in my time here," he said. "It may be the highest we've had." He smiled at me, a dead ringer for the actor Tom Skerritt. "Let's get you into the city doctor for an eye test before we do anything more, okay?"

I passed the eye exam with flying colors, pleasantly surprising the doctor and myself, thanks to forty-eight hours of enforced farsightedness without glasses or contacts. I was working at a local running shoe store, and it hadn't been easy selling shoes that weekend sans sight, but my employers understood my mission.

In my interview with Sergeant Murray Day, I had to weigh how much personal information I should share and how much I need not. Since arriving in Vancouver, I'd managed—as usual—to put my issues of gender identity and sexual orientation on the back burner and busy myself with the matter of making a living and forging my future. But I did not want to be caught in a deception and had a strong desire to be completely transparent and forthcoming. As I answered question after question without emotion or elaboration, I felt little rapport building between the two of us. I assumed he was trying to be objective.

"Do you have a boyfriend?" he asked, clearly uncomfortable.

"No," I answered.

"When was your last boyfriend?" I didn't want to discuss the three or four guys I'd dated—even that word was a stretch for most of them over the past eight or so years. My love life had consisted largely of my getting drunk enough with my friends to forget I might want a love life one day, with the occasional ill-considered drunken trysts with guys thrown in.

"Well, I wouldn't say any of them have been at all serious," I offered.

"Why is that?"

"Oh, I guess I just haven't met the right guy." I shrugged, wincing inside at my answer. "I was traveling a lot for my work." He gazed at me over his reading glasses for a few seconds. I *am so done*, I thought. Fortunately, he moved on to other areas, such as my education, work history, and family background.

"Okay, I think we're just about done here," he said, leafing through his papers. "Let's see. Have you ever been depressed?"

"Well, I think I had some depression as a teenager."

"Have you ever seen a psychologist?"

"Yes."

"Can you elaborate on why?" He looked up over his glasses again.

"I've had some issues about, you know, my femininity, I guess you could say," I said, wondering if that was sufficient but feeling somehow it wouldn't be. "I just went to talk to someone about not being your typical girl, you know, I like sports, I like jeans." I stopped myself before I became a total after school special, knowing how painfully inadequate an explanation it was without getting into a dissertation on gender theory. He nodded. I imagined he had never had a conversation like this before, and I wasn't prepared to blow this poor man's mind.

"And how are you now?" he asked. "Do you still suffer from depression?"

"Nope," I said. "I feel really good. I think I've worked it out."

"Any medication? For the depression, that is?"

"No, never."

"Okay, good." Clearly, he very much wanted that to be my answer, and I was happy it was true. "Detective Hawthorne* will handle your file." He rose and motioned for me to follow him. He led me into an adjoining office, where a forty-something-year-old woman with blunt, dark bobbed hair, wearing a navy-blue blazer and skirt sat at a desk talking on the phone. She finished her call quickly. Sergeant Day introduced us.

"Detective Hawthorne, this is Lori Shenher." He gestured to me. Detective Hawthorne rose from her desk and we shook hands. "Thanks for coming in. I'll leave you to Detective Hawthorne," he said to me, looking much more comfortable than he had been in our interview. He exuded relief.

If Detective Beach and Sergeant Day had given me the impression they thought I was an excellent candidate,

Detective Corrine Hawthorne seemed determined to let me know I was nothing special. She needn't have worried about that: throughout the recruiting process I had felt like an imposter waiting to be exposed. She shut the door and sat down at her desk, looking me over.

"Women on this job have to work much, much harder than men to be respected," she began. I listened keenly. "We have to conduct ourselves as professionals at all times. If we don't act like professionals, dress like professionals, work like professionals, no one will treat us as professionals. Do you understand?" I nodded, suppressing a gulp, trying to ascertain whether I had done something unprofessional in the last two minutes to draw her ire. I soon realized this was just how she was. I remembered my father's definition of a professional as someone who worked until the job was done, not someone who stopped when the whistle blew. In his world as a school principal, overtime pay did not exist. I decided to keep this gem to myself.

"Whenever you come here, you will dress in business attire. Whenever you call this office, you will identify yourself immediately and let the person on the phone know I am handling your file. Do you understand?" She raised her eyebrows. I nodded vigorously, beginning to think this could be some kind of joke. It wasn't.

She went on to explain the next steps: the Police Officers' Physical Abilities Test (POPAT) and the Justice Institute of British Columbia (JIBC) Recruit Level Assessment. I worried I wouldn't be able to remember all the acronyms. Would there be a test on those? She led me out of her office to the front counter, where she instructed the clerk to schedule me for each test.

The physical testing for applicants consisted of three components: a timed twelve-minute run known in the athletic world as the Cooper test or Cooper run; two pool tests, including a fifty-meter swim followed by a submersion exercise where you were required to retrieve a rubber brick from the bottom of the diving tank, which was probably about fifteen or twenty feet deep; and then the POPAT. Surprisingly, many people fail to retrieve the brick and their policing hopes are dashed.

The POPAT is a circuit performed indoors where—one at a time—participants complete six laps of what can best be described as an obstacle course that includes a gap jump, stair climb, and push/pull station designed to simulate dealing with a noncompliant man of medium weight. The entire process must be completed in less than four minutes and raises subjects' heart rates to an anaerobic level to test their ability to function under cardiovascular strain. After a brief rest, they are required to carry a one-hundred-pound bag a distance of ten meters and back, a task designed to simulate carrying an uncooperative person to the wagon, away from a protest, or something similar.

As a keen athlete all of my life, I felt fairly confident I could pass all of these tests, but I trained hard for the run because not only did I wish to pass, I wanted to be competitive. For several weeks beforehand, I ran weekly twelve-minute runs as fast as I could on a treadmill at an incline in addition to longer runs. When I arrived at the Brockton Oval in Stanley Park on that cloudy March morning, I felt as ready as I would ever be.

When the run began, I was shocked by the pace of the other fifteen participants—twelve of them men. How could I have so seriously misjudged these people when I'd assessed their fitness while watching them warm up? They were killing me after only four hundred meters, and I knew I was fit. *How could they be smoking me like this?*

I decided I had no choice; this pace would finish me if I maintained it. I forced myself to adjust to a less painful pace and accept my position in dead last place. But, one by one, I began to reel them in as I sprinted toward the final few hundred meters. As I raced to the finish line, I calculated rightly that I would finish third, mere seconds behind two fit guys. My time was just under nine minutes, which had been my goal, even though anything less than twelve minutes was a pass. I watched many of the people who had blazed around the track ahead of me walk over the finish line, out of breath and unsure of what had just hit them.

The rest of the day went well. I had no problem with the swim and retrieving the sunken brick, and I completed the POPAT, though the latter confirmed for me that I had to work on my upper body strength for the push/pull portion if I were to improve my time and confidence. Later, I learned I was the only one hired from that day.

A few days later, Detective Hawthorne called me.

"Lorraine, it's Corrine Hawthorne," she said. The "Corrine" threw me, since she had always called herself Detective Hawthorne when we spoke, and her voice was unfamiliar because it sounded so chipper and non-threatening. "I have *excellent* news for you." She took a long dramatic pause, and I wondered if she thought I was an idiot and really couldn't see what was coming next. I played my part and waited, determined not to ask *What, Corrine? What could this excellent news possibly be?*

"I'm very pleased to tell you we have decided to hire you, and you will be starting in the coming academy class next week." There was no hint of a job *offer*; this was a proclamation, and I imagined that no one ever turned the job down. As a backup plan, I had been considering a job coaching basketball at a local community college, but I thought the choice would be made for me. I pondered what words to use to accept and wondered if I even wanted to. There was so much about coaching basketball and working with young people that appealed to me. The college job was mine if I wanted it. Still, something stopped me from turning Detective Hawthorne and the VPD job down.

"We're expecting very big things from you, Lorraine," she said. I realized she was still in the midst of her speech and I wasn't expected to respond or actually accept. "We know how smart you are—your scores have been exceptional, some of the highest we've ever seen—and we know you won't disappoint us."

"Thank you," I managed. I had been so sure I would be bounced from the process along the way, it never occurred to me I'd have to decide whether I wanted to work there. Saying nothing felt easier than saying no, and that was that. This was my mind's first betrayal of the gut that had served me so well to this point in my life. It felt so strange, talking like this to my new best friend, who was so sisterly and gregarious, when just days before she had been harsh and suspicious of my abilities and motives. I understood that her change from the humorless, stern, hard-assed cop I had come to know meant that I was in. I was no longer an asshole in her mind. I was one of *them*.

2

Paid to Play in the Strike Force

• • •

*"As George Orwell pointed out, people sleep peacefully
in their beds at night only because rough men stand ready
to do violence on their behalf."*
RICHARD GRENIER, WASHINGTON TIMES

IN NOVEMBER 1991, on my graduation from the police academy, the VPD assigned me to a patrol unit on the Downtown Eastside. Shootings, break-ins, robberies, stabbings, suicides, and sexual assaults filled the hours of my shifts. In 1993, I was pulled from my squad to work a special assignment with the now-defunct Prostitution Task Force (PTF), a two-man unit given the dual assignment of identifying Downtown Eastside sex workers and conducting undercover "John Stings."

I posed as a sex worker two nights a week for six months, standing on the cold streets between six and ten hours at a time, making verbal deals with men to exchange sex for money. Over that rainy Vancouver winter, my life was threatened, objects were tossed at me from cars, I was nearly abducted at gunpoint, and I endured the less dramatic indignities of shivering in a too-short dress and suffering in high heels. I did not know the pain of drug withdrawal, addiction, loneliness, hunger, spousal abuse, or sleeping rough that other sex workers deal with, but still, I felt miserable. In 1994, I was assigned to a patrol unit on Vancouver's west side, where I remained until the Strike Force beckoned.

In early 1996, I began working for the Strike Force, the VPD's elite surveillance unit. The Strike Force of my era was the police department's answer to *Lord of the Flies*; although a reputation as a team player was the number one quality needed for admission, once inside, many operated as though success could only be achieved off someone else's back. I had expected a cooperative, collegial atmosphere where we all united in our common goal of catching bad guys, but our leadership consisted of manipulative types striving to make names for their own protégés. Like handlers in a dogfighting ring, they touted their "guy" as "the best foot" or "the best driver," as though those faux titles held any meaning or relevance in the real world.

Those who didn't aspire to these artificial distinctions often found themselves targets of the leaders, who would sniff out any perceived weaknesses in the others. Still, there were some great people in the Strike Force, and we formed bonds over the intense work and the hard celebration after we'd put our targets in jail. There weren't many bullies, but they wielded an inordinate amount of influence over the rest of us. As a result, the work suffered and professional development was slower than it should have been.

Surveillance is heady stuff that involves high-risk driving, skulking around in the darkness, and rubbing elbows with low-life thugs and big players in the crime world, all while trying not to be identified as a cop. I loved it. I had loved hide-and-seek as a kid, and as far as I could tell, this was just big-boy hide-and-seek, a kind of capture the flag with cocaine and automatic weapons thrown in for good measure. I couldn't believe I got paid for doing this.

Surveillance came easily and naturally to me. I kept a low profile and avoided being targeted as someone the others would try to force out of the section as incompetent. I watched as others—mostly men, because they made up the majority of the Strike Force—were taunted, criticized, and bullied if they showed an iota of weakness or need for mentoring. Strangely, in my time with the Strike Force I didn't see any women bullied, probably because there weren't many of us and each squad had to have at least one female member so that the men would have a woman to drink with in bars when doing inside coverage on targets. It also seemed that the women who made it into the Strike Force were capable, socially functional, and decent-looking, so I expect we were deemed easy to have around.

I came onto the Strike Force with the highest ranking in the 1996 Surveillance Tactics and Resources (STAR) course. Several of my closest friends took the course with me, and these were the most fun three weeks of my career. One evening, during one of our regular mock training exercises, we were told our targets planned to do a break-and-enter of a commercial building somewhere in the Lower Mainland. We knew little more than what the men's faces looked like, where they lived, that they had criminal pasts, and what kind of vehicle they drove.

In the Strike Force, you are part of a team of eight to ten people in four to five cars, each with a driver and another officer known as a "foot," who is there to follow and watch when the target is walking or stationary. The feet call all the target's movements when the target isn't in a vehicle. When the target gets into a vehicle or on public transit, the surveillance picks up speed and drivers often take huge risks at breakneck pace to catch up if circumstances or traffic put them out of the game for any length of time.

On this dark November early evening, the surveillance became fast and intense, and our team struggled to keep sight of the target vehicle. My driver dropped me near Main Street and East 2nd Avenue to observe the direction of the target's turn around the corner and broadcast it to the rest of the team, but when I'd done the job, rather than pick me up on Main, my driver roared past me in his excitement to follow the bad guys. We were all still learning the rhythm of surveillance, and everyone was so excited. No one noticed that "the feet are up" message indicating that everyone who was on foot had been picked up had not been sent out over the radio.

My sense was our bad guys were close to doing their crime, so rather than trying to get on the crowded air to tell my team I was still out there, I decided to follow the surveillance on the radio and run to get myself back into it somehow. Portable radios have a far shorter range than vehicle radios, however, and I felt a growing dismay when the reception became ever fainter as the distance increased between me and the south-bound surveillance. As I reached the peak of the south slope of the city, I regained radio reception and heard someone on my team say the targets looked interested in a warehouse on the Fraser River at the very south end of Vancouver, more than forty blocks from where I'd started running. I began looking around me for a bus or a cab, desperate to get there before the crime was committed, but seeing none, I kept on running, grateful for the steeper downhill grade after running uphill for so many blocks. As I ran, I heard someone come over the air and say, "Anyone got Shenher, yet?" followed by dead air. Just as I was about to respond that I was coming, someone else came on and said, "Heads up, targets are parking." This was followed by a mad flurry of voices on air, people advising they were taking this position and that, so I just kept on running, hoping I'd be able to figure out exactly where they were when I got there.

Piecing together odd bits of communications, I found the target vehicle and, to my surprise, located the two bad guys working on a side door of the warehouse. I buried myself in a bush and peered out. Our road boss came over the air, asking, "Anyone got an eye yet?" Dead silence. An "eye" was what we called the surveillance person on foot trying to get a visual on the target. This person on foot will have a front eye watching the front of a location, and another will hold a rear eye position, watching in case the target goes in or comes out the back. This ensures that the target won't see obvious undercover cops sitting in cars directly outside. The cars remain in "sets" a couple of blocks from the target, ready to roll if the target comes out and drives off in a vehicle.

"I got it," I said calmly.

"Shen?" exclaimed a surprised road boss. I was about to click my radio twice to indicate affirmative, but just then the bad guys forced their way through the warehouse door.

"Heads up—targets just kicked in the warehouse door. We have crime," I said.

Everything went a little crazy. Discipline at takedown time is hard to orchestrate and maintain in surveillance, but the team managed to hold it together long enough for me to organize the takedown and then call the targets coming back out carrying stolen goods. I radioed, "Targets are out. Take down! Take down!" and watched as my team jumped on the bad guys and arrested them.

I crawled out from my hiding spot and walked toward the team as they backslapped and high-fived each other. When they saw me approach across the parking lot, the conversation stopped.

"Shen! Holy shit! Did you *run* here?" our road boss asked. I nodded, suddenly feeling the chill settling into my bones. I stood there in my heavy black Dayton boots, sweat soaked through my outer jacket and jeans, my hair wet and straggly.

"You fucking guys owe me a beer," I said.

ON THE LAST night of our STAR course, we went to the old VPD bar called the PAC, or Police Athletic Club, apparently named for the athleticism required to carry a beer and play pool at the same time. Only VPD employees and their signed-in guests were allowed entry. Wherever the name came from, in the few years it remained open early in my career, I found it next to impossible to go there and not drink too much, and I was one of the more controlled drinkers. It wasn't uncommon to see guys passed out under the tables, and many a marriage was ruined in the back stairwell. Had that club not closed down in the late '90s, I might not have survived, and I know others who wouldn't have. I'm pleased to report that the levels of impaired driving by off-duty police are nowhere near where they used to be and the new crop of police officers is far more responsible than we were.

Police of my era were—and I'm deeply ashamed to say myself included—a fairly entitled bunch, and many of us held the unspoken belief that we were better drivers drunk than civilians were sober, an obviously ludicrous and dangerous belief. The hypocrisy of this thinking is not lost on me, and I have no rational explanation for it. We were supposed to hold ourselves to a higher standard, and I know I failed miserably. I'm repulsed by my behavior in those days, and we lost a couple of colleagues to impaired driving crashes but fortunately didn't kill or hurt anyone else.

At the bar, Mike Porteous, widely considered the best surveillance person and instructor the VPD has ever known, racked up the billiard balls, and I broke to begin a game of eight ball. Afterward, he motioned me to bring my beer and join him at an empty table.

"Listen, I want to talk to you about something," he said, looking at me with a somber expression. I'd never seen him drunk, and he wasn't on this night. I was still in good shape after two or three pints.

"Okay," I said.

"I want you to promise me you'll come to me if anyone gives you a hard time," he said quietly. I searched his face for clues he might be joking but saw none.

"Thanks. I think I'll be fine," I said. I thought it was sweet of him to look out for me, even though it was clearly unnecessary.

"No, I'm serious." He took a long sip of his beer. "I had a partner in the Strike Force, Jill*—you know her a little, I think— and she was the best person I'd trained until you, and they broke her spirit. She was better than the guys, they didn't like it, and she was never the same. She left the job shortly after. I don't want that to happen to you."

"Okay." I thought it highly unlikely that anything like that would happen to me. I was tough, I was capable, and surely, any problems Jill, whom I barely knew, had were because she couldn't take it and must have somehow invited their abuse. Only wimps succumbed to sexism.

"So come to me with anything, okay?"

"Okay. Thanks." I thought I never would, but I appreciated how concerned he was. Later, I once considered seeking his help when the missing women file was floundering badly, but even though our desks were within spitting distance, he remained immersed in his homicide files and I in my own misery. I decided against it, and he didn't offer again.

When we were out there doing real surveillance, I lived for the rush of having someone walk perilously close to me in my hiding place and not see me there. I had some awareness, obviously, that the people we were following were dangerous criminals, often looking for the right opportunities to commit serious crimes, but I viewed surveillance as a game to be won. Losing was not an option.

Surveillance isn't glamorous. You pee in alleys. You dehydrate yourself to avoid peeing in alleys. You either go hungry for extended periods or grab bad food from twenty-four-hour drive-throughs when you can't get back to the car and your lunch box. If you carry food into the eye with you, as one of my colleagues once tried with near-disastrous consequences, dogs and coyotes follow you, and the most feared outcome is that they cause enough distraction around you to cause you to get burned, or found out by the target. You run for blocks at a time, soaking your several layers of rainwear, fleece, and winter clothing in sweat, only to stop short, take up an eye position in the cold and shiver for your hour as the sweat dries and the chill sets in.

I have stood for hours forty feet aboveground on the branches of a fir tree watching a bank robber's house, waiting for him to come out. I have crouched still as a statue, spine twisted, underneath stairwells and bushes and garbage cans. I have squatted behind a Dumpster full of rotting food during a summer garbage strike, the Dumpster situated across the alley from a chicken rendering plant on the Downtown East-side, fighting the bile rising in my throat and the perverse urge to watch the strangely Zen-like cascade of poultry guts fall from a conveyor belt—all in the name of pursuing a violent sex offender whose friend worked there. I lay on my belly for more than an hour in a three-inch-deep, eight-foot-wide puddle of cold water on a patio, soaked to the skin, in November, watching through the knots in a fence as a crook broke into a basement suite. I drank beer from glasses of dubious cleanliness in skid row hotel bars, a table away from some of the most hard-core and violent outlaw motorcycle gang members in town. And I loved every second of it.

What few people love are the debriefings, referred to as "debriefs." At the end of every surveillance shift, no matter the time, the team conducts a debrief, usually led by the road boss. At the start of the surveillance, one person is assigned to keep notes of each shift, chronicling every twist and turn of the day. These are reviewed in the debrief, theoretically in the name of reducing errors and helping everyone perform better. Invariably, it descends into personal attacks and petty points made off the backs of the tactically weaker or more junior members of the squad. I tolerated debriefs only because my abilities spared me any unwarranted criticism, but in many ways that made them even more intolerable to me. I tried to defend people whenever I felt a debrief was disintegrating into pure bullying, but those responsible were strong personalities, often in tight with the sergeants or corporals, and I felt powerless as a junior member.

It took me two years after leaving the Strike Force to stop running red lights and speeding in my own car on a quiet day off, and it's only through pure grace that I never hurt anyone. I was eventually frightened out of this behavior by my realization that the average citizen couldn't do these things and I didn't want to kill an innocent person. What made us special? What made *me* special? When I had to honestly answer "nothing," I knew my behavior had to change and I began to notice that sense of entitlement more in others.

In early 1998, big changes loomed on the horizon for the Strike Force, forcing many of us to make tough decisions. The new chief constable, Bruce Chambers, was hired in August 1997 as an outsider tasked with making sweeping changes to the VPD. He was not welcomed by many of the top executives, and his tenure was very short, culminating in his firing in May 1999.

Chief Chambers wanted to restructure and send ten Strike Force members to fill vacancies in the Major Crime Section. The openings existed in Robbery, the Sexual Offence Squad (SOS), Drugs, and Missing Persons, which was part of the Homicide Unit. This was a time when gang murders were a significant problem in the city, and that entire section was understaffed. The Strike Force would be downsized from three squads of ten to two squads. We were given the first chance to request one of these Major Crime spots, or we would be placed elsewhere.

I took some time to decide my next move. Before I left the Strike Force, I worried that I would be lost without my teammates and the elitist feeling the Strike Force affords. I had been lobbying to move into the role of road boss, the person on the squad who leads the entire show, meets with investigators on serious files, and makes all of the decisions in the heat of the surveillance. It is a high-pressure, high-risk position, and the adrenaline—as with most roles in surveillance—is incredibly addictive. If you can road-boss, you can do anything.

I could road-boss. I had done it a couple of times on lesser files as training. But I realized that because of the particular makeup of my squad, I would get few chances to road-boss if I stayed. My squad had several senior officers who were adequate road bosses, and when the squads merged there would be even more candidates senior to me, so my turn would not come soon. I loved surveillance and had always said if I could do it for the rest of my career, I would. However, like everything else I had experienced in policing to that point, the Strike Force was far from what I had hoped it would be.

One of the occupational hazards of policing, surveillance, and specifically road-bossing was that to be successful you constantly engaged in "worst-case-scenario" thinking. You always had to ask yourself what was the worst possible thing that could happen next in the surveillance, within some level of reason. For example, if we were following a bank robber, we had to allow him or her to enter the bank and carry out the robbery unless we had intelligence indicating that this person was unusually unstable or was planning to injure anyone inside without provocation. Obviously, this was a tough call to make. As a road boss—and ideally all team members were thinking along these lines, too—you needed to form fluid plans in your mind for what to do if a customer challenged the robber and a hostage-taking ensued or if the target jumped on the counter, gun waving, or myriad other possible scenarios.

As road boss, you also had to create action plans and be calm enough to communicate them to the team in times of extreme tension. This type of worst-case thinking became habit and poisoned my mind for many years. I suffered from anxiety because I could rarely take an experience at face value; I became obsessed with envisioning what horrible thing would or could happen next and how I might respond. Rarely could I appreciate the present moment. As with many of my policing experiences, I had no idea then how damaging this would be to my mental health as time went on and this style of thinking mixed with the post-traumatic stress disorder (PTSD) I was suffering from.

I decided to speak to Peter Ditchfield, the inspector in charge of the Strike Force, Gang Squad, and Emergency Response Team. Peter had recruited me for the Strike Force, and he was respectful and supportive of my career. He was one of the few senior managers I had worked with who seemed unafraid to make decisions. Shortly after the restructuring of the Strike Force, he left the VPD to join the Organized Crime Agency of British Columbia.

"What can I help you with, Lori?" Peter asked when I went to see him.

"Well, I'm thinking of going for one of these Major Crime spots," I answered, watching his face for a reaction. At only seven and a half years on the job and the most junior member of the Strike Force at the time, I still felt like a new recruit and was worried that people might view my ambition as premature. "I'm kind of intrigued by the Missing Persons job."

"Yes, that would be an interesting job, and I understand they're looking to add a second detective to the office." He stroked his chin thoughtfully. "Robbery, sos, Drugs, and Vice are all fairly senior squads," he said. I could sense disappointment coming. "I should tell you that several of the others have expressed interest in those, so they would all have seniority over you for them."

"Yeah, we've all been talking, and I kind of figured that," I said, trying not to sound overly discouraged. This wasn't a surprise.

"However, no one has expressed an interest in Missing Persons, and I think you would do an excellent job there." He looked at me pointedly. "They need someone to look at a rise in missing women, and that could very well turn into a serial killer investigation. It would be an excellent learning experience for you."

"I've always wanted to work Homicide," I told him. "Missing Persons seems like a good place to start, and it would have a lot of real mysteries to hunt down. I think it would be cool."

"Do you want to think about it, or should I let them know you're interested?"

Homicide had always been the pinnacle of police work in my mind; I just never imagined I could be that close that soon. Missing Persons had traditionally been the training ground for Homicide, with an average stay of two years before you made the jump. Here I was with less than eight years of service and my goal was within reach; it seemed too good to be true. I was idealistic and ambitious, but everything I had wanted in my career to that point had happened—usually ahead of schedule—so I asked myself why this should be any different.

"Okay, that would be great if you told them I'm interested."

I left Peter's office feeling that mixture of excitement and anxiety that would become all too familiar as my career progressed.

It did concern me that the VPD was willing to allow someone of my status to head up what could prove to be a major investigation, but again, my naïveté, idealism, and belief in my own competence clouded my judgment. I assumed if I uncovered something truly sinister, the department would bring in bigger guns to help me. I believed I had the ability and the energy to take this investigation and run with it, and what I lacked in experience I would make up for in dogged determination and persistence. I had never been too proud or too afraid to seek help and guidance from more experienced members, and with twenty homicide investigators just down the hall, I figured I couldn't go too far wrong. And Peter thought I'd be fine.

Looking back, I doubt that the managers in the Major Crime Section gave any thought to who was joining Missing Persons other than to be glad there was a warm body in the position, someone junior and ambitious enough not to book off sick frequently, someone who would put a bright face on this investigation and assure the Downtown Eastside community that it was in safe hands. This was a pattern that would repeat throughout this investigation, and it took me more than a year to figure it out. Over time, I would see that strategic planning was not at the fore of these kinds of decisions. Policing is a reactive business, and the management of the people doing the work is equally reactive. Long-term planning around running and staffing the missing women investigation was essentially nonexistent.

In the beginning, I saw this investigation as a stepping-stone, a way to make myself known both within the VPD and beyond as a solid investigator. I was able to view these victims with a certain amount of detachment—not with indifference but with a healthy set of boundaries. They were the victims, and I was the investigator. It was when I began to view them as people not very different from me that I would struggle.

3

How It All Began

*"No one can tell you what goes on in between the person
you were and the person you become. No one can chart that
blue and lonely section of hell. There are no maps of the
change. You just come out the other side. Or you don't."*

STEPHEN KING, THE STAND

I BOUGHT TWO PAIRS of John Fluevog Angel Michael
brogues—one black, one burgundy—with soles bearing
little rubber angels, guaranteed Satan-resistant for my first
real detective assignment. As a recovering Catholic, I figured
any extra Devil-proofing couldn't hurt, and my purchases felt
right as I embarked on my career as a gumshoe fighting evil
and injustice.

In the spring of 1998, VPD civilian Missing Persons clerk
Sandra Cameron had reported that drug-addicted women
working in the Downtown Eastside sex trade were going
missing at a higher rate than normal. July 27, 1998, was my
first day in Missing Persons, and I would mostly be working
on the files of the missing women. I sat down at my desk in

the tiny office and inadvertently kicked a plastic box at my feet. I reached down and pulled the black rectangular tray out into the light, reading the raised letters "Rat Poison—Danger Toxic" above a skull-and-crossbones insignia. Nice. Binders of files with the pages falling out lined the messy bookshelves. I opened a file drawer hoping to find paper and instead caused a small avalanche of dental molds of varying ages, some labeled, others not.

I was thrilled to learn my supervisor would be homicide sergeant Geramy Field. I had worked alongside Geramy on several files when she was a supervisor in the Sexual Offence Squad and I was in the Strike Force, and I respected her a great deal. She was the VPD's—and Canada's—first female police dog handler and a trailblazer for women in policing. Geramy brought a calm, assured presence to whatever team she worked on, and she was a natural leader. Geramy supervised our four-member Missing Persons office, in addition to one of the VPD's two overworked homicide squads during the height of a gang war.

My partner was Detective Al Howlett, a highly principled man and oddly brilliant investigator burned out from too many years investigating bad cops in the Internal Investigation Section (IIS). As I got to know him, I learned that Al was frustrated because he knew that even if he proved a case against a corrupt or negligent member of the force, often little or no action was taken and that person would be back working in the community before the ink had dried on Al's report. Al's desk was an oasis of order in a desert of disorganization. Each night before leaving, he made certain the entire surface of his desk was free of everything but his telephone. A couple of hours into our first day together, Al casually looked up from his file and spoke for the first time since we had introduced ourselves.

"This is what they call a sick building, you know. They won't tell you that, but a lot of the guys who've worked in the DO (Detective Office) for years get cancer when they retire." He gazed down at his file.

"Is there anything you can do about it?" I asked. "Like, to protect yourself?"

"Nope." I sat waiting for more, but when I saw no further information was forthcoming, I went back to organizing my desk.

Al was an excellent detective, and he taught me how to put a file together in an orderly, organized way. I also learned that he would not willingly act as my mentor; the missing women files would become predominantly *my* thing, but he would help me when I needed it. What he didn't know was that I would learn a great deal from him, and he was an excellent mentor. His note-taking and record-keeping were flawless, and although I never reached his high standard, I did improve my record-keeping from passable to more than acceptable. He had been the investigator on several of the first missing women files and felt there would be no happy ending to their stories. He found working on these files frustrating dead-end work, and he was at a loss—as was I—about how to take the investigations further. He was extremely capable, but policing had sucked him dry long ago.

In those days, I felt a certain pity for Al, thinking how sad it was that a man so close to retirement could have so little good feeling about his work or the organization he worked for, clinging only to his unwavering routines and idiosyncrasies. In less than three years, I would become Al. Now I recognize all the signs of burnout that Al suffered, brought on by doing a horrible job for an organization ill equipped to support him, because I have suffered from them, too. I understand the look of panic I would see on his face when our day's plan would suddenly

change and we would be forced to do something or go somewhere out of the ordinary. I understand why he wouldn't bring
his gun, that mine would be enough. I know now how much
strength it took for Al to make it to retirement, and it saddens
me to think of what this job has cost him and others like him.
I only hope he has found peace in his retirement.

IN APRIL 1998, a woman named Sarah de Vries had disappeared,
and a friend of hers, Wayne Leng, had set up a 1-800 tip line.
Wayne was a single middle-aged man who worked in the auto-
motive industry and had an interest in computers. On July 27,
1998—my first day working in the VPD Missing Persons
Unit—a man named Bill Hiscox phoned Wayne's tip line suggesting that Robert William Pickton be considered a suspect
in the disappearance of Sarah and the other missing women. It
would be several days before this information would reach me,
and I would work feverishly to interview Hiscox myself and
search for any links between the victims and the Pickton farm.

As I worked to follow up on the Hiscox tip in early August
1998, I also began setting up our investigative office and scouring the missing women's files for clues surrounding their
disappearances. These first few weeks were a strange mix of
investigation and administration that would come to charac-
terize my job for the next two years.

In addition, I was surprised to learn I would be responsible for covering the Coroner's Liaison Unit (CLU) officer's job
every Friday. We shared our office with the CLU officer, who
worked to identify deceased people and to coordinate with
the morgue and next of kin, and it was viewed as important
enough to warrant five-day-per-week coverage. But the officer
only worked four days a week, so 20 percent of my time searching for the missing women would now be spent at the morgue,
determining the identities and collecting the personal effects

of Vancouver's deceased. Taking valuable time away from my investigation to give another detective a four-day workweek seemed shortsighted to me.

When I began, there were seventeen women on my list. My approach was clinical, and I had not yet turned my mind to the bigger philosophical and political pictures, but those would begin to intrude on my thoughts, both awake and in sleep. In those first months, I strove for efficiency, well aware that one detective working on seventeen files needed to stick to the germane. My initial goal was to assess just how large the number of missing was and how much of an anomaly this number was in comparison with a normal year for Vancouver missing persons from a similar demographic.

One of my first tasks was to re-interview the people who had reported the women missing. I wanted to closely study each case so that I could identify any links or common threads. The obvious similarities were there—the women were adults, addicted to drugs, working in the sex trade, living on the Downtown Eastside—but I needed to look beyond those similarities for information about where they hung out, who they bought their dope from, who they had ripped off over the years, *who they were.*

As I worked on the files, I remained alive to anything I could use to bolster the credibility of the information about the Pickton farm and strove to identify and locate Bill Hiscox for an interview. Whenever I had a spare moment, I read the files over and over. I sought out the women's families, social workers, landlords, mental health workers, street nurses, friends, drug dealers, boyfriends, and ex-boyfriends to try to get a sense of their daily lives and activities. There had to be something beyond their lifestyle and neighborhood that linked them: a place, a person, an activity aside from drug use. But what was the link?

My initial work involved database searches. The VPD record management system itemized interactions with police to assist with the creation of timelines, but the majority of this intelligence was still on paper index cards, and the work was slow. The Canadian Police Information Centre (CPIC) computer system outlined criminal charges, convictions, and jail sentences served.

Once I possessed a basic grasp of the victim files, I had Wayne Leng come in for an interview, in mid-August of 1998. All of our telephone dealings to that point had been uneventful. Wayne was small and compact and wore glasses. He spoke softly, with a slightly high-pitched voice, and he seemed gentle and kind. I found him to be helpful, conscientious, and knowledgeable about the Downtown Eastside—all traits that alternately comforted and worried me. I continued to ask myself if he could be a serial killer. The only way to rule him in or out was to go at him hard, and I did. I questioned him about why he would put everything in his life on the back burner for this woman who had such problems, who so clearly couldn't give Wayne the kind of love that he had to give. He simply said he was patient and knew she had the potential to live a good life and be a solid citizen. Try as I might, I couldn't anger him— specifically, I couldn't bring him to express anger at Sarah.

I asked Wayne if he would be willing to take a polygraph, and he agreed, saying he would do whatever I asked if it would help. He would call me several times a week with information, and I enlisted him to help me get the only possible witness to Sarah's disappearance—Samantha Moore*—to come in for an interview. This would be the first time I would seriously question Wayne's judgment.

Samantha was supposedly working near Sarah on April 14, 1998, the night Sarah disappeared. One of the first things I did when I began reviewing Sarah's file was to go out on the stroll and try to locate Samantha, because she could be a key witness. She wasn't hard to find, and I pulled over next to her. From talking with her, it was immediately clear to me that Samantha was fairly astute and her faculties were not completely destroyed by drugs or mental illness, as is so common on the Downtown Eastside. She was high and working, and I hoped to build some rapport with her by making an appointment to talk at another time so that she could make the money she needed that day and not have her clientele scared off by my unmarked police car. This would turn out to be a mistake.

I knew the chances of her showing up were slim, but I felt the risk was worth it because the quality of a street interview in the Vancouver drizzle is so low when a woman is in a hurry to get back to work. Time spent talking to the cops was time wasted, so I felt an interview was best planned for when she wasn't working. If I was going to take her statement, I wanted to do it properly, and that meant audio and videotaping it. She agreed to see me at my office a few days later. She never showed up. I called her cell number and was unable to reach her for several days, until, finally, she answered. We again made a date to talk, and again, she failed to show up. A few weeks later, I drove past her again on the street and stopped to talk. At this point, she told me she really hadn't seen anything the night Sarah went missing and an interview wouldn't be very useful. I implored her to come in and allow me to do a cognitive interview with her that can very often help to jog a witness's memory, and she said she would try. She never came in.

Throughout this time, I had been in contact with Wayne because he and Samantha kept in touch and I hoped he could encourage her to talk to me. He told me he was doing all he could to persuade her to be interviewed, but somehow she was not getting in the door. Some months later, I went onto Wayne's website www.missingpeople.net, as was my custom every few months to see whether there was anything of interest. I was horrified to discover the "statement" of Samantha Moore, a *National Enquirer*–style account of the night Sarah went missing, complete with all sorts of detail that had been absent from our conversations. Furthermore, there was a preamble attached in which Samantha was quoted as saying the VPD had not tried to contact her and was not interested in hearing what she had to say. It seemed her entire take on this course of events was markedly different from my experience with her.

It was clear to me that Samantha's story had become more and more elaborate and incredible with each retelling, and it would be impossible to tell truth from fantasy. I called Wayne, furious he would publish this online "statement" rather than continue to encourage Samantha to come to me with what she thought she knew. He stood by his actions, fueled by his new role as webmaster, determined to make public everything he learned about the investigation, even if it compromised the integrity of that investigation. Samantha was ruined as a witness, and I was left asking myself what more I could have done to get her statement while the events were still fresh in her mind.

In the summer and fall of 1998, as I worked in that tiny Missing Persons office, reports of new missing sex workers piled up at an alarming rate, each one a seemingly more hopeless and impossible case than the last. Kerri Koski, missing in January 1998; Inga Hall, missing in February; Sarah de Vries, April; Sheila Egan, July; Angela Jardine, November; Michelle Gurney, December; Marcella Creison, December; Cindy Beck, missing in August 1997 but not reported until April 1998; Helen Hallmark, missing in June 1997 but not reported until September 1998; Jacquie Murdock, missing in September 1997 but not reported until October 1998. All gone. Vanished. Ten women. An entire basketball team.

When I began, I was unaware there was interest in forming a missing women's working group. In September 1998,
soon after I began in Missing Persons, Inspector Gary Greer,
who was in charge of the Downtown Eastside, and Detective
Inspector Kim Rossmo, the lone member of the Geographic
Profiling Unit, invited me to a meeting. The Geographic
Profiling Unit had been underused since Rossmo created it
nearly five years earlier, after completing his PhD in criminology. Rossmo's promotion from constable straight to detective
inspector—an unprecedented jump to a special VPD rank created just for Rossmo—and his installation as the head of this
one-man unit ruffled many feathers. Since his promotion, he
had been ostracized by the detectives and many in management. My manager, Major Crime inspector Fred Biddlecombe;
SOS Sergeant Axel Hovbrender; Downtown Eastside neighborhood safety officer Constable Dave Dickson; and I attended
the meeting.

There was a surreal quality to the invitation for me. For
some six weeks, I'd been toiling away in my office, completely
unaware that anyone else in the VPD was interested in or
working on the missing women cases. I had sent out bulletins
to patrol members, other sections of the VPD, and police agencies across the country asking for information and received no
indication that others sensed a problem. My first reaction was
enthusiasm: here were others I could work with, people I could
share my theories and ideas with. I envisioned a cohesive team
setting where we would band together toward a common goal:
finding the women.

From the meeting's opening, tension hung in the air.
Rossmo and Greer took the lead, while Biddlecombe sat back
with his arms folded, a scowl on his face. Fred Biddlecombe
was a dour, intense man who rarely smiled. He wasn't given to
casual conversation, and it seemed the pressures of his position were great.

"We see this as an opportunity to—" Greer began, before Biddlecombe cut him off.

"I know exactly what opportunity you two," he gestured toward Greer and Rossmo, "see in all this. But I won't have my people paraded around in your dog and pony show. Lori's barely been here a month, and she needs the chance to see where her investigation leads before we start sounding alarm bells that will have every quack in the city calling her."

Dave Dickson passed around a handout: two sheets of paper filled with more than fifty names of mostly Indigenous women from the Vancouver area who had gone missing or been murdered. Biddlecombe looked at it quickly and turned on Dickson.

"Where did you get this?" he demanded. I sat there wondering the same thing. I'd been working for six weeks to compile a comprehensive list of the missing women. Most of these names were new to me, and I worried I'd missed even more. "That's not current. A good number of those women have been found," Biddlecombe finished, visibly upset.

"Yes, sir, you're right. Unsolved accounted for all those first ones I brought to them. This is a new list from the Vancouver area," Dickson replied.

Biddlecombe pushed the handout back toward Dickson as he spoke. "And when Unsolved did start working on locating them, important information was leaked to the press, which is why I'm not thrilled to devote any of my people to this working group." He looked pointedly at Dickson, but it was as though he hadn't heard him. "I don't want to open Major Crime files to people I can't trust not to run to the press. I don't want this investigation moving outside of Major Crime."

I sat there, openmouthed, watching the back and forth like a spectator at a tennis match.

When he spoke of "opportunity," I suspected Biddlecombe was alluding to Greer's less-than-secret desire to be the next

chief and Rossmo's need to justify the existence of his fledg-
ling Geographic Profiling Unit. Now nearing the end of his
five-year contract, Rossmo seemed to be looking for a life raft.
I failed to understand why singling out Dave Dickson or airing
dirty laundry was fair or served any purpose.

Rossmo and Greer had composed a press release for this
meeting, warning of the possibility that a serial killer was at
work on the Downtown Eastside, and they wanted it issued
immediately. The rest of us in this newly created working
group were opposed—not because we didn't agree there was
probably a serial killer. We felt it was premature, given that I
hadn't yet fully investigated many of the missing women files
to rule out any other possible fates. In hindsight, there would
have been little harm in issuing the release, but most of us felt
it would cause more trouble than it would prevent.

Specifically, we thought the language of the release was
inflammatory and likely to meet indifference from the sex
workers while inciting panic among many outside the community. Typically, these women knew better than anyone the
dangers associated with working the streets, and news of the
operation of a serial killer would not come as a surprise to
them. Warning the women would not stop them from working and putting themselves at risk; it would merely satisfy
Downtown Eastside community leaders that we were doing
something. Greer and Rossmo agreed to hold off on the release.

After Biddlecombe left the room, I approached Rossmo.

"Can you help me with something?" I asked.

"Sure."

"I need to analyze the number of missing women I have so
far, to show it's statistically unusual and a real problem, not just
a strange blip or something. Can you do that?" His eyes lit up.

"I can do an epidemiological analysis of the numbers to look
for patterns or anomalies over the years," he answered.

"Perfect. Come and see me and I'll give you what you need." I lowered my voice. "And keep it between us. Biddlecombe will have an aneurism if he knows I'm showing you the files."

After this meeting, two of the participants, Sergeant Axel Hovbrender of the Sexual Offence Squad and Constable Dave Dickson, joined me back at my office. I'd known Dave from my time on patrol, and he would prove to be an invaluable ally and friend over the years. He deserves an entire book on his own; his work with the youth and sex workers in the Downtown Eastside is legendary and his compassion boundless. We talked for a few minutes about the meeting before Dave begged off to get back on the road, responding to his constantly vibrating pager for which so many desperate, disadvantaged kids had the number. As always, he left me with strict orders to call him if I needed anything. Everybody calls Dave when they need anything.

Axel sat quietly for several long moments. I didn't know him well, but my experience of him had always been as someone who didn't speak often, but when he did, people listened.

"Lor, I don't have a lot of advice for you. You seem to know where you're going with this." He paused. "But I will tell you this: document everything, *every single thing*, and ask for help, ask for what you need to do the job. Document it every time you ask for help and document it when they turn you down." He looked meaningfully into my eyes, and I swallowed hard, feeling a weight descend upon me. I knew he was sending me an important message in the only way he could, without scaring me right off the entire police department. He *knew* how this was very likely to go, and he was trying to protect me.

More than any other moment in this investigation, I am grateful for those words, because they woke me up and forced me to see what I was getting into. It wasn't perfect by any stretch, but I took Axel's advice and documented everything

I did as well as I could. I asked for help, and I wrote it down when help was denied. I even kept a list of what I'd written down so that when many of my most important documents seemed to disappear before the Missing Women Commission of Inquiry, I could at least say I had had them at some point. As someone told me during my legal prep for the inquiry: *He with the most notes wins.* No one wins in this story. But I was able to stand up for my work, or at least that which wasn't misplaced years later by Project Evenhanded, the RCMP's exploration of missing and murdered women in British Columbia.

4

The Initial Pickton Information

• • •

"If there be light, then there is darkness; if cold, heat;
if height, depth; if solid, fluid; if hard, soft; if rough, smooth;
if calm, tempest; if prosperity, adversity; if life, death."

PYTHAGORAS

IN A JULY 1998 conversation with Wayne Leng, Bill Hiscox said that a "Willie" Pickton had a large farm in Port
Coquitlam, a suburb of Vancouver, and often bragged
about his ability to grind up bodies and dispose of them. He
knew a woman who had been in Pickton's trailer and had seen
several women's purses and identification cards and "bloody
clothing in bags." Leng encouraged Hiscox to call me, but
instead he called Crime Stoppers and left a tip that Pickton
was someone we should look at. A few weeks later, he left a
second tip with the same message. As is typical with Crime
Stoppers tips, Hiscox left these anonymously. When the tips
reached me, I immediately researched everything I could get
my hands on about the man I would come to know as Robert
William Pickton.

A week or so before talking to Hiscox, Leng had received an eerie call to his tip line. An older man or possibly a woman with a raspy, wheezy voice said that if Leng was looking for Sarah, he wouldn't find her because she was dead, and that's what was going to happen to more girls just like her; every Friday one would end up dead.

Leng released this taped message to the media, and it was played repeatedly the same week I began my new job in Missing Persons. I was inundated with calls, faxes, and anonymous letters from people with tips about whose voice it might be. Excited by so many potentially fruitful leads to pursue, I dove into the work. But after interviewing twenty suspects, I was able to quickly rule them all out. All of their voices were distinctly different from that of the caller, none of them behaved at all suspiciously, and almost none had links to any of the missing women. I found out later that the call had been made as a prank. Little did I know this would be the only point in the investigation that the public would become involved in trying to solve the mystery of the missing women.

When I received Hiscox's first Crime Stoppers tip, I ran the few short steps from the Missing Persons office to Crime Stoppers next door, breathless with excitement and determined to get the tipster's information. Within moments, the constable in Crime Stoppers, Linda Malcolm, patiently explained to me that she could not identify the caller.

"Lori, I completely understand why you're asking, but you know I can't give you the name, even if I had one." She smiled, her blue eyes kind.

"Can't you even give me a hint?" I pleaded, my hands in prayer position in front of my chest. She laughed. "Not even for you."

"Can you show me how to use PIRS?"

"That I can do!"

I sat down at the RCMP Police Information Retrieval System (PIRS) terminal and entered Pickton's name and date of birth. Electrified, I read that he had one entry on his criminal record—a 1997 stay of proceedings for attempted murder and forcible confinement in Port Coquitlam. As I searched through the details, I learned the victim was a sex worker picked up from Vancouver's Downtown Eastside, and both she and Pickton had nearly died from knife wounds that night.

"BINGO!" I shouted, nearly jumping up out of the chair, thinking, *This is what a serial killer looks like!* Linda showed me how to find the lead investigator's name and contact information.

I racked my brain for a way to learn the caller's identity that would be both legal and admissible in court. I couldn't conceive of all the ways it might play out, but I knew every step I took leading to Pickton would be scrutinized later. I waited for the caller to come forward, and when I wasn't interviewing men in an attempt to identify the voice on the tape, I used my time to research Pickton and connect with the Coquitlam RCMP officers who had arrested him. During this brief time, I felt the most alive, the most useful, the most certain the work I was doing *mattered*.

From this research, I tracked down the Coquitlam RCMP officer who had been in charge of the file, Corporal Mike Connor. A couple of days after we received Hiscox's tip, I reached Mike on the phone. It was obvious that Pickton was someone he wanted in jail and thought about often, and that this particular event bothered him deeply.

He told me that Pickton had picked up Anderson*, an Indigenous woman and Downtown Eastside sex worker, and taken her to his farm in Port Coquitlam for sex. Somehow, the date had gone wrong, and Pickton and Anderson ended up in a life-and-death struggle in which they each received serious stab wounds—Pickton a single wound, Anderson multiple wounds. Both managed to get themselves to the hospital, and despite having cardiac arrest twice on the operating table, Anderson lived. Pickton's injuries were less severe, but he later alleged that the interaction with Anderson had left him with hepatitis.

"Do you know why the charges were stayed?" I asked Mike, certain he'd be able to tell me the reasons behind the Crown's decision to drop the case.

"No. It seemed as though it had something to do with her drug use, that they didn't think she'd make a credible witness because of her habit."

"What does that have to do with anything?" I asked, incredulous.

"I don't know. I'll go out and have a talk with the Crown prosecutor again now that this has come up," he went on. "I never really understood it, either. If she'd died on the table, we'd have had him cold for murder."

We agreed that we would keep in touch and that I would let him know if I tracked down the Crime Stoppers caller we would come to know as Hiscox. After talking to Mike, I was certain Pickton was worth pursuing. In the meantime, Leng continued to push Hiscox until he finally agreed to contact me.

Of all the people in Pickton's circle, it is Hiscox I have the most respect for, because he is the one person who seemed driven by altruism. He became involved at his own peril and without any personal agenda that I'm aware of. He had his own problems, including drug addiction, alcohol abuse, and difficulties with his marriage. Work was scarce and he was collecting welfare benefits. For more than a decade, his substance abuse had frequently landed him in jail for violence or property crimes, and his record was long. He has since spoken quite openly about his struggles.

But Bill Hiscox understood the concept of doing the right thing, and among the vast number of men who had been on the Pickton property over the past twenty years, he was the only one who put himself on the line and told me when we first spoke, "What's going on at this place is wrong, and if girls are getting killed, he [Pickton] needs to be stopped." Despite the scores of men and women who had heard the rumors, had seen the oddities, had been to the parties and participated— perhaps unwillingly, perhaps not—in the depraved games we learned about after Pickton's 2002 arrest, Hiscox was the only one who felt it was important enough to say something, even if that meant the party would be over.

I have never viewed human sources as "rats." Over the course of my career—before and long after I dealt with Hiscox—I saw some police officers treat sources as roadkill to be driven over on the way to a criminal conviction, no matter how serious the crime. Too often, these people are criminals themselves and seen by the police as a means to an end, treated as though any further damage to them and their lives as a result of helping us is simply the cost of doing business. The higher the stakes—organized crime is a perfect example—the more pressure police place on human sources to perform without regard for their future lives.

Within these short weeks, I'd been led to an excellent potential suspect, and I could barely contain my excitement. This was exactly the type of tip I had envisioned receiving when I took this case, and I eagerly followed it up. I imagined what could be happening on that farm. I knew Pickton possessed at least one backhoe, and I pictured him digging bunkers, perhaps to hold his captives alive or to bury them. My mind ran through all sorts of possibilities as I prepared myself to question Hiscox about what he knew of the place. I researched other cases like this in the U.S. and the U.K. and

knew that hidden rooms and torture chambers were not outside the realm of possibility for such depraved killers. I felt an
urgency to get on the farm in case there was a chance that any
of the women might be rescued. I lay awake at night plotting
legal ways we could get on the farm to learn more.

I ruminated on my conversation with Mike Connor about
why the 1997 charges against Pickton had been stayed. He was
obviously frustrated by his impression that Crown counsel
hadn't felt confident of a conviction because of Anderson's
drug use and alleged unreliability. I found this bizarre. One
hundred percent of my court experience had been in the Provincial Court of British Columbia and the B.C. Supreme Court,
and if every case involving offenders and victims with drug
problems or credibility issues were thrown out, those court-
rooms would be vacant.

I also knew from my time on the Downtown Eastside that
a drug problem didn't automatically turn a person into an idiot
or a liar or give them amnesia. We agreed that had Anderson
died from her injuries, the case would be a slam-dunk murder or at least manslaughter conviction. Mike told me he was
exploring ways to have that case reopened, and I sensed he
was understating how important this was to him. We agreed
to meet and review the file, which we did a bit later in August,
after Mike returned from summer vacation.

Reading Mike's file filled me with a deep sense of forebod-
ing. I felt even more strongly that we were onto something
with Pickton. Over and over, I kept thinking, *Nobody tries this the
first time out of the gate; he's done it before.* I viewed the entire case
rather clinically at this point; there was no room for emotion
or thinking of my victims as real people. I felt the protective
professional detachment from emotion that had served me so
well in my career thus far—though that wouldn't last.

As I looked more closely at the files of the missing women
reported to our office, I saw the spike in numbers starting in

1995. From 1978 to 1992, six women remained missing and I couldn't see any who were missing from 1993 to 1995. With a jolt, I realized there were three women still missing from 1995, two from 1996, and five from 1997. And 1998 was shaping up to surpass them all with eleven, and the year wasn't over. Twenty-one Downtown Eastside women missing since 1995. I didn't need Rossmo's analysis to tell me someone was killing these women, but backing up my suspicions with science might help me get the resources I was going to need.

I became more convinced that Pickton was our man. Mike and I agreed to place an entry in the Canadian Police Information Centre (CPIC) system flagging Robert Pickton as a person of interest in the missing women investigation and asking any police members who came in contact with Pickton to page both Mike and me at any time, twenty-four hours a day.

FROM THE TIME I first became aware of Pickton, in July, I had been trying to locate Anderson for an interview, but she had been living on the street, and whenever I would find out where she had slept the previous night, she'd be gone by the time I got there. On August 21, my opportunity finally arrived. Anderson had been arrested. After a wild cocaine binge in skid row, she resisted arrest and drove off in a police car left running at the scene when the officers it belonged to—one of them a very good friend of mine—had tried to arrest her. She drove into a wall in the same block and found herself facing a number of charges in the Burnaby Correctional Centre for Women.

Anderson and I knew each other from my patrol days on the Downtown Eastside, and when I asked to interview her at the correctional center, she was cooperative and affable; she had been there several days, free of the drugs that made her paranoid and violent. We talked for nearly two hours, and she told me about that fateful night in March 1997 when she had met Robert Pickton. Her story was riveting. I had no doubt that she was telling the truth and that she had been in a fight for her life.

Her recollection of the events mirrored her previous statement perfectly—typical for someone who has been through significant trauma and is telling the truth. Lies are easy to tell once, but they are almost impossible to retell identically. Listening to her, I couldn't understand why anyone wouldn't find her or her story credible. She would have made an excellent witness in court; she just would have needed someone to take care of her and ensure that she wasn't using drugs the days of her testimony.

In those days, before I had learned that the taped message was a hoax, I recorded a voice "lineup" cassette tape to try to determine who the mystery person on Wayne Leng's tip line could be. I reasoned that if photo lineups worked, there was no reason a vocal lineup couldn't be used the same way. I knew it might not be admissible in court, but I carried on, believing it might still have some investigative value. I recorded several of the homicide detectives in my office speaking the same lines as the raspy-voiced person for comparison with the original caller.

Anderson believed she would know Pickton's voice if she heard it again. I played the tape for her in our interview and asked her to stop me if she heard any voice she knew. She listened intently as each of the six men said there would be more women "just like Sarah"—dead—every Friday. When the tape was done, I asked her if she recognized any of the voices. She shook her head sadly, so eager to help, not wanting to be wrong. She didn't recognize any of the voices.

I tried to impress on her how important it would be for her not to return to the streets on her release from the correctional center, because I believed there was a real possibility Pickton would try to pick her up again. She was genuinely afraid, but her addiction would prove far more powerful than her fear. In less than a year, she was back smoking crack and getting into cars with strange men to support herself, a little more cautious but every bit as much at risk. I felt sick with worry for her, but I was powerless to do anything more.

A Letter to Anderson

* * *

DEAR ANDERSON,

It's been years since we last spoke, but I think of you often. *Resilient. Feisty. Indomitable.* All words that describe you. All words that describe many of your sisters now inconceivably missing and dead.

I know you're haunted by them.

I'm thinking back to that 1998 morning I was driving into work, listening to the news. As I heard the announcer tell the story of a woman—high on cocaine and running in and out of traffic on the Downtown Eastside—I wondered if she could be you. Several cops tried to get hold of her, and finally they did. But she was not to be held. She escaped. Jumped into a running police car, drove a few yards, and crashed into a building. The woman's name was Anderson, and I shouted *Bingo!* knowing I had finally found you. You were in custody.

I laughed hearing this story. Knowing you a little, feeling a sense of wonder at the very strength of your survival instinct, thinking you'd probably get a kick out of making those poor young policemen look like Keystone Cops. Looking forward to our meeting.

You were staying at the Burnaby Correctional Centre for Women. They told me you'd be there for a few weeks at least, so I gave you some time to clean up, knowing we'd have a much better talk if you weren't in the throes of detox.

I fought to contain my excitement, for you were a key piece to this puzzle I was trying to solve. The more I tried to learn about Robert Pickton and his pig farm, the less ground I seemed to be able to cover. But you had been there. You had been with him. And you had *survived him*. Did you have any clue back then what that really meant?

You were smaller than I remembered, almost mouselike. Half-Indigenous, half-white, with wild curly dark hair and a small shy smile, despite your apparent dislike of police, whom you saw as just one more obstacle in the way of your getting high and escaping the demons in your own head. Nothing personal, you said.

I told you the truth—that you didn't have to talk to me if you weren't up for it, that I had arrested you a couple of times in the past, that I was very interested in your story and wanted to go over it again with you if you felt you could handle that. You agreed. You said you were pissed; you couldn't understand why that prick wasn't in jail. I asked you what you thought the reason for that was. You said the Crown said you weren't credible. On account of your drug addiction, you explained. As though that was typical.

You looked up at me timidly and said, "That's not right, is it?" I replied that in my experience, it's usually up to a judge and jury to make a decision about the credibility of a witness. You nodded and I was reminded again of all the ways that poor, drug-addicted women are dismissed.

We talked about the missing women, about how many of them you had known—Sarah, Helen—and about your fear.

You avoided the corner of Princess and Cordova, where he had picked you up that night, afraid he would return to find you. Did you know he tried to pay friends to finish you off? To kill you so that you would be forever silenced, unable to tell, unable to point a finger at him and say, "Yes, Your Honor, that's the man"? He knew this wasn't over with you. He was so right.

That's the man who offered you $100 for a "lay"—a pretty decent date back in 1997 for the low track, where the most desperate and unprotected women worked. You said the word with the nonchalance and slight disdain of someone for whom sex had long ago ceased to be anything other than a quid pro quo arrangement. "Lay," "blow job," "half and half"—all mechanical, locker room, porn site terms devoid of any feeling or illusion of closeness. I wondered if you had ever been fortunate enough to have sex out of love, if you had ever wanted to be with someone as much as they wanted to be with you. I worried I was stereotyping you by even wondering that.

So you jumped into the truck, despite a small but persistent voice in your head telling you something about this guy was off. You said this feeling grew stronger as he drove you east along the Lougheed Highway, but still you carried on.

A hundred bucks. A hundred bucks.

You asked where he was taking you and he said he had a place in Port Coquitlam. You suggested a hotel or even an alley might be better. He said nothing and just drove on in the night, never fully stopping for red lights, merely coasting as he approached and timing them so the truck never slowed enough for you to chance a leap out the door. By then, you were thinking about it.

This is why I don't leave the skids.

You noticed a bra on the floor beneath your feet. *What's this?* Silence. You looked out the window for some magical way to escape. He drove on through the night.

He pulled onto a large junk-filled property—but he didn't drive to the house. You were afraid and again asked him where you were going. He told you he had a trailer near the back of the property. He drove on in the darkness.

He parked alongside a dirty construction-type trailer and helped you out. Then, he suddenly stopped you, telling you to wait right there as he pulled a large sheet of plywood from somewhere near the trailer and laid it down on the ground outside the trailer door. You thought that was odd because it wasn't raining out, the ground was dry, and there was nothing but a little gravel to track inside. It wasn't like the place was clean or anything. Weird.

Okay, come on in. You did. *A hundred bucks.*

Every girl has her limit, you said. But sometimes you get yourself into spots, situations, and it's hard to say no, to tell them you've changed your mind, that it doesn't feel right. They already think they own you. The deal's already been made, and you know how these guys can get if you piss them off.

You had sex on a filthy mattress on the floor. Mona Wilson would be killed on this mattress. How many others were there? When he was done, you asked for your money and he said no.

Here we go.

You asked if he would at least drive you back into Vancouver.

No.

You asked if you could use the phone.

No.

So you reached for the phone book and before you could begin thumbing through it, he grabbed one of your arms and clamped a handcuff around your wrist—so quickly you hadn't even seen the handcuffs. Immediately, you knew you were fighting for your life.

He tried to grab your free arm, but you fought harder than he could have imagined you would and he couldn't get the second cuff on you. You saw a knife on the counter and struggled to reach it like a drowning person lunging for a life raft. Got it. You lashed out at his neck, slicing him from one ear to Adam's apple. You dropped the knife and ran for the door.

He bled heavily but still managed to grab you again. You grappled for a few moments; he now had the knife. He shoved it hard into your abdomen and then pushed it *up*. You both flailed about as you each lost blood and consciousness. Finally, he indicated you could go, pointing to the door. You felt gratitude that he let you go.

As you turned to stagger out—your guard down and now focused merely on survival—he grabbed you once again around your neck and pulled you back into the trailer. *He tricked me.* He plunged the knife into your lower chest. Then he passed out.

Hands pressed against your body to hold your organs in, you ran the hundred or so yards back to Dominion Road, looking about wildly for anyone to help. You crossed the road and pounded on the door of a darkened farmhouse, but no one was home. Did anyone ever tell you that home belonged to his aunt? You smashed your fist through a window, trying to get in, thinking, *He must be coming after me.*

Then you saw the lights of a car.

Half-naked, bleeding, and still holding the knife, you flagged the car down, screaming that someone had tried to kill you. Amazingly, the couple stopped—and politely implored you to put the knife down, which you did. You hadn't even known you were carrying it. *How did I get it back from him?* You cried, telling them someone tried to kill you and you feel bad because you think you stabbed him, *you had to stab him.* You were already worried they would find some way to make it your fault.

It was always the girl's fault. *They asked for it, making these choices, working the streets—what did you think would happen when you got in the car with a stranger?*

The people in the car called 9-1-1 and arranged to meet an ambulance on the way to the hospital. They put you on board and the paramedics went to work, trying to stop the blood loss that had reached a very dangerous point. You had to tell them all you didn't mean to stab him, because you were sure you were dying and didn't want to have this on your slate if there was actually an afterlife. They told you, *Shhhh, save your energy,* but this was important and they had to know you didn't mean it. You would die twice on the operating table, but you hung on.

He managed to drive himself to the hospital shortly after you. Bleeding out. Quickly, the police would put two and two together.

You lifted your T-shirt and revealed several long jagged scars crisscrossing your midsection and lower chest. I was amazed you survived. I told you of how I had seen the property and could not understand how you could have possibly run that distance from the trailer to the road. It was easily the length of a football field and a half.

I told you I believed you were the only one who had got away.

You nodded slowly.

We went over some details again, and I asked you what your plans were once you got out. You said you had kids living with your mom and you wanted to clean up and get them back living with you. You said you didn't know he had tried to find you and that itself was enough motivation to get through detox and make a new start. You hugged me and I wished you the best of luck.

The guard came to take you back to the open living unit and you paused, turned back to me, and said, "Catch him, okay?" I said I'd do my best.

During the investigation, I'd often talk to the people walking the beat, asking if you were still around, hoping you had found the strength to overcome your addictions. Last I'd heard, you were doing really well.

It really is about luck—that you're where you are and I'm where I am. A mere coin toss.

How must you feel now? Do you feel vindicated in some way or just disgusted that your story wasn't heard and it had to go on so long? Do you still feel outrage, or was that beaten out of you through years of violence and scratching out an existence in the constant soul-sucking world of the Downtown Eastside? Do you wonder about all the women who died needlessly? Do you think about how easily you could have died that March night? Do you feel survivor's guilt? I know many of the girls do.

I wonder if you know how brave you are.

5

Working with Bill Hiscox

●　●　●

"The pendulum of the mind alternates between sense and
nonsense, not between right and wrong."
CARL JUNG, MEMORIES, DREAMS, REFLECTIONS

OSSMO TOLD ME he felt the offender (or offenders) had
the ability to dispose of bodies in privacy, was probably
Caucasian, and probably used a vehicle—all things I
had surmised early in the investigation and reasons that the
Pickton tip resonated so strongly with me from the outset. Early
in the missing women investigation, I discounted nothing—
I met with anyone who wanted to talk—and remained open
to anything that might help us find these women, including
Rossmo's theories. Unfortunately, none of these led us
anywhere.

In August 1998, I made several unsuccessful attempts to
reach Bill Hiscox at the number he left Leng, and we finally
spoke on the phone early in September after I tracked him
down to a men's shelter. I left him a message, and he returned
my call later that night. A phone conversation is never optimal

when dealing with a source, but it marked a beginning I hoped would lead me to a face-to-face meeting so that I could better determine his credibility and his motivation for coming forward.

We spoke easily, and I found him to be reasonable and lucid. He made no mention of a reward—not that one had been offered yet—and he did not ask for payment. He spoke intelligently and answered thoughtfully, and I liked him.

"I'm not working out there anymore," Hiscox told me. "He's a creep, odd duck, you know? Like, we just never got on that well. I think he just put up with me because Lee said I was okay."

"How did the grinder thing come up?" I asked.

"I dunno. We'd be sitting around, shooting the shit, and Willie'd say, 'Hey, if any of you guys ever need to get rid of a body, I got this here grinder works like a hot damn. You're welcome to it.' And that was Willie, always giving people his stuff, then getting pissed if people took advantage."

"Did he only offer the grinder the one time?"

"No, I remember him saying it a few times, like to other people. He seemed kinda proud of it."

"So, why were you so hot to talk to the police about him?" I wanted to test him a little, see if he was motivated by money or a grudge.

"Well, why do you think?" He seemed annoyed at my question. "If he's killin' girls, he needs to be stopped. I may be a lot of things, but I know what's right, you know? What Willie's doing, it isn't right. If that was my sister, I'd sure as shit want someone speaking out to stop it."

He told me he was trying to clean up his life and get his own place. He told me about his friend Lisa Yelds, nicknamed Lee, a good friend of Pickton's who arranged for Hiscox to work on the farm as a laborer. This was typical of Pickton—he seemed to have platonic relationships with women living on his property and sexual relationships with sex workers.

Although Hiscox characterized Yelds as a close friend of Pickton's, he said she had expressed concerns to Hiscox that Pickton might be drugging her and possibly touching her while she was unconscious, but she wasn't certain. Neither she nor Pickton drank alcohol or used drugs. Hiscox often described Pickton as a "creepy guy" and told me how Pickton had picked up a sex worker downtown, taken her back to his place for sex, then stabbed her. I knew he was talking about Anderson.

"Did you know the girl he stabbed?" I asked.

"Nah, no idea. Some girl he picked up downtown, I think. He was pissed, said she gave him hepatitis. Said he'd pay us to bring her back to the farm so he could finish her off."

"You heard him say that?"

"Oh yeah, a few times to different people. Lee said he asked people to find her all the time. He blamed her for his being sick."

I was keenly interested in having a conversation with Lisa Yelds or finding a way to place an undercover operator in a position to befriend her, but Hiscox was certain she would not want to talk. From Hiscox's description of her, it was clear that she was at best incredibly antipolice and was not interested in helping anyone other than her closest longtime friends. It was obvious that Hiscox felt affection and loyalty toward her, in part because their friendship extended back many years.

Both Yelds and Hiscox were afraid of the Picktons' biker associates and of being known as police informants within their own peer group. In the 1980s and '90s, the Picktons were well known in the community. Their parties were notorious in the Port Coquitlam area. The family owned several large properties that they would eventually sell to the city, which subdivided them for developments and big-box stores such as

Home Depot. Before that, Robert and his brother, Dave, lived on one property, and on another property a mile down the road there was a large barn known as Piggie's Palace, where, according to local lore, those parties took place and were well attended by many in the community, including elected officials and police. Although there were rumblings of illegal after-hours liquor activity, for the most part it sounded like relatively good clean fun, at least on the surface.

Down the road from Piggie's Palace was quite another story. Robert lived in the small dirty mobile office trailer farther back from the road, and Dave inhabited the house near the front of the large lot. Large mounds of recently moved earth, piles of junk metal and lumber, derelict cars, and numerous backhoes littered the property. The brothers owned and operated P&B Salvage company and the farmland was their storage area. There was also a barn and attached slaughterhouse where Robert butchered his pigs and lambs, selling the meat to friends and local sellers.

None of the sex workers I spoke with agreed to go on the record with what they saw and experienced on the property shared by Robert and Dave, but several told me stories of depraved sex "games," many involving non-consensual sex acts and torture; drugs laced with unknown hallucinogens; and pigs exhibiting an unnatural interest in humans. As one woman described to me shortly after the Pickton search began in 2002:

"I was in the trailer, you know, we were partying and some of the guys were getting pretty into it, taking girls into the other room and around the side. Dope everywhere. I was using a lot back then, so my memory isn't the best, but I knew what I was doin'. Someone gave me some smack and as soon as I shot it, I felt sick, really weird, not like trippin', more like sick. Just not the way a high feels.

"So, I say I'm going out for some air and no one really stops me, so much is going on and everyone's fucked up, right? And I go around the trailer, it's a really nice night, not raining for once. My head's swimming, so I just walk. I'd never been out there before, so I walk for some air and I turn a corner and there's a pigpen. I grew up in the country, I know pigs, so I walk over to the fence to have a look, I'm feeling a little better. And out of fucking nowhere these pigs are throwing themselves at the fence where I'm standing like they want to get at me. I never seen pigs act like that, pigs are gentle. But it was like they could smell me, smell my woman-ness. They scared the shit out of me and I got the fuck away from there."

Hiscox agreed to think of ways to obtain more information from Yelds but wasn't confident she would cooperate. He offered to try to spend some time on the farm, but I suggested he do so only if it was convenient for him and if that appeared normal to Yelds and Pickton. I didn't want him doing anything outside of his normal routine, and I didn't want to give him the impression that I was directing him. At this point, I didn't know enough about him to have him acting as an agent for the police, and I didn't want him doing anything to put himself at risk or to tip Pickton off that he might be a police source. We agreed to speak again in a few days, and I continued to assess his true involvement in the activities on the Pickton farm.

A few days later, I arranged to meet Hiscox, but he called on the morning of our meeting to say he couldn't make it but would come at one or two that day. Two o'clock came and went and no Hiscox—no call, no show. I was mildly annoyed but tried to be patient and reassure myself this was typical of sources—especially those with addictions.

About ten days later, Hiscox called to apologize, saying he had been in the hospital and unable to meet me. I told him I would come to see him in the hospital that same morning.

I blasted out to a hospital outside of Vancouver around nine thirty and searched for his ward. A nurse directed me to his room, and when I asked, she told me why he was there but implored me not to say she had told me, because I wasn't family. I assured her I would not say a thing. I found him in his bed and sat down to talk. A second bed filled the room, but it was empty.

"You're a tough man to track down," I said, smiling. "You doing okay?"

"Yeah, sorry." He shifted in his bed, wincing. "I'm just going through a rough time. Stuff with my old lady isn't good, I lost my job again, got arrested. Kind of messing up here big time."

"Are they helping you here?" I took off my coat.

"Yeah, it helps to rest a bit. The counselor is good."

"Good."

"You know, I really don't need this shit with Willie in my life. I got a lot on my plate, but if he's a killer, I wouldn't be able to live with myself if I didn't tell what I know and try to stop him." He shrugged sheepishly.

"I know. I appreciate you talking to me. I know things are really hard for you right now."

"It's no problem."

I marveled at his dedication to trying to do the right thing, even when it was less than convenient for him. I never got the sense it was about money; he received no money from me or from the VPD during the investigation, and he never asked me for anything that might have been available to him as a source. The most he ever got before Pickton's arrest was a cup of coffee from Mike and me.

My goal that day was to get to know as much about Hiscox, Yelds, and Pickton as possible. Hiscox responded fully and thoughtfully to my questions and gave me personal details about his life, his history, and his hopes for the future. He told me he was the tipster to Crime Stoppers and also said that

Wayne Leng had given some members of the media his name. He had been contacted in July for information, but he did not provide any, and eventually they stopped hounding him. He clearly wasn't after public notoriety.

Hiscox had met Pickton and his brother, Dave "Piggy" Pickton, through Lisa Yelds, who also arranged for Hiscox to work for the brothers for a couple of months at P&B Salvage. He found Robert Pickton very quiet, with no sense of humor, and didn't like being around him, but he assured me he had no problems with Pickton; there was no money owed between them, and they were not involved in drugs or other criminal activities together. Since sources often minimize their business dealings with other shady characters, I took this information with a grain of salt and remained open to the idea that they could be more closely connected.

Yelds and Pickton used to date and still got together here and there. Pickton had no other girlfriend that Hiscox knew of and used the services of sex workers regularly, a piece of information Hiscox also learned from Yelds. He characterized Yelds and Pickton as "best friends."

"Lee said Willie asked her to get him syringes; she always gets him things in exchange for meat. She's like his contact for stuff."

"What are the syringes for? She doesn't use, right?"

"No. She said he wants them for a girl named Anderson, half clean and half dirty needles."

"Any idea why?"

"No idea. I never heard of that before, the clean and used thing. Lee says Willie wants to get this girl. Lee thinks to hurt her in some way. I think this Anderson might be the girl who gave him hep, maybe. I don't know."

Hiscox felt certain Lisa Yelds wouldn't talk to me because she was loyal to Pickton as a friend and business associate.

Yelds was a longtime biker associate and someone who would never "rat out" a friend—especially to the cops. Hiscox characterized Yelds as someone who "just doesn't give a crap" and was a borderline "psycho" at times herself. He said someone could be lying on the ground bleeding and she'd just step over him or her and carry on. He said she was generally quite cold but was loyal to Hiscox because they grew up in foster care together and she had stuck up for and protected him when he was a kid. Hiscox reiterated several times how much she hated cops.

Despite the volume of information he gave me about Yelds, I got the feeling he didn't want me to know too much about her. He gave me her phone number but said he doubted she would talk to me. He didn't feel he could even approach her to let her decide, but he said if I went with him and met her casually and we didn't tell her I was a cop, she would probably relay a lot of this info about Pickton in front of me.

I hesitated to call Yelds, since I was afraid that might put Hiscox at risk if he returned to the farm. He agreed to introduce an undercover operator to Yelds if we asked him to—perhaps portraying her as a new girlfriend if we decided to use him as an agent. He assured me that Yelds would not be suspicious; apparently, she did not like Hiscox's estranged wife and would not think it odd for him to bring a new girl around to meet her. We didn't discuss the details or implications of the operation, but I got the sense that Hiscox hoped I could be the undercover operator.

Although I had had numerous undercover assignments in my career, I hadn't undertaken one that might turn into a days- or weeks-long operation. I was an investigator now, and although the prospect was enticing, I knew there were better people for the job. Six months earlier, I'd have jumped at an offer, but I felt a strong commitment to the work I'd begun with the missing women. I decided I would turn down the offer if asked and maintain my role as file coordinator and lead investigator.

Hiscox said Yelds told him within that past week that Pickton had some "weird things around the house," and this led to her divulging he had several women's purses, items of jewelry, and bloody clothing in bags and that her impression was he kept them as trophies.

"She says she thinks he could be responsible for those missing Vancouver girls," Hiscox told me.

"Is she scared of him?" Hiscox laughed at this.

"What's so funny?" I asked.

"You just gotta know Lee," he said, shaking his head, still chuckling. "It doesn't surprise me she'd still hang with him. That's just how she is. She doesn't give a damn."

"Do you think she's in danger? Are you worried about her?"

"Nah. You gotta know Lee. She'll be cautious. She said she keeps one eye open around him now."

This type of thirdhand information was interesting, but I couldn't verify the truth of any of it; it was not going to help me obtain a search warrant to get on the farm. As I continued to listen to Hiscox, I felt a growing frustration that we needed more and hoped an undercover operation would be the key.

"I'll call you Tuesday morning, assuming you'll be released, okay?" I said.

"Sounds good. I don't know if they'll let me go back home or what. My wife came to see me last night, so maybe we can work things out."

"I hope so. I hope it goes well for you," I said. "Can you call me and let me know where you'll be staying?"

"Sure."

I drove back to Vancouver feeling hopeful we could make some inroads into Pickton's activities through Lisa Yelds.

When I got back to my office, I told Al Boyd—who was now my supervisor, since Geramy had been seconded to another investigation—about my dealings with Hiscox, and we agreed that this should be an RCMP investigation, since the farm was in the Coquitlam RCMP jurisdiction. I had already phoned and left a message for Mike Connor on my way home.

Mike and I played phone tag for several days and finally spoke in late September. He was excited by this new information and the progress I was making with Hiscox, but he was also deeply concerned about the threat to Anderson. We felt it was imperative that he find her and warn her she could be in danger. We also agreed that Mike would request the services of Special O—the RCMP surveillance unit—to follow Robert Pickton. Within two days, Mike had arranged for surveillance coverage on Pickton from four o'clock in the afternoon until whatever time they "put him to bed"—surveillance jargon for when the team members feel the likelihood that the target will go out again before dawn is minimal. For a man suspected of picking up sex workers in the later hours, this would not be easy.

We also had to consider whether we should allow a man suspected of killing sex workers to pick a woman up on the street. It presented a surveillance catch-22—we couldn't guarantee that a woman would be safe or that the team wouldn't lose Pickton's vehicle, but if we arranged to have Pickton stopped by a marked patrol car every time he picked up a woman, he would quickly suspect surveillance. It's similar to following a sex offender, which we did several times during my tenure in the Strike Force. You can't allow him to break into a home and assault anyone to secure your charge, so often the team must settle for a trespassing arrest, stopping the suspect in the yard or on the front steps of a potential victim's home.

The downside is that the suspect ends up being charged with a much less serious offense than the one we know or strongly suspect he had every intention of committing. At any rate, we were given three days of Special O's time, and Pickton did little to arouse suspicion. He did not try to pick anyone up; nor did he spend any significant time on the Downtown Eastside other than to conduct what appeared to be business relating to his farm.

In the meantime, I had heard from Mike that many members of the Coquitlam RCMP knew the players in a well-established criminal group in Coquitlam, including Yelds. He asked me whether my source had mentioned her, and I had to tell him yes. On October 13, I tracked Hiscox down to a Maple Ridge drug treatment center. I left a message for him, and he returned my call within an hour. Mike also told me that his superiors had no appetite for an undercover operation. At least Mike was there to advocate for the file and protect Hiscox, and that was somewhat comforting to me.

Hiscox was not happy when I told him that the RCMP wanted to contact Yelds directly, but he agreed to meet with Mike and me. He remained very concerned Yelds would discover he'd been talking to the police. He said he would trust whatever I decided and would do what I thought was best. I felt the weight of responsibility that he would place this degree of faith in me, and I vowed to do everything I could to look out for his interests as long as he continued to be on the level with me. I told him that I thought passing him over to the RCMP—ideally, Mike would handle him—would be better than them going straight to Yelds, and he agreed. But he wanted to be out of the picture sooner than later, and he didn't want Yelds to know that he had led the cops to her.

6

Watching Our
Investigation Stall

• • •

"I feel as if I were a piece in a game of chess, when my
opponent says of it: That is a piece that cannot be moved."
SØREN KIERKEGAARD, EITHER/OR

IN MID-OCTOBER, MIKE and I picked Hiscox up from his
treatment facility and drove to Starbucks for a coffee, then
sat in the car in a parking lot and talked. Hiscox looked far
better than when I'd seen him last; his complexion had some
color, and he appeared more rested. He was in his early forties, Caucasian, medium height, and wiry fit in that way men
who've lived and fought hard can be. His face bore scars like a
boxer's over his brow, chin, and bridge of the nose, and he carried himself like an aging hockey player, strong and sure but
sore. He wore a faded ball cap, mackinaw jacket, blue jeans, and
work boots and looked like any other Vancouver area laborer.
I played him the voice lineup I'd created.

"Does that sound like anyone you know?" I asked.

"No, definitely not Willie. More like Dave, but Dave talks kinda like Elmer Fudd, and I don't think it's him," Hiscox responded.

"Can you go through everything that happened that led you to contact Lori, from the beginning for me? I know it's repetitive for you, but it'll help me know where we're at," Mike asked.

Hiscox repeated what he'd told me and delved further into Yelds's contacts than he had with me, because Mike was much more familiar than I was with the players in the Coquitlam outlaw motorcycle gang scene of years gone by. I could tell immediately that Mike saw that Hiscox was the real deal and knew all the players and history.

"Lee saw IDs and bloody clothing in bags when she was cleaning in Willie's trailer, that's what got her to tell me about it," Hiscox said. "She put two and two together with the offer to get rid of bodies in the grinder and the stories about the missing girls on the news and the girl who he stabbed who he says gave him hep. She thinks Willie could be a serial killer, but she's no rat and doesn't want to do anything about it." He snorted lightly. "So, she tells me—and me, I can't just sit on this, I have a duty to do something and I can't live with my conscience and stay quiet about it." He continued telling Mike all he had shared with me.

"Anything else you can think of?" Mike asked. "Anything new?"

"Yeah, Lee also said she saw a purse she thought belonged to a native girl, like it had one of those dream catchers hanging off it. Said she saw that one a couple of years ago now."

The only Indigenous female we had as missing from the Downtown Eastside from around that time was Janet Henry, last seen in July 1997. Janet had frequented the same area as Anderson, and they both were short and had short dark hair. There had been no trace of Janet and no sightings of her, and her welfare checks had gone uncollected since June 1997.

"How do you think we should approach Lisa if we were going to?" Mike asked.

"You have to know Lee. She's tough and she's no rat. It'd have to be undercover. You couldn't, like, knock on her door and say, 'We're the cops, can we talk to you for a sec.'" Hiscox laughed. "Yeah, she wouldn't go for that. She'd slam the door in your face. She hates cops."

"So, you think an undercover operation is the way to go with her." Mike asked. "Would she trust a new person in her life?"

"Not easily, for sure. But if they came with me, she'd let them in."

But when Mike and I spoke alone later, we were both concerned about going this route. An agent essentially works for the police and is directed by the investigators to get what is needed on a case. Once someone agrees to become an agent, they become a compellable witness in any court proceeding and lose their status as a confidential source.

Acting as a police agent is incredibly emotionally demanding, and even the most stable and composed sources can struggle in that role. I had always felt my first responsibility to Bill Hiscox was to him as a person. Although finding the women was extremely important, I didn't want to make him another victim of the investigation. I just couldn't guarantee that making him an agent wouldn't ruin the personal life he was working so hard to rebuild. Mike knew more of the players in Yelds's world and agreed that involving Hiscox in an operation posed risks for him.

We drove Hiscox back to his treatment center.

"We need to figure some stuff out on our end about Lisa," Mike told him. "We'll probably have to contact her one way or another, but we want it to be in a way that doesn't cause you any grief."

"Good." Hiscox hesitated before climbing out of the car. "But you know, if my name comes out, so be it. It's the price to pay for doing the right thing."

After this meeting, I received what I felt was a significant show of support for this investigation from the VPD Major Crime management. Acting Staff Sergeant Brock Giles and I met, and he told me he was committed to providing money to advance the Pickton investigation and help pay for things such as an undercover operation, witness protection, aerial forward looking infrared (FLIR) photography, and land photos. He also offered the VPD's assistance in putting together a joint submission to the Provincial Unsolved Homicide Unit (PUHU).

I called Mike Connor and told him about this offer, but something had happened on the Coquitlam RCMP end. They no longer seemed hot to speak to Yelds, for reasons unknown to me. Mike didn't know what had changed.

It was at this point in the investigation that I began to realize how priorities shifted from one minute to the next in policing organizations—both the RCMP and the VPD—and how something that seemed to be the most pressing matter one minute could be moved to the back burner the next. It seemed that someone could just decide a file wasn't important anymore, with no real basis in fact for that decision and no documentation, certainly none that I would be shown. This was the first of many deaths of the Pickton investigation during my time working on it.

Hiscox contacted me in December 1998 to let me know he was out of detox, clean and sober, and still willing to help us with Pickton. He hadn't seen Yelds since before rehab but offered to get back in touch with her if we wanted him to. He had been staying away from his old crowd in the interests of his rehabilitation, and I told him to focus on his recovery and to let me know if he happened to hear anything. I would contact Mike, and we'd figure out where to go from there. We agreed to let each other know about any new developments. It's unclear to me how Mike got the impression we were out of contact with Hiscox, as he later testified at the Missing Women Commission of Inquiry, because that wasn't the case on my end. When I was able to track Hiscox down and speak with him, he simply didn't have any new information to offer about Pickton. In hindsight, this was another misunderstanding between the RCMP and the VPD, because Mike and I had an excellent working relationship.

I tried to reach Hiscox again in February 1999, but he didn't call me back. I tried again a week later, but still no reply. I became concerned and ran his name through CPIC and PIRS— the RCMP record management system—which indicated he had been in some recent difficulty and would not be available to help us until the end of February. My heart sank. Not knowing what kind of mental shape he would be in, I began to accept that perhaps we had all the information we would get from him.

That same day, we held a meeting about Pickton with members of the Provincial Unsolved Homicide Unit, the Coquitlam RCMP, and the VPD Major Crime and Missing Persons units. We decided to take the unusual step of conducting a photo blitz with the Downtown Eastside sex workers to see whether any of them recognized Pickton from his photograph. Several VPD members completed this assignment after the Coquitlam members were called away on an emergency investigation and were unable to work with us.

We showed Pickton's photograph to eighty sex workers and asked whether they knew him, had dated him, or had any dealings with him of any kind. The answer was always no, no, and no. Later, members of Project Amelia, the Missing Persons Review Team (MWRT) formed in 1999, repeated the procedure at the WISH Drop-In Centre for sex workers and spoke to another fifty women, with the same results. No one batted an eye looking at the photo—an excellent likeness of Pickton and one certain to be recognized by anyone who knew him. Nothing.

It seemed inconceivable to me that none of these women knew Pickton or had been to his property. How could it be that not one would risk blowing the whistle on a killer, even if he did own a great place to party, make some money, and score free dope?

In the meantime, Hiscox's personal difficulties with substance abuse and the law continued, and he told me he was not in touch with the people on the Pickton farm. I realized he would not be of much future help to the investigation if this continued. We were to meet that day at a trailer on a Surrey property, and as I pulled my car up on the dirty, heavily wooded rural lot on the edge of the Fraser River, a chill passed through me and I questioned my decision to come here alone.

I parked several yards from the decrepit office trailer—not unlike the trailer on Pickton's farm—and as I walked toward it, the door opened. Two very rough-looking Indo-Canadian men and a hard-bitten Caucasian woman stepped out and stood in front of me, arms crossed, scowling. They were all in their late thirties or early forties, poorly groomed and dressed in dirty nondescript clothing. I imagined they could be brewing moonshine and breeding fighting dogs out behind the trailer.

"Oh, hey," I said. "I'm looking for a guy named Bill. Is he around?" They stared at me. Scenes from *Deliverance* flashed through my mind. No one moved. I knew it wouldn't do Hiscox any favors if I let these people know we were working together. "Okay, here's my card. Can you have him call me if you see him? I need to talk to him." I stepped toward the nearest man and held out my card. He didn't raise a hand, didn't even look at it, just held his cool gaze on me. I let the card float to the dirt. "Tell him it'll be better for him if he calls me."

I turned and walked back to the car. Within about ten minutes of leaving the property, I received the first of a series of bizarre pages in which a male spoke of a person named Mercury. He also mentioned the name of a very violent and dangerous man I had arrested in the Downtown Eastside in my first years on patrol, and hearing this name after all these years both baffled and unnerved me, so random and seemingly unrelated was this information. The caller referred to the pig farmer and dirty cops, and I felt dismayed because it sounded a lot like Hiscox. He mentioned an RCMP inspector working in Richmond, but his voice cut out on the name and it wasn't clear what his involvement was.

Hiscox had either gone off the rails or was trying to pass me a message in some convoluted way. I also suspected that someone from the trailer was unhappy about my visit and had contacted him. Just as I was about to give up and head back to Vancouver, my pager went off again. It was a voice message from Hiscox letting me know he'd been arrested and was being held in Surrey pretrial and we could meet there. I turned the car around.

When I arrived at pretrial, I asked Hiscox who Mercury was and he feigned shock that I would know the name. The meeting was not a good one, and I questioned his mental fitness. He looked rough, and he told me he'd been injured during his arrest. I wanted to forget about the strange Mercury messages because I suspected they weren't relevant to the investigation and I needed to remain focused. But I couldn't rule anything out, no matter how far-fetched it seemed, until I was certain the information wasn't germane.

The Mercury red herring became a strange and annoying detour for a few weeks and left me even more concerned that

Hiscox was no longer credible because of his paranoid mental state. I couldn't confirm that he was behind the strange pages, but I did not feel confident about involving him in any future undercover operations or introductions and worried that this would further limit our ability to get closer to Pickton and Yelds. I was disappointed, but I continued to look for ways to get on the Pickton farm.

That was the extent of my dealings with Bill Hiscox until February 2002, though I made regular attempts to check in with him. Whenever we spoke, he was eager to try to help, but he had no new information to offer.

7

The Missing Women

• • •

*"If the misery of the poor be caused not by the laws of
nature, but by our institutions, great is our sin."*
CHARLES DARWIN, THE VOYAGE OF THE BEAGLE

*F THEY WERE from Kerrisdale or UBC, you'd be doing more to
find them.*

Repeatedly, this cry arose from various sources—sometimes
as an observation, more often as a direct criticism. I responded
to it with force, vigorously denying—both inwardly and out-
wardly—that we would ever make such a distinction between
the people we served.

*There's no difference; we treat all people the same. We have to
because it's the right and just thing.*

Not only did I desperately want to believe this, I did believe
it, deep in my heart. Anyone who said or thought we would
make this distinction didn't know us, didn't know the way we
worked. It was only as the investigation wore on that I saw
that only some of us worked that way and that there were
whole institutions, an entire justice system, an economic and

political system that did not see the victims in the same light as UBC students or young women living in the upscale communities of Kerrisdale or Point Grey or Kitsilano.

For the first eight months, I fell into the role of unofficial spokesperson for the VPD on this investigation, partly of my own initiative because our media spokesperson, Anne Drennan, was busy and it took more of my time to brief her fully than to simply talk with the media myself. This was in no way a criticism of Anne, but we worked in different buildings, we were both very busy, the investigation was complex, and meeting to discuss it was difficult.

Repeatedly, I would answer this criticism with an earnest explanation of all we were doing to find these women. And I believed it. I believed we were doing all we could because I was working harder than I had ever worked in my life to determine what could have happened to these women and why women kept disappearing. I explained that with other women we would have homes to search—offices, date books, PalmPilots, and purses to sift through for clues. We would interview coworkers who worried when the women didn't show up at the office, spouses who expected them to walk in the door with the groceries for dinner, children left standing in front of school waiting to be picked up. All baffled by these disappearances that would be totally out of character and had never happened before.

The victims lived on the fringes of what many viewed as normal society, and although they were known and valued in their Downtown Eastside community, their lives looked very different from the lives of UBC students or Kerrisdale women. Days could pass without friends or street sisters seeing them, and boyfriends might not hear from them for a week or two and assume they were in jail or had found a situation with drugs and a couch where they could pass some time. Street workers and nurses might miss them for a few days, but they rarely became alarmed until more time passed. Cell phones weren't common among sex workers in the late 1990s, and they made calls on pay phones or from a friend's place. Not even family members the women called regularly would worry if one or two expected calls didn't come. After years of worrying needlessly, they rarely became alarmed if they didn't speak for a few days or even weeks. Many of the missing women continued to manage calls to family on special occasions, however, and when these stopped their children, sisters, and mothers knew something was wrong.

Even though I was searching for people comprising part of the highest risk group in society, my investigation was not subject to scrutiny or oversight. No one demanded I report regularly on any progress; every bit of information I passed up the chain of command was of my own initiative, rarely in response to any query from above. I was given the assignment to assess the missing women cases but little guidance beyond that.

One afternoon in late 1998, Detective Ron Lepine of the Homicide section entered the Missing Persons office and sat down. I didn't know him well then—this was before he would join us on Project Amelia the following spring. He always said hello, and he had a warm paternal bearing, a kind face and a slightly nasal voice. He was probably five years away from retirement by then but remained energetic and enthusiastic.

"What do you think has happened to these ladies?" he asked as he looked at their photos above my desk.

"Well, Ron, I just don't know," I began. "My list keeps getting longer, and no one seems to know why. No even seems to keep track of sex workers, they just fall through the cracks and no one seems to think that's a concern. But they haven't picked up their checks—some of them for months and months—and that makes me think they aren't alive anymore."

He nodded thoughtfully. "You know, before Homicide, I worked in Vice for a long time." He leaned forward, elbows on his knees. "The sex trade has changed a lot in a very short time. Mostly because of crack, I think. These ladies used to work circuits, like the Calgary Stampede, Klondike Days. Some even went to Hawaii occasionally to work. They could sit on a plane for five hours without fixing. They could function at that kind of level. But the low track has evolved into something where they aren't going anywhere and the bosses, especially if they're old Vice squad guys who haven't kept up, they don't understand that. They still think these ladies have pulled up stakes and moved somewhere, and I just don't see that happening in this day and age."

"That makes sense, because no one seems to think their going missing means much. No one seems to think they're really 'missing,' you know?" I said.

He nodded again. "And if they don't think that, they won't treat this like the crisis it is. You can't change these old dinosaurs' minds easily," he said.

Ron was right. This mistaken knowledge of our victim demographic contributed greatly to our inability to garner support and resources for the investigation. I couldn't seem to gather the proof I needed to show this was a crisis and women were dying.

Most of the victims had gone missing before for varying lengths of time. During these periods, many were never actually missing—some had gone underground to hide out from a violent ex or a ripped-off drug dealer or had entered detox for another attempt at getting clean. Others simply left town for a while and hadn't thought it important to tell anyone because no one had cared what they did or where they were to this point, so why should they now? However, for many this time proved different. They were missing for growing periods of time, none was showing up alive or dead, and the numbers were unusual and rising.

Slowly, I would begin to see that the critics were right. If these women were from any other walk of life, there would be total outrage—search parties, volunteers, roadblocks. If they were a group of loggers or accountants, the hunt would be on to find them. But they were sex workers, drug addicts, and somewhere in all of this, that bell continued to ring—*They chose this life, they chose the risk.* On a very deep level, a large segment of society and the policing community didn't feel these women were worth searching for, and many people questioned whether they even wanted to be found. The sense in many circles was they knowingly put themselves in harm's way. They were on their own. Many of my colleagues felt this way:

They're like bad pennies. They'll turn up.

She probably found love and has gone off to start a family.

No doubt she's ripped someone off again and is hiding out somewhere.

They come and go from the reserves all the time, that's where you'll find them.

Have you checked detox? Lots of 'em go to detox, you know.

I'd respond to these comments with the questions: Then why aren't they calling their families? Why aren't they picking up their welfare checks? I'd get a shrug in return. *Don't know. Don't care.*

Years later, we would learn that several more were *actually* missing at that time, but we were not yet aware of them because they hadn't been reported missing by anyone, the missing persons reports were filed in jurisdictions outside of Vancouver, or our own Missing Persons office had misfiled, misplaced, or otherwise mishandled the case. This posed an obvious problem: the police agencies in the Lower Mainland, B.C., and Canada were not linked by any reliable information management system at that time. One of the first things I did, in July 1998, was send out a CPIC message to all Canadian municipal policing agencies and RCMP detachments.

I explained I was investigating the mysterious disappearances of women who worked on the street. I asked that they contact me if any of these agencies carried any similar files in which the last known location of their victim was Vancouver and we could determine if that woman belonged on our list. I also asked whether any other jurisdictions had a missing sex worker problem. The responses—when I received any response at all—were shocking.

Many of the agencies were confused by my request because they didn't keep statistics on such people, since they went missing all the time and led very transient lives. The Toronto Police Service said they didn't classify their missing people by "occupation" and therefore could not say whether they had a particular problem with missing sex workers. The intelligence officer there told me they didn't search for missing street people and would only be alerted to a problem if the media discovered one. The media. I began to get a sense of what I was up against, or so I thought.

I saw no indication among most experienced police officers that they felt these missing women—who numbered in the high teens at that point—were missing as a result of foul play. The unofficial but pervasive feeling within policing circles was that they had gone on one of several prostitution circuits, met men known as "marks" who were willing to take them away from street life, left the life of their own accord, or just picked up sticks and moved on to another location.

I began my career working on the Downtown Eastside in both patrol and in the now-defunct Prostitution Task Force and got to know several of the women on the list. For six months in 1992–93, I stood on a cold lonely corner of the industrial district and turned tricks to arrest johns as an undercover operator. I wasn't an expert, but I knew in my gut none of these scenarios represented what was really going on. But what was? Just because my victims engaged with their community differently from a university student or suburban housewife didn't mean they didn't engage. They moved throughout their community and availed themselves of various services; they just weren't always predictable or dependable, which made tracking them more difficult.

Through my CPIC search, I did find two files I determined fit our victim profile: women, survival sex workers, with serious drug addictions living in the Downtown Eastside. Survival sex work is exchanging sexual acts for money to sustain and support one's basic survival needs. Many underage runaways and drug addicts use sex work to support themselves and avoid homelessness. I requested these files be sent to me for inclusion on our list. They were Marnie Frey and Taressa Williams.

Marnie was from Campbell River, B.C., but had been a resident of the Downtown Eastside for years. Her stepmother, Lynn Frey, had reported Marnie missing to the Campbell River RCMP in 1997, after Marnie uncharacteristically failed to call home as she had regularly done, despite her troubles. Taressa was a woman from the Semiahmoo First Nation in White Rock, B.C. A runaway from the age of fourteen, she seemed to have no one searching for her other than a concerned and conscientious Mountie who felt certain she had met with foul play, but his investigation had hit a dead end.

I felt a great deal of unease surrounding the victims. Were there others out there we were unaware of or had written off for some reason or another? I lost sleep wondering whether that one unknown woman might hold the key, but I moved forward with the files I had. Once I felt reasonably sure we had as many victims as we could possibly be aware of on our list, I began to review their files yet again, looking for links or anything I might have missed the first time through.

A Letter to Sarah de Vries

* * *

DEAR SARAH,

I feel as though you and I have somehow been partners on this strange journey. We both came to this investigation in 1998, you a couple of short months before me—the mentor, a big sister of sorts, much in the same way you were one to so many of the girls on the street.

I had known you on the street but not nearly as well as I would come to know you after you left. You were a writer, a gifted, educated, articulate young woman defeated by a world that seemed unable to allow you to just be—to be a woman of color in a white family, to be different and beautiful and yet not be seen as some sort of commodity or jewel to be had, possessed. You struggled valiantly, but in the end, your pain brought you to the Downtown Eastside, and it was that pain that made you such a compassionate friend to so many.

The men who used you, the men who purported to love you—it was nearly impossible to tell the difference between them. Could you? Did you ever know which to trust? I had always got the sense you saw above and beyond the bullshit.

You knew who was giving you a line and who really wanted to see you do well—you worked the middle ground and got what you needed without giving up too much of yourself. Was that how it was for you?

You and your family—Maggie; your mom, Pat; your aunt Jean; Jeanie; Ben—are all so inextricably tied into these years for me. I feel in many ways you are—or should be—the poster child for this tragedy. You are every daughter, every person's schoolmate, every young girl's best friend from Brownies—perhaps you represent just how vulnerable we all are, our children all are. And it scares us, doesn't it? We don't want to say, *Look what happened to Sarah. She came from a good neighborhood, went to a good school, had two parents at home, every advantage—look what happened to her.*

More than with any other family, I have wanted to open up to yours. Perhaps it's because yours is a family of writers, or because I've found them to be so even, so thoughtful and balanced, even in their assessment of this case, this heartbreak, this world. They are phenomenal women, your mom, Jean, Maggie, Jeanie. I often bump up against that keen awareness that I must walk that line between speaking from the heart and speaking as a part of this goddamn investigation that makes us all walk and talk like automatons.

When I called your mom to tell her about Pickton's arrest, she was out and your aunt Jean answered. You'd get a kick out of this, I know. Her first question to me was *What are you reading these days?* And we entered into a lengthy discussion of the latest mystery writers—not really my thing, but she assumed as a cop it would be, and I was just thrilled to talk to someone about something other than this horrible man and the horrible things he'd done. Maggie was equally warm, wanting to know how I was after I had just given her this oddly bittersweet news. In her quiet voice she whispered the words to me I will never forget: *This is that man you had told me about, isn't it?*

When I think of you, I think of that fit, well-groomed young woman rollerblading around the Downtown Eastside, grooving to her Walkman—you always reminded me of those images we often see from war-torn countries of children playing a game of soccer or basketball in the midst of mass destruction and total disarray. It was as though you were able to transport yourself away from that filth, back to Kits Beach or UBC. Back to somewhere supposedly safe.

You touched a great many people. I think those people have a difficult time accepting you didn't survive your journey. I think everyone expected you would be someone who would hit bottom, then bounce back to do amazing things and teach others what you had learned about yourself and this often harsh world. In the back of my mind, I guess I felt about you the way some parents feel about a favorite child—that you more than anyone would be okay, that you would turn up, that in some way, I wouldn't have to worry for you the way I did the others because *you would make it.*

I still half-expect to see you come rollerblading around the corner, world tuned out, earphones on.

8

Looking for Links

• • •

"Justice must always question itself, just as society can exist only by means of the work it does on itself and on its institutions."
MICHEL FOUCAULT, LIBÉRATION

ONE OF THE first things I set out to do was link as many of the missing women's files as I could. I scanned each one, hoping to find a name, a place, a contact each of the women might have shared, but the only name was drug addiction, the only place the Downtown Eastside, and the only shared contacts an endless parade of men in cars and on foot buying their bodies by the hour or by the act.

Common sense dictated that victims sharing a lifestyle, a neighborhood, and an occupation were linked. But something inside me strained against the assumption that these three things completely defined any of these women. To lump them together simply because they were "junkie hookers" would be to ignore potentially relevant details. I knew I had to examine their individual circumstances and personalities—their uniqueness.

File by file, I read about the families they were estranged from and marveled at how long it took for anyone to file a missing persons report. I would learn of all the reasons for this: the women were transient, they often did not keep in touch with loved ones, and those who did file a missing persons report would often receive inconsistent information and face indifference from the police. It was like a giant game of pass the buck. Families assumed the girls were just in transition, police assumed they didn't want to be located for various reasons, and street workers in the Downtown Eastside community who knew these women best wrung their hands in frustration because they knew something was wrong and no one was listening. It was a vicious cycle, and precious time was wasted.

My work delving into the women's files ran parallel to my ongoing investigation of Robert Pickton, and I searched to find places where the victims might have connected with him. Left home at thirteen. Four children before the age of twenty-five. Sexually abused by some variation of parents, adoptive parents, stepparents, foster parents, siblings, relatives, family friends, and strangers. Criminal convictions for everything from prostitution to drug possession to assault to break-and-enter to robbery. Infected with HIV, AIDS, hepatitis, tuberculosis. What the files did not contain were words like *bright, intelligent, athletic, tough, resourceful, artistic, talented, sensitive, funny, afraid.*

I read and reread the files—nearly twenty at that time. I began to notice that none of these women was under the age of twenty at the time they went missing. Each was known as street-smart and was a relatively longtime resident of the Downtown Eastside. When I was a new constable working in the area, a social worker told me that the average life expectancy of a person living on the Downtown Eastside was seven years. Many of these women had been down there four, five, six years or more. These women had not survived this long by being stupid; they obviously had skills and savvy.

Each of these women was seriously drug addicted, sick to such an extent that to leave the heart of an area where drugs and services were readily available caused them panic, anxiety, and emotional and physical breakdown. They seldom strayed from the core of the Downtown Eastside other than for a rare visit with family, to attend detox, to escape the threat of an angry boyfriend or someone they had ripped off, or to party where drugs would be a sure thing. They were sick, addicted, dirty, and scarred, and they knew they were not marketable anywhere but on the filthy, desperate streets of the Downtown Eastside.

A very small number of the victims seemed to work or live in the Mount Pleasant area, in those days a sort of drug addict's bedroom community south of the Downtown Eastside that has since become a trendy and much more expensive area. Many of the drug users in Vancouver lived there and came to the Downtown Eastside to work the streets and buy their drugs. The area was cleaner and safer and resembled many of the areas of East Vancouver, with a mixture of low-rise apartments and run-down houses split into rental suites.

It was a short, often perilous walk or bus ride along Main Street from the Downtown Eastside to Mount Pleasant. Along the way, there were several cheap beer parlors and hotels, each with its own subculture and cliques—all potentially dangerous for a woman who might owe money or anger the wrong person at the wrong time. The remainder of the victims seemed to live right down in the five- or six-square-block area surrounding the heart of the Downtown Eastside—Main and Hastings, or Pain and Wastings, as many locals referred to it.

We had no information that any one of the missing women had disappeared from a particular location or even a certain area of the city. Aside from Inga Hall and Sarah de Vries, we were unable to pin down disappearances to a specific day, and in many cases, the last cashed welfare check was our best indication of when they had last been safe—a window of a month.

Inga Hall had been working the street with her daughter Violet* early one morning in 1998. Violet returned from a trick and was keen to go home to their East Vancouver apartment and fix, but Inga wanted to hold out for one more date, so Violet went home without her. Violet never saw her mother again. When we began seeking out the families of the victims to provide DNA samples, Violet was Inga's only immediate family member. I had been in contact with another family member who had been searching for Inga to give her an inheritance, but when she learned of Inga's disappearance, she gave up her investigation.

My heart broke when I met with Violet. She was thin, wasted, and heavily addicted. Her mind virtually gone, she had trouble following our conversation. She agreed to give me a buccal swab for DNA testing, and I met her in her room, thinking it was lucky I had reached her when I did because she wouldn't be alive much longer given her current health. She had no concept of what DNA testing was or even that Inga wasn't coming back. I worried that Violet was probably incapable of consciously consenting to provide me with her saliva sample, but she signed the form and I took the sample anyway, believing that what I was doing was for the greater good.

Three locations kept popping up in my work—the corner of Princess and Cordova Streets, the Astoria Hotel, and a run-down rooming house on East Hastings that doubled as a brothel and a shooting gallery for heroin users. Still, all I knew was that many of the women had been to these places or had ties there.

This would prove typical of this investigation—all sorts of arrows would point in a certain direction, but then there was nothing more, despite my digging and looking into potential leads and possible links, nothing to indicate I was on the right track and should carry on with a particular track. Each lead would just fizzle out and dry up no matter how much I struggled to make it into something—*anything*—of value. Each lead floated like a gigantic cartoon balloon over my head emblazoned with the words YEAH, SO? So many times, I would have to decide whether to continue what seemed like flogging a dead horse or to move on to some other seemingly more promising lead. Without the time, personnel, or resources to go down every rabbit hole, I moved on.

All I could confirm was that each of these women had at some time frequented at least one of these three places, but that was hardly unusual for residents of the Downtown Eastside with drug addictions and was comparable to saying that each of the women had a drug problem or lived in poverty. The community was small and fluid; many of the residents moved from one rooming house, hotel, or corner to the next, spending varying amounts of time in a particular spot. The bottom line was each of these women was no more likely to meet someone dangerous in one of these locations than anywhere else on the Downtown Eastside—they were at risk everywhere, and a chance meeting with a predator could go unnoticed in the strange drug-and-alcohol-addled parade that went on twenty-four hours a day.

I learned that even among the low-track workers of the Downtown Eastside there was a pecking order, and I was dismayed to hear about what are known as "beer whores" in the skid row area. These poor women worked in the relative safety of the beer parlors and scummy bars in the three or four blocks surrounding the notorious Balmoral Hotel, hanging around men they hoped would buy them glasses of draft in exchange for sex acts in the bar washrooms or the rooms of adjoining hotels.

As I looked at the women's lives individually, I hoped to find someone with an axe to grind, an unresolved child custody dispute, past convictions for violence against them—anything to warrant an interview with an actual person who might have had a reason to want to harm any of them. This was a path that had to be explored, despite the question nagging at me: *If they were killed individually by different men, why weren't we finding bodies?* None of the so-called suspects who warranted an interview were particularly sophisticated; nor did many of them have the means to dispose of a body—or twenty to thirty bodies— without someone seeing or knowing something. It is not an easy thing to commit a murder and not leave a body that will eventually be found, even after elaborate attempts to dispose of it, as even reportedly highly intelligent killers soon discover.

Investigators interviewed many of these men when the women were first reported missing. Others were dead, and a small number had never been interviewed for reasons unknown to me. One by one, I began to locate and interview these men, and after each interview, I would conclude that several were disturbed, with histories of violence, but there was no evidence to take me any further, no real motive to indicate they had killed or contributed to the disappearances of these women. They had their own problems, their own addictions, their own sorry lives to deal with, and I found that man after man, no one stood out to me as having anything obvious to hide or any need to be bothered with killing anyone. Still, they had to be ruled out, and I certainly couldn't do that based on one interview.

Scouring file after file, I saw no clear indication that any more than two or three of these women definitely went missing from within the confines of Vancouver. For all anyone knew, they could have disappeared from Vancouver Island, from the U.S., from the Interior of B.C.—there were no clues and no information saying so-and-so was last seen in such and such a place. None of these women told family and friends they were going anywhere. I knew they probably had gone missing from Vancouver streets, but I couldn't confirm this and, therefore, had no logical starting point for any type of search or canvass, no place to begin collecting surveillance videotapes or speaking to business owners who might have seen something. Nothing.

I also had little idea of what date any of them disappeared, with the exceptions of Sarah de Vries and Inga Hall. A good example was Helen Hallmark, who we later determined through her welfare file had disappeared sometime around August 1997 but was not reported missing until September 1998. Most of the other cases were less extreme, but the window of time was usually wide—often several months passed between the time a family member had last spoken to a woman and the time the police were notified of her disappearance. There was really no one to blame—the families were used to this sort of sporadic contact and had long ago learned to worry in solitude, since the girls always showed up eventually. How were they to know that this time they wouldn't show up? That those lost hours and days would be precious if there was any hope of finding them?

Checking rooming house records proved much less helpful than looking at welfare files. Many of the hotels on the Downtown Eastside fudged records, double-booked, and charged extra to allow drug dealing and prostitution in the rooms. Typically, the management was not strong on documentation, and lists of occupants were kept in a hodgepodge, with just enough detail to satisfy a police beat team who might ask to see them but hardly the type of log to help track someone down. Many of the lodgers used false names and identification to avoid detection by either the police or creditors. When occupants failed to show up for a few days, they weren't missed, but management usually tossed their belongings out to make room for new paying residents. Few stopped to wonder where an old tenant might be, and if the belongings weren't claimed within a few more days, they were sent to the dump.

These missing women were on their own—those who did stay in touch with family often only told them the good news and spared them the sordid details of their lives, such as who was looking to lay a beating on them, what despicable thing a bad date had done to them last night, where they were getting their money, and who their friends and boyfriends were that week. By attempting to spare their families, these women isolated themselves even further.

Yet another obstacle was our inability to access medical records. This was part of a larger problem. Since we could not prove that any of the women had been victims of crime, they were considered missing and as such government agencies and hospitals treated this as a privacy issue, refusing to release any information without the victims' consent. I made attempts to have the families request this information, but this was not acceptable for a variety of very understandable reasons again relating to privacy law. I began to wonder if some of these women had died—in hospital or extended care facilities somewhere under aliases—and we simply hadn't been notified because no one had made the connection and fingerprinted them.

I found an ally in provincial chief coroner Larry Campbell. Together, we decided in mid-1999 to enlist the broad powers of the Coroners Act to investigate these women's medical histories and see whether there might be some reason why they had not been located. This enabled Larry to assert our belief that the women had been the victims of foul play and that they were probably dead. In this way, Larry could argue that these files were the responsibility of the Coroners Service because they had a duty to try to identify them if they were deceased.

Many of the victims had been known to use aliases to avoid arrest for outstanding warrants, but we were only aware of what some of those names were. I began to investigate what steps hospitals used to identify patients who were admitted unconscious and without identification. The results were not encouraging. I could not convince anyone I spoke with in the provincial government to go on the record for my file, but several officials advised me that hospitals were not in the business of identifying people. Essentially, if someone came in with a library card, B.C. Identification Card, or something similarly lacking official standing bearing the name Sally Smith, the hospitals would be satisfied this was Sally Smith. If this woman died in hospital, the police would not be called to fingerprint her as is the procedure when someone dies without any identification—she would die as Sally Smith unless someone came forward to say otherwise, which was nearly impossible considering no one who knew this woman would be likely to know she was in hospital in the first place.

Hundreds of people die indigent every year in British Columbia. Several agencies deal with these deaths—the Ministry of Children and Family Development, the Public Guardian and Trustee, the Ministry of Social Development and Social Innovation—but they all work under the assumption that the deceased is the person they believe him or her to be. Often it is impossible to locate next of kin, so the deceased is interred by Glenhaven funeral home in Vancouver. Some of the missing women could have died in hospital using false identities and no one would ever have known what became of them.

This situation poked one potentially gaping hole in my assertion that body disposal was very difficult for a criminal:

if some of the victims died through noncriminal means and fell through this crack, we would never be informed. I couldn't imagine that this scenario accounted for all the victims. Nor could it account for the sudden spike in numbers of missing women specifically; if women were dying and falling through this crack in the system, surely men would fall victim in the same way consistently over time. Yet we had no similar problem with men missing from the Downtown Eastside.

9

Project Amelia
(the Missing Persons Review Team)

• • •

*"Why, if it was an illusion, not praise the catastrophe, whatever
it was, that destroyed illusion and put truth in its place?"*
VIRGINIA WOOLF, A ROOM OF ONE'S OWN

IN MAY 1999, we formed Project Amelia, the Missing Persons
Review Team (MWRT), and I was thrilled. The spring and
summer of 1999 proved to be the most dynamic period
during my time searching for the missing women, and it felt as
though we were making real progress. We were actively investigating the information we had about Pickton, investigating
each of the women's files individually, liaising with the coroner's office, and tracking unidentified human remains through
the RCMP. I became the administrative lead, or file coordinator,
in addition to the lead investigator, both roles that, according
to the tenets of the Major Crime case management system,
were never intended to be performed by one person.

The VPD of 1998 did not employ the major case management system. Indeed, only one member of our department,

Doug LePard, had even been trained, and none of the principles were addressed in VPD policy at that time. I had no training and no idea each role was to be filled by a different investigator. The B.C. RCMP developed this system in the late '90s, and it was primitive in comparison with the well-oiled major case machine police use today. Because our victims were missing but not known to have been abducted or murdered, the cases never fit the requirements for consideration as a "major case." Ridiculously, under these old or nonexistent definitions, their risky lifestyles were not considered when assessing their vulnerability or applicability as a major case.

The file coordinator is essentially the overseer of the investigation, responsible for setting up administrative systems to collect, manage, and process all the information and evidence brought into the investigation in a manner acceptable for court. Their role is to take a long view of the case and troubleshoot any legal and investigative concerns to ensure everything is as per proper police procedure. The lead investigator determines where the evidence is leading and oversees the other detectives as they track down leads, interview witnesses, and interrogate suspects. The file coordinator conducts a more administrative function, whereas the lead investigator performs more of the hands-on sleuthing. Together, they chart the strategic course for the investigation.

Following the advice from Axel Hovbrender, I asked for help and documented everything. He was the first supervisor—besides Peter Ditchfield, my former Strike Force Inspector—who shared my sense of doom about this case. Axel had been around long enough to know that the right things weren't just magically going to happen and the most I could do was try my best for these women and try to protect myself.

In spring 1999, I made an official request for personnel, and Detective Constable Alex Clarke, Constable Dave Dickson,

Detective Constable Mark Chernoff, Detective Ron Lepine, and Sergeant Geramy Field were assigned to help in our search. Robbery clerk Dorothy Alford would be our support and data entry person. Finally, there seemed to be an acknowledgment of the seriousness of this case and the need for more resources, so now we could make a concerted effort to solve these disappearances. Once again, how naïve I was and how sadly misguided my optimism.

Alex Clarke would help me with the file coordinator's role and partner with me should we need to go out on the road to conduct follow-up work. Mark Chernoff and Ron Lepine were partners normally assigned to Homicide, and their first task would be to review the unsolved murder files of several Downtown Eastside women whose bodies had been found in outlying RCMP jurisdictions: Tracy Olajide, Tammy Pipe, Mary Lidguerre, Carrie Gordon, and Victoria Younker.

Dave Dickson remained a VPD patrol constable and long-time Downtown Eastside soldier well known for his work with sex workers and children. Over the years, Dave had built an excellent rapport with and reputation in the community and gave our group some much-needed credibility on the street. He would be available to us half time; the other half he would devote to his duties working closely with social workers and children's advocates to keep young people from joining our growing list of victims in years to come.

Geramy was one of the two homicide sergeants and would be our supervisor under Inspector Fred Biddlecombe and Staff Sergeant Brock Giles. Unfortunately, Geramy, Mark, and Ron would be expected to continue their duties in Homicide and could easily be pulled away from Project Amelia at any given time if they were assigned a new murder case. Initially, I didn't foresee the problems that would be caused by the fact that several of us were essentially doing two jobs, and the stress placed on those of us working with inadequate supervision weighed heavily. This lack of departmental commitment to our project meant that we couldn't properly investigate the women's disappearances and would contribute greatly to the failure of the project.

I had requested nine additional investigators and received what was effectively two, considering that only Alex and I were assigned full time to the project. I was told we would be getting two more people soon, but they had not been identified. I had envisioned that we would receive two people of the caliber of those working in the Home Invasion Task Force, originally headed by Sergeant Doug LePard, the only VPD member at the time who had received any formal training in major case management. Doug put this group together—an investigative dream team—and once they were up and running, he returned to his position supervising the Domestic Violence and Criminal Harassment Unit. Detective Constable Tom McCluskie, another highly experienced investigator, took over as the acting sergeant supervising the Home Invasion Task Force.

At its peak, the Home Invasion Task Force had between eight and twelve investigators—all highly competent detectives normally assigned to various sections of the Investigation Division. This group received funding and equipment from several outside sources, including B.C. Tel, all of which provided them with cell phones, call display office phones, extra vehicles, and a video display terminal for use at local malls as a public information booth both warning of the dangers of home invasion and showing video of suspects in the hope that someone could identify them.

Granted, the two investigations were markedly different, and Project Amelia did receive office phones when the Home Invasion group downsized from two offices to one, enabling us to occupy that first project room. As time passed, I would

peer into their office longingly, trying to imagine how different
our investigation would be if we had the same type of support
from management, if we had the same type of enthusiasm and
full-time commitment from experienced investigators, if we
had the same engagement and commitment from the community. New detectives dreamed of being asked to join the Home
Invasion Task Force; those same people avoided Project Amelia
like the plague, uninterested in searching for a bunch of missing "whores," as several referred to them. It was particularly
discouraging to see the bandwagon-jumping that occurred
once the search on the Pickton farm began in earnest in 2002.

Suddenly, many of these same investigators scrambled for
invitations to work on "the farm," and what was previously
thought to be the Siberia of investigative work was now considered the sexiest case out there, a career maker. I happened to
overhear Tom McCluskie speaking with some other members
in the building a few days after he had been seconded to Surrey
to work on the Pickton file, describing it as "a great investigation." He was right, of course. The old me could have easily
been that person calling it a great investigation. It had always
been a great investigation for an eager detective. *Where were
these people when we needed them?* Investigators who didn't know
I had been the lead investigator of this fiasco for more than
two years would say things to me like *You should try to get out to
the farm. It's the case of a lifetime,* or *This would be a great place for your
career. You should try to get out there.* I just stared at them, glassy-
eyed, mumbled something to the effect of *You can have it* and
walked away. How greatly these two years would change me.

When Project Amelia was being set up, I was concerned
that I lacked the experience of a Tom McCluskie or a Doug
LePard, but I began to feel a certain degree of confidence in my
knowledge of this investigation and the things I had learned
over the past year. I felt that with the right people involved,

Project Amelia could be successful, and I had high expectations of finding our victims and making arrests. What Alex, Dave, and I lacked in Homicide experience, Mark, Ron, and Geramy could provide, and I naïvely assumed the two new people coming in would be competent. Little did I know that Project Amelia would have no mandate from management, no budget, and little guidance, just a token show of VPD support for a project that no one cared about and even fewer felt any long-term responsibility for.

My immediate concern was to establish a case management system to maintain and analyze what I knew would be volumes and volumes of information collected by Project Amelia. I had only ever put together individual case files, and now I needed to know how to document, collect, and store complex information in a way that could be easily analyzed, searched, and presented in court—because from the start I envisioned that we would arrest someone and that the case would be brought before the courts. We had to be ready. Otherwise, why were we here?

Biddlecombe had been negotiating to purchase a computer system called SIUSS—Special Investigative Unit Support System—that was billed as the latest and greatest in criminal case management systems. I was told it would have the capability to track and link information about suspects, vehicles, locations, investigators, and evidence and prepare it in a comprehensible manner for presentation in court when the time came. The RCMP had used SIUSS successfully in a murder case in Abbotsford, but I would later learn that investigators had had concerns about SIUSS and ended up designing their own system, Evidence and Report I (E&R I), which the RCMP and other departments would use for all such cases.

The VPD purchased several SIUSS licenses, and training began for the people chosen to operate the system. Three VPD detective constables in other departments were the only investigators to receive the training, because they were all currently working in analyst positions. I requested the training because I felt it was important as the file coordinator to understand the system, but my admission was denied because of the cost. Our administrative person, Dorothy Alford, and Sexual Offence Squad administrative assistant Emer Fitzgerald also received training, because they would be involved in data entry using SIUSS, but theirs was a cheaper lite version and not very comprehensive. Dorothy would become the person we most relied upon for SIUSS entry, yet her training was far from adequate and hardly fair to her.

I made the mistake of trusting in and relying heavily on this system to collect all of the information gathered over the next year and a half, as well as store what had been collected in our victim files in previous years. The promised support contract that supposedly came with the system never materialized, and when SIUSS changed the platform for the program we were not notified. One morning, our staff logged in and found a completely foreign system. Little follow-up training was ever provided.

We had a huge backlog of information from the twenty-some victim files that formed the foundation of our case and needed to be entered in SIUSS. Without this vital information, we might miss a link that could be key to solving the case. Dorothy, who was working hard to enter information into SIUSS, assured me that this would be done, but she later told me that the data entry team had decided to only enter the "bare bones" victim information and return to those files later to enter the rest more completely. At the time, the lack of SIUSS personnel assigned to Project Amelia was at the root of this problem, and over time, this vital victim information did not get into the SIUSS system.

Management would not reassign additional siuss people temporarily or full time, and I was tasked with trying to recruit them on overtime to come in and help us when they could. This situation prevented any continuity or systematic entry of data. Few people wanted to work overtime, especially in a windowless room in summer. As a detective constable, I had no authority to reassign anyone, and no one in management would take the initiative, because they didn't want to fight with these people's managers to bring them over from another understaffed unit to help us.

Geramy and Fred told me this was simply how it was, despite my explanation of the obvious problems with this situation. This was one of the many times I should have put my foot down harder and demand that a proper job be done, but whenever I did, I was always told there was no money or no people available and I'd have to understand that this was the way things were. I voiced my concern that what we were doing was tantamount to building a house with only a fraction of a proper foundation, but they merely shook their heads and said that was the best they could do. How were we to find links and common threads when most of our known information—the contents of the victims' files—was not entered into the database? It seemed ludicrous and incredibly shortsighted to me.

Shortly after setup, we received news that our new investigators would be coming to us in a matter of days. Geramy told me that Deputy Chief Constable Brian McGuinness himself handpicked Wayne Myers* and Gary Fisk* to join our team. I was surprised. Not only did they have even less experience dealing with major files than I had, they brought with them a dubious reputation, both on the street and among their fellow officers. Geramy shared some of my concerns but told me this was who we were getting and we would have to make the most of it. I went to speak to Biddlecombe about my misgivings, and he told me he shared them. He knew the two well from his days leading the Internal Investigation Section and was not happy they were joining our team.

We heard they had a hot potential suspect—Person of Interest (POI) 390, as he became known throughout the Missing Women Commission of Inquiry—and they pitched this guy to the RCMP Provincial Unsolved Homicide Unit in Surrey in an attempt to have themselves assigned out there to work on catching him, circumventing the VPD and the chain of command. Our team had no idea who this suspect might be, and I couldn't understand why they wouldn't have shared this information with our investigation from the start. This was my first indication that they weren't team players.

The RCMP told them to take their suspect and their information back to the VPD, since that was where the investigation had originated and where all of the victims seem to have disappeared. They appealed to their only ally in the VPD upper management—Deputy Chief Constable Brian McGuinness—who gave them an audience. After hearing their story about POI 390 and how a routine traffic stop of him caused the hairs on Myers's neck to stand up, McGuinness was convinced and essentially ordered Biddlecombe to take them on in Project Amelia, despite Biddlecombe's vehement protests.

In our meeting, Biddlecombe was visibly upset and told me his hands were tied, but he would speak with Fisk and Myers when they arrived and put them on notice that he didn't trust them, didn't like them, and would be watching them closely. I walked out of his office crestfallen but trying to keep an open mind. The dedicated team of crack investigators I had imagined assembling was fast becoming a mishmash of well-intentioned inexperienced people or part-timers and problem children, but I remained determined to make the best of the situation. The experienced and professional people we did have were tied up either working homicides or doing administrative desk duty. Still, this had to be better than it had been, working alone with no help and no supervision. It had to be—if not, what were we doing?

We assigned desks and phones to all the team members, and I placed enlarged photos of the missing women on the big white boards that covered the thin walls of the project room. Every day for more than a year, I looked into those sad, tired faces and tried to imagine where they could be, what those eyes had seen that mine could not, and I made those photos a silent promise to stand up for them and advocate for them and find them. I made lists of what had been done, what remained to be done, and who our top persons of interest were. We worked doggedly, crammed into our airless, windowless room.

During that time, one of my homicide detective pals gave me a book he said was required reading on Canadian case law and interviewing murderers—*Convicting the Guilty* by Steve Sherriff, a respected Ontario Crown prosecutor. After I'd finished reading it—and learning a great deal—I passed it around to our team and made sure everyone had a chance to read it. A few weeks after Fisk and Myers joined us, I handed it to Myers, telling him it was the most informative and helpful thing I'd seen on interviewing suspects and the case law surrounding interview techniques. He tossed it onto my desk, where it landed with a thud.

"I don't need that," he said.

"Have you already read it?" I asked eagerly. "It's great, huh?" I was keen to talk about it with everyone, and I fully intended to include him as part of our new team. "If you have, maybe Fisk'll want to have a look."

Myers pushed the book farther away from him toward me.

"I don't need that academic bullshit," he growled. I glanced over at Alex. *Okeydokey.* Conversation over.

Alex and I sat at desks beside each other, Myers was directly across from me—so close I could dial his phone—and Fisk sat across from Alex. There was no space dividing any of our desks from the others. Dorothy sat at the end of the room behind the largest of the desks, because she had two computer terminals and needed access to the large filing cabinets we had brought in for the mounting paper files we were accumulating. Geramy had a desk but rarely used it as she was almost always working in the Homicide office at her desk there some forty feet outside our door.

We were all in each other's back pockets, and privacy was nonexistent. This would have been fine under normal circumstances, but both Fisk and Myers seemed to think they were speaking to the South Pole every time they got on the phone and their booming, guffawing voices made it impossible to concentrate on anything else. Often, the detectives outside in the Homicide section would close our door to try to silence the idiocy, but we were trapped inside with it.

Mark Chernoff and Ron Lepine occupied desks on the other side of Alex and Fisk, but they avoided the project room whenever possible, working outside at their Homicide desks and coming in only for meetings or to talk to me when Fisk and Myers were on the road. Chernoff and Lepine were suspicious of Fisk and Myers, and Fisk and Myers considered Chernoff and Lepine Homicide Squad prima donnas. It was hardly the beginning of a cohesive, cooperative team.

In our first meetings, after I had had extensive discussions with people conversant in major case management principles, I explained how information would be organized and stressed the importance of proper documentation for court. I also provided the team members with handouts detailing how information should flow into the office and how it should be handled and formatted so that I could see and read everything and then prepare it for entry into SIUSS. This instruction was not necessary for Chernoff and Lepine, both highly organized and conscientious investigators, and Alex and Dave were learning quickly and wouldn't be a problem. However, Fisk and Myers rolled their eyes and showed little indication that they would stray from their normal routine, which appeared to consist of conducting informal "street interviews" of witnesses and keeping few, if any, notes.

As we sat discussing how searches should be documented for SIUSS, they inexplicably began telling Alex, Dorothy, and me about their days working the Vietnamese dial-a-dopers in the Downtown Eastside and Mount Pleasant. They laughed uproariously as they described searching the apartments of these men and dumping flour on suspects' heads during their searches for drugs, telling the men, "There you go, now you know what it's like to be white!"

They did not understand how anyone would find this a blatant and offensive disregard for these men's rights and personal dignity. What drugs they did find were often tossed—by their own admission—into the nearest Dumpster or storm drain after the search was completed, and it seemed that little Fisk and Myers did was ever documented or ended up before the courts. These lapses proved to be a dark predictor of the future.

I was amazed that they apparently hadn't been disciplined for any of these so-called searches and that each of them—Fisk especially—had secured relatively comfortable positions in specialty squads over the years, despite several internal investigation complaints. It looked as though they had somehow managed to create their own reputations as knowledgeable investigators, but had anyone ever looked further into their work, they would have found this was nothing but smoke and mirrors. Neither had the kind of knowledge or tact one would expect them to gain in nearly thirty-five combined years of policing.

Geramy asked me to name the project—it was customary to use a word beginning with the letter V for any Vancouver Police Department project, but I couldn't think of anything I liked that wasn't Vanish or Vixen or some other flippant reference to these women. I chose Project Amelia, in homage to Amelia Earhart, the world's best-known woman who had disappeared without a trace. That she had not been found bothered me somewhat, but I felt confident that we would find our Amelias somewhere, somehow.

But, like that ill-fated flight, Project Amelia began with high hopes and little indication of how very wrong things could go.

10

Other Cases, Other Avenues

• • •

"What is wanted is not the will to believe but the will to find out,
which is the exact opposite."
BERTRAND RUSSELL, SCEPTICAL ESSAYS

IN MID-JUNE 1999, we met with investigators from Spokane, Washington, in what would prove to be a valuable two days. They generously agreed to Geramy's invitation to come to Vancouver and share their experiences with us, which helped us understand our case and how under-resourced it was on many levels. Spokane had several missing and murdered female sex workers—close to fifteen at the time their investigators met with us. Their task force was grappling with both the Spokane murdered sex worker cases and Seattle's Green River Killer case, in which victims' bodies were found dumped along that waterway. The absence of bodies in our cases put us in a different position, but I felt certain we could learn from these investigators.

The Spokane case sparked the formation of a task force drawing from law enforcement agencies and FBI across the state.

We paled in comparison; their members were shocked we were not a task force. We learned they had developed their own case management system specific to the case, their own dedicated media liaison, and a specific strategy for both using and manipulating the media when necessary to the case. Staffed with numerous seasoned homicide detectives, some of whom were brought out of retirement to assist, they were highly organized with full managerial support from each agency.

We spent two days behind closed doors at the VPD, sharing suspect information during the day and war stories over beer in the evening. I learned so much from those hours, and both Geramy and I felt a renewed sense that we were on the right track with Pickton after discussing him with the Washington detectives.

Some months later, their task force's hard work would pay off and they would arrest Robert Lee Yates, a U.S. Army National Guard helicopter pilot and family man for several of the Spokane murders. Shortly after that, Gary Leon Ridgway would be arrested for the Green River murders. He was ultimately convicted of the murders of forty-eight women and later confessed to killing nearly twice that number. Task forces worked.

I traveled to Tacoma, Washington, a few weeks later to attend a meeting of law enforcement from around the Pacific Northwest to discuss the details of the case and gather information about Yates's timeline to determine whether he had spent much—if any—time in Canada. It didn't appear that he had. Two members of the RCMP's Violent Crime Linkage Analysis System (VICLAS) Section also attended the meeting, and I asked them what was happening with the Pickton file. Police officers are required to complete VICLAS reports on serious violent crimes, including unsolved homicides and child abductions, as well as missing person cases. VICLAS matches suspect modi operandi, DNA profiles, and other common elements to find linkages and solve serial crimes. RCMP ViCLAS members worked closely with the Serious Crime Section and the Behavioural Sciences profiling people. I told them I didn't know who was assigned to the file or what was happening with it, but as happened so often, everyone agreed that it should be looked at and that Pickton was an intriguing potential suspect. I couldn't count how many such conversations just like that one I'd had surrounding the Pickton file over the years.

The last case I came into contact with was in Poughkeepsie, New York, in the late 1990s. The police in that small town estimated they were aware of approximately seventy sex workers—and eight had gone missing. Like us, they had no bodies, no trail, and no evidence for several months. Speaking with their lead investigator felt like coming home to me—finally someone who understood the frustrations of working on such a file.

The detective I spoke with was sympathetic and offered some advice based on his department's success. His team ultimately caught their suspect through information about the street from the women themselves. They created a sex worker questionnaire and asked every woman on their strip to fill one out with an investigator. The questions ranged from recent bad dates to what sorts of acts would the women do and what would they never do to when they work to how well they knew any of the missing women.

What arose from this were repeated mentions of a man many of them—fifty out of seventy-two—had been out with on repeat dates. They said the man wasn't particularly violent but was known to "flip out" occasionally. Several of the women mentioned that he would offer them more money if they would accompany him to his home, but most said no and he would drive them back to the strip without a problem. Many of the victims were known to *never* go to a john's home, but investigators discovered that if the price was high enough, some would.

Eventually, police set up surveillance on this man and legally entered his home—a large house he shared with his mother, father, and sister in a pleasant middle-class area— and found all eight victims dead in the rafters. Inexplicably, although the house was filthy, the family swore up and down they couldn't smell the badly decaying bodies. His parents were professionals, yet they lived in complete and utter filth. It was a bizarre scenario.

I decided we needed such a questionnaire for our sex workers and a well-orchestrated plan to help as many of them fill one out as possible. Later, during the Missing Women Commission of Inquiry, this questionnaire would be criticized and perceived as an abuse of the women's rights and privacy. We treated those women who agreed to fill out our questionnaire with the utmost respect and sensitivity, and no one was pressured to participate.

The Project Amelia members struggled to get the questionnaires filled out or even present them to the women. We made trips to the WISH safe house and did our best to blanket as many of the women there as we could. I knew there were at least four hundred women working the Downtown Eastside, but we only collected sixty questionnaires. I implored Geramy to help me impress upon those members of the team who were on the street most to use this tool, but it just didn't fly. Everyone agreed it was potentially useful, but only Dave, Alex, and I used them. The other suggestions Poughkeepsie investigators provided all involved forming a multi-jurisdictional task force and assigning vast increases in manpower the VPD was simply unwilling to provide, despite my repeated requests.

When Project Amelia was formed in the spring of 1999, Alex agreed to go to Glenhaven funeral home to search manually through the thousands of records of indigent deaths in the hope that we might find some women who matched the victims. Alex had experience as a patrol officer on the Downtown Eastside, and her firsthand knowledge of many of the missing women proved invaluable to our team.

Since searching by name would be useless, Alex broke every death down by age, gender, date, and physical description—an incredibly tedious task that took her several days because none of the records were automated, much less computerized. The only saving grace was that there were relatively few young women of the missing women's ages in the records—most were elderly—and Alex felt satisfied that if anyone seemed to be a possible fit with one of the victims, she would have been able to determine if it was her. No such luck.

One daunting part of this process was that Glenhaven only dealt with indigent burials in the Vancouver area, and we couldn't be certain that one of the women hadn't died in some other area in the Lower Mainland, the rest of the province, or the entire country. Without the resources to expand this aspect of the search, it died in the water. The best we were able to do was enlist Larry Campbell to search each province's Coroners Service records for the names on our list and confirm that none of them had died. But, again, we weren't able to search for aliases we didn't know.

If nothing else, examining the women's medical records was helpful in narrowing the window of time in which the women had disappeared. Several of the women had visited a hospital or a doctor sometime between the time someone last saw or spoke to them and the dates their last welfare checks went unclaimed. I encountered several sympathetic doctors who were able to at least confirm that the women weren't in dire physical shape on their last visits and hadn't been admitted to hospital for lengthy stays, even though many of them suffered from HIV, AIDS, hepatitis, or tuberculosis. Nearly all of the women seemed to have used their own B.C. CareCards

for medical treatment before they disappeared—a strong indication that they were unlikely to have started using a fake or
stolen card in that short time. Still, I couldn't place my full confidence in that likelihood.

I ran the victims' names through this system again months
later to find that none of them had received any medical treatment in the intervening months since I had last checked. This
led me to two ominous conclusions: no one had stolen their
cards and was now using them, and none of these women, all
of whom were heavily dependent on the medical system, had
received any health care whatsoever after the time we believed
they had disappeared. This was another clear indication that
they were no longer alive.

Our miraculous discovery of missing Vancouver woman
Amy Guerin* in an Arizona mental hospital in 1999 opened
the door to speculation about the myriad other places some of
the victims might be. I contacted the U.S. government for lists
of all the state and privately run hospitals and mental health
facilities in the country. Unfortunately, the U.S. was not much
better organized than Canada, and because of the autonomy
given each state, no one was able to provide such a list to me,
let alone contact information for each facility.

All we managed to obtain was a growing list of places where
these women *weren't* but no clearer idea of where they were.
Our list of violent men grew almost daily, but again, there was
little or nothing to link them to the missing women. None of
this represented new information. We considered this information but usually concluded that there was not enough
evidence to justify stretching our already taxed resources to
look into their activities further. I do know that some of these
men were reexamined as potential killers when Project Evenhanded began in 2001. Robert Pickton was another matter.

A Letter to Janet Henry

• • •

DEAR JANET,

I know this may seem strange, but I'm writing to you to tell
you about the amazing spirit that is your sister, Sandie. I
think you knew, but you would be so proud of this woman
and all she has done to try to find you and lay you to rest.

Never have I heard of a family that has borne the degree
and depth of tragedy that your family has—sadly, your disappearance has not been the only pain they have known, and
even as Sandie has coped with your loss, the losses continue
to mount for her and your family.

Where does the pain end? Sandie asked me that once,
and I had no answer. This soft-spoken, beautiful, dignified,
gracious woman has fought on through the loudest, ugliest,
most undignified and ungracious moments a human being
can ever imagine. She—more than anyone I have ever
known—deserves an answer to that question.

She is my hero. Sandra Gagnon. Your sister. A warrior
fighting for your memory, for your dignity. A truly coura-
geous person. I worry about her daily, hoping her faith and

strength will endure, that her life will somehow get easier, that she will find some sort of meaning under this avalanche of pain that has been her existence for much too long.

Hers is a light that must never go out.

11

The Families

* * *

*"It's so much darker when a light goes out than it
would have been had it never shone."*

JOHN STEINBECK, THE WINTER OF OUR DISCONTENT

N MID-1999, WE planned a meeting of the families of the
missing women to bring them up to speed and introduce them to the other members of Project Amelia. One
of the promises I had made to myself was to do my utmost to
keep the families of the women apprised of the status of the
investigation, despite how busy we were with the coroners'
investigations, hospital searches, and liaising with detectives
from other agencies and task forces. Many of the files I had
inherited came with the same complaints from loved ones—
no one talked to them, no one returned their calls, no one cared,
and no one seemed interested in what they knew about their
missing daughter, sister, or mother.

Although I knew I would have to be mindful of the time I
spent in liaison with the families, I felt we owed them at the
very least the courtesy of returning their calls within a few days.

The more I spoke with them, the more I learned that we had some serious fence-mending to do and trust to earn. Many shared their early experiences, which included hurtful and dismissive comments about their poor parenting and their loved one's lifestyle, as well as racism on the part of the Missing Persons clerk. One parent told me she was shocked when this clerk told her perhaps her daughter wouldn't be missing if she had been a better parent. These interactions would color their perceptions of the VPD and our commitment for years to come. I believe a good part of the difficulties we had in gaining the trust of the families and keeping them from leaking information to the media was the result of this long-standing mistrust—and I couldn't blame them one bit.

If we had had the manpower, I would have assigned each investigator to deal with a certain number of the families so that the task could be shared by all of the members of the team and the investigators would still have time to follow up on leads. Because only a few people were available and I only trusted some of them to deal sensitively with the families, I made the first of many classic management errors in dealing with a case of this magnitude, errors that would quickly lead to my own burnout. I didn't trust anyone else to liaise with the families, and so I became the contact person for all of them. Like many of the roles I took on, I won this one by default.

Some of the missing women's families had lost touch with the Missing Persons office long before I'd been assigned in 1998, and I wondered whether this was out of frustration or whether there were other reasons. Like many of the victims, some of their families were troubled and some were transient. Still others simply accepted that their loved one wasn't coming back or didn't want to be found and moved on. There was a core of five or six out of the twenty to thirty on our growing list who would remain in regular contact with me, whereas many of the others were satisfied with the occasional call from me to update them on our progress, or lack thereof, every few months.

The families of Sarah de Vries, Marnie Frey, Janet Henry, and Catherine Knight maintained the most regular contact with me throughout the investigation, sometimes calling to offer some forgotten bit of potentially pertinent information, other times just to speak to someone associated to their loved one, to gain some reassurance that someone out there was still looking. I grew to depend on these calls in many ways, for they renewed my focus and sense of who I was working for when my frustration level would grow too high.

I also struggled to maintain some professional distance. There were so many things I wanted to share with the families, so many times I wanted to tell them to lobby harder, push further, because so little was happening in the investigation on the police end. They placed their faith in me, and as time went by, it became more and more apparent to me that my position on the case made it impossible for me to advocate for the women and their families, and my views and feelings placed me in a position of potential disloyalty or at least in conflict with the organization I worked for. This contradiction wore on me.

My fear wasn't that I would be ostracized or scorned for speaking out in support of these disenfranchised women; it was much less easily defined. I was afraid that if I were perceived as sharing some of the views of the families and the community, a worse thing would happen: I would be dismissed within the VPD as a bleeding heart, as too emotionally involved in my own case. If that happened, it would be impossible for me to advocate for anyone and I wouldn't be taken seriously within my own organization—and that would be very damaging to the future of the investigation. At that point, I still felt I would be of more assistance to these women and their families by continuing with the investigation, with limited capacity as an advocate, than if I weren't there at all. So I continued this strange balancing act, maintaining some distance from the families and the community and not saying many things I wanted to say.

Because of the history these families had with the VPD, I couldn't trust them not to run to the press with anything I might want to share with them. It was simply too risky—for me personally and professionally, as well as for the integrity of the investigation itself. The information about Pickton was never far from my mind, yet I couldn't share it with the families short of asking very vague questions—such as *Did your sister/daughter/mother ever mention a farm?*—for fear of tipping him off. In hindsight, perhaps tipping him off would have made him stop killing, and this thought would torture me for years. What would tipping him off have looked like? How might that have changed things?

When the matter of the reward came up in spring 1999, I made a decision. By this point, my level of frustration had reached new heights, and I felt the only way to generate the kind of attention this tragedy warranted was to bring the public into it. Maggie de Vries, Sarah's sister, seemed the only person I could confide in, not because I didn't trust some of the other family members, but because Maggie was one person I felt would not use the information to right all the wrongs that might have been propagated against her family by the VPD. I thought she would take a balanced and considered view of what I would tell her and make a sound plan as to how best to use it.

The VPD did not support the idea of offering a reward to help find the person or persons responsible for these disappearances, and for good reason. Rewards seldom prove useful and often divert valuable police time and resources away from the investigation to deal with false claims, red herrings, and crazies trying to cash in on someone else's misery. However, underlying this sound reasoning was another line of thought: to offer a reward was to admit we thought these women had not disappeared willingly, and that was a theory I do not believe the VPD was ready to adopt. However, in July 1999, the Vancouver Police Board approved a $100,000 reward for information leading to the arrest and conviction of "the person or persons responsible for the unlawful confinement, kidnapping or murder of any one or all of the listed women missing from the streets of Vancouver."

Despite the fact I had been quoted in the media as far back as 1998 saying that I thought these women had met with foul play and that the possibility of a serial killer or killers was a real one, Anne Drennan maintained a much more neutral stance as the department media spokesperson. This was no doubt through the direction of the Major Crime Section and VPD senior management; in all matters, Anne was only as informed as they allowed her to be. Her voice was the voice people listened to most, and so the community continued to cry that the VPD was not acknowledging the possibility these women had been murdered, even though both Geramy and I said publicly we believed the women were murder victims.

For all of the families, the length of the investigation was extremely traumatic. Hope, denial, dread, and fear would cycle around in their minds as they tried to reassure themselves their family member had just taken off or left the area to try to get off drugs. Then news of a violent predator would come to their attention, convincing them she had been murdered. Either way, not knowing where her body was or how much she may have suffered played havoc with their imaginations. Theirs was a hell that went on for years and for many has not ended.

Many of the families took an occasional hiatus from the investigation—insofar as they could when the fate of their mother or daughter or sister weighed on their minds constantly. Some would call me or wait for me to make one of my occasional update calls and tell me they wished to be out of the loop for a while, asking me to call only if I had something concrete to tell them. They needed a break, some time away from the immediacy of what was—and wasn't—happening, and I respected this completely.

Several of my relationships with the family members grew. Maggie de Vries, Lynn Frey, Susanna Knight, and Sandra Gagnon would call often, and I found these late-afternoon chats helpful. They would often bring me tidbits of information I wouldn't otherwise be privy to, things these women had picked up in their own intrepid searches for their daughter and sisters. We would toss theories around, lament the lack of support for the women on the street, and acknowledge the inevitability of their meeting a tragic end considering how society treats them and ignores the men who buy sex from them.

One of the main reasons behind the spring 1999 family meeting was to explain the need to collect DNA samples from as many of the blood relatives as we could. At that time, it was the only way we knew to obtain samples of DNA similar to that of the victims to use for testing should we find a body or body part. In the end, it would prove to be less crucial as newer technology assisted us, but it was a start and gave the families a sense that we knew what the hell we were doing.

One of the few things I am proud of in this investigation was coming up with the idea of using PAP smear tests to obtain DNA profiles on the missing women. I continued to believe it was only a matter of time before we started finding bodies or body parts, and as time passed, identification would become more difficult, especially for those women who were without family or who had been adopted at birth. In this way, we were guaranteed of having victim DNA on all but two of the twenty-seven women on our list—and we were able to obtain familial DNA for those two.

I made an excellent contact at the B.C. Cancer Agency—which collects and stores slides for comparison against newer tests—and she agreed to put aside the most recent PAP smear slides of all the missing women who had had the test and save them indefinitely, rather than just for the required seven years. She also informed me there was a policy change afoot to reduce this hold period from seven to five years. Several of the missing women were fast approaching the five-year mark, so I was pleased to discover this resource when I did.

My contact there was wonderful to deal with, one of the few medical administrators I worked with who balanced privacy concerns with the practical need to identify these women should DNA evidence arise down the road. We agreed that the agency would not release any personal medical information about the women, but the slides would be available if we were able to show we had a reasonable belief that we had found the DNA of one of them and needed to test it against the known sample. This was extremely helpful—the familial DNA would help to show a likely match, but to be able to test against a known sample of the actual victim vastly decreased the likelihood of a misidentification.

In the meantime—before we knew about the B.C. Cancer Agency's storehouse of DNA—we held the family meeting and I explained DNA testing in layperson's terms in a way that I hoped wouldn't be too upsetting to everyone. The families were very receptive, and everyone who could provided a sample. We used saliva on a buccal swab, because hair was unreliable and blood was considered invasive. Saliva would provide an effective basis of comparison against the found sample.

There were strong divisions within some of the families that I suspect arose from feelings of blame for their loved ones' fate. Some family members who had not been there for their missing loved one when she needed them suddenly showed up, claiming concern and putting themselves forward as the family spokesperson. This proved a minefield to navigate, and I had to make assessments of several people before determining who might be the best contact person for that family. I made mistakes in the beginning, trusting that a brother, sister, or parent I had been in touch with actually cared about their missing relative. Later, I would discover that this person had not been supportive at all or had been the abuser responsible for the woman's being on the street in the first place.

I encountered several men in these files who had abused their sisters or daughters in the family home, then later pushed to be the family representative, presumably so that they could have some element of control over what information about the missing woman's past reached the police. These incidents were impossible to prove, as many historical sexual assault claims are, but it was easy to sniff these men out, and once I stopped dealing with them as the family contact, they faded from the scene, no longer interested in finding their sister or daughter. In a couple of cases, the victim's mother sold her very young daughter to men for sex, pimping her out on a regular basis, often in the family home. That discovery overwhelmed me with sadness; I knew these things happened, but it made me sick to come face-to-face with fathers and mothers who so horribly abused their daughters and now were calling me professing their love and concern.

Over time, many of these families began to seek each other out for support. They met at the various events staged to bring attention to and memorialize the women, as well as online through the website Wayne Leng set up. After a honeymoon period of a few months, signs of strain became obvious. Disagreements arose over everything from who got to do media interviews to board appointments on various Downtown Eastside committees to memorial events to what to do with funds raised in the names of the missing women. Some of these people shunned the spotlight, whereas others sought it. Clearly, for some, their association with this case was the closest to the center of attention they had ever been, and some handled that better than others.

Lynn Frey, Marnie's stepmother, called me one or two afternoons a week on her drive to pick up Marnie's daughter from school. I became aware of Marnie's case through my July 1998 CPIC search across Canada for related files of women who had disappeared from the Downtown Eastside under similar circumstances. Her family knew from the onset we were investigating Marnie's disappearance as potentially linked to our other missing women, and Lynn and I discussed this frequently.

Lynn would tell me of her efforts to find Marnie, and she made frequent trips from her Campbell River home to the Downtown Eastside to seek more information. These midafternoon chats lifted my spirits, and I came to value Lynn's information greatly. Her dogged persistence and determination to find Marnie inspired me to press on during the especially difficult days.

A Letter to Marnie Frey

* * *

DEAR MARNIE,

Finally, your parents received the news they dreaded—you were on that farm. Over the years, they clung to that ever-fading glimmer of hope that maybe—just maybe—you had avoided a violent and painful death. Maybe you had died in the midst of feeling the only peace and comfort you had known in your last few years, that euphoric rush as the dope hit your vein.

Your stepmom, Lynn, searched high and low for you, proving that blood ties aren't always the strongest. She and your dad did all they could to find you, spending most of the time turning over stones, walking skid row, and searching the Internet for you—and the rest of the time out fishing to make their living, wondering out on the water if you'd turn up while they were away and they'd miss seeing you. Or worrying I'd try to reach them to tell them I'd found *something* and forget where they were. But I always knew how to find them if I had something—anything—to tell. But there was rarely anything to tell. From that August you went missing, there'd been nothing.

Lynn and I talked for hours on the phone. She always amazed me with her ability to ask how I was doing with "all this" when she was suffering so much over not seeing you. Through our talks, I felt as though I got to know you and the struggles you faced. You were a firecracker, that much I could figure out. No one could tell you what to do or how to do it— but one thing controlled you. If not for the drugs, perhaps you would have harnessed that energy and strength and been the kind of mother and person you always wanted to be, the kind you had wanted your birth mom to be, the kind Lynn had been to you. Perhaps—unlike many of the other women—your own sense of invincibility was your savior for so long, convincing you that you could rise above your problems and take care of yourself, even among the parasites and lowlifes you dealt with every day on the Downtown Eastside.

I looked at photographs of you—taken by a customer in a bank machine vestibule. You smiled like a model, feeling beautiful in a thrift store coat, red lipstick, and vinyl, mid-calf boots—you were still pretty despite your hard living, and your sparkling eyes and smile radiated hope. What were you hoping for, Marnie? Your big break? Some kind of break? That this sleazy man would be the first to come through with promises of the kind of life you always felt you were destined to live? Was it these dreams that got you through your day, your week, your life?

You didn't have a chance: from a very young age, you were addicted to heroin, and by the time many kids were just beginning to experiment, you were already gone—the legacy passed on to you by your birth mother and her twisted belief that drugs would make you feel better and ease your pain as they did hers.

No chance. You had no chance.

Lynn would tell me of how she walked into the lobbies of scummy skid row hotels and rooming houses, showing desk clerks your photo and asking if they knew you. She told me of the one man who said he could tell her something for ten bucks. She passed over the money only to be told he knew nothing, and it was right then she felt the kind of cruelty and humiliation you must have felt in your years of working the street—of men offering, then taking away—people dangling those carrots they would never let you hold in your hand.

The day Pickton was arrested, I asked to be the one to call and let Lynn and your dad know. Even in the midst of this news, she expressed concern for me, that I had been unfairly portrayed in the media. She apologized to me and wanted me to know she shared no part of your aunt Joyce's criticisms of me. She told me she was proud of me, the way a mother might say it, and I thought of you and how lucky you were to have an advocate like her on your side. She and I share that, I suppose. We share that sense of trying so hard to advocate on behalf of all of you and of failing so miserably to have made any kind of difference or save any of you from this horrific end.

Lynn knows how hard she tried. She never stopped believing she would find you.

12

The Second Pickton Tip

• • •

*"From a certain point onward there is no longer any turning
back. That is the point that must be reached."*
FRANZ KAFKA, THE TRIAL

IN APRIL 1999, Pickton resurfaced as a suspect in a sexual
assault and strangulation attempt on a New Westminster
sex worker. Although Mike Connor and I had attempted to
track his activities through the Canadian Police Information
Centre (CPIC) flag, we had received next to no information
about his activities. Finally, we had something.

Because Pickton fit the description of the attacker, a meeting was held at the New Westminster Police Department with
members of the NWPD, the Burnaby RCMP, the Coquitlam
RCMP, the Provincial Unsolved Homicide Unit, and the VPD.
We discussed Pickton's viability as a suspect in the missing
women files and we agreed that his photo should be shown
to as many sex workers as possible in all the jurisdictions with
an active sex trade. Again, Special O was assigned to conduct
surveillance and obtain a discard DNA sample—an item such

as a cigarette butt, condom, drinking straw, or dirty Kleenex used by the suspect from which a DNA profile can be taken—from Pickton to use in comparison with DNA found in three murders around Agassiz, B.C., of women who fit our victim profile—Tammy Pipe, Tracy Olajide, and Victoria Younker.

The RCMP's Special O surveillance unit observed Pickton from May 5 to 11 and saw nothing unusual or apparently significant. He was followed to West Coast Reduction Ltd., an animal-product rendering plant on the Downtown Eastside waterfront, where it was later determined he regularly brought pig entrails. Aside from that, there was little activity. Pickton seemed to attract minimal police attention, and despite the CPIC flag, we were receiving no reports of his being stopped in areas frequented by sex workers. There was not enough evidence in the New Westminster assault to charge him, and he continued with his day-to-day activities.

May came and went quickly. The formation of Project Amelia occupied every moment. Hiscox and I played phone tag briefly but did not speak, and it was becoming clear to me that in the interests of his own recovery he was no longer in direct contact with anyone on the Pickton farm. I was reluctant to press him further or encourage him to return to a lifestyle that might promote or restart his drug use, so I accepted the limitations of his new life, hoping he would call if there was anything new.

I took most of July 1999 off for vacation—the first time in my career I used all my vacation time in a single block. Already, I felt I needed a break from the impossible task of trying to build a 747 from wood and a few nails, and I needed to recharge my batteries. Digestive problems, headaches, and recurring nightmares began to plague me early in 1999, and I hoped all I needed was some time off. This investigation didn't feel to me the way hard work felt; I knew hard work and welcomed a challenge, but I was becoming more and more aware that my efforts were making little difference to the victims, and that tugged at my spirit in a way I'd never experienced before. The tiniest seeds of scepticism and doubt—in what I was doing, in the support for our work, in *everything I used to believe about pursuing murderers*—grew slowly and silently. I hoped this just meant I needed a little time away.

The rest of the Project Amelia team remained at work, and Alex took over my role as file coordinator in my absence. Little did I know the most vital tip of the file would come in when I was on holiday.

While I was away, Geramy took a call from Jim Brown, a Coquitlam RCMP constable. He wanted to pass on information he'd received from a source about a male and female—and perhaps others—killing Downtown Eastside prostitutes. It quickly became evident that Brown wanted to pass on to us not only the information but also the source himself, which was highly unusual, if not unheard of, for an RCMP officer to do. Geramy assigned Mark Chernoff to follow up on the tip.

On July 19, Mark met with the confidential source, Ross Caldwell. He told Mark about a murder that occurred on the Picktons' Dominion Avenue property sometime between February and April. Caldwell explained that a close associate of Pickton's, Lynn Ellingsen, had told him this story, and it was through her that Caldwell had come to know and occasionally work for Pickton. Ellingsen told Caldwell she and Pickton had gone downtown in a Chevy S-10 pickup truck and enticed a sex worker with drugs, booze, and money to come with them to the Port Coquitlam farm.

Mark called me at home to tell me about this new break, and I immediately wanted to rush back to work. I felt invigorated and filled with a renewed sense of purpose. I knew this was exactly the boost I—and our team—needed. We shared our various theories excitedly, agreeing that this was too eerily similar to the Hiscox tip and we just had to be on the right track with Pickton.

As with any source information, there were obvious problems with the story. The first order of business was to confirm that Caldwell was not somehow Hiscox—especially since the information was similar. We compared notes and began to realize this was probably a separate circle of people around Pickton, probably known to Hiscox and Yelds but not closely related. This information elevated Pickton from a strong possible suspect to a highly likely suspect in my opinion—we had smelled smoke before; now we could see the inferno.

Immediately, Mark rightly wondered whether Ellingsen's involvement could be more than what she was relating, but he also recognized that the first step would be getting her to tell us that story. According to Caldwell, Ellingsen's story was that Pickton gave them each some money—hers was for helping to bring the woman out there, and the sex worker was paid for her time. According to Ellingsen, she went into a separate room in the trailer so that Pickton and the woman could be alone, presumably to complete the sexual arrangement. Sometime later, Ellingsen said she went out on the property to look for Pickton, wondering where he had gone. As she approached the slaughterhouse, she saw what she believed was a female human body hanging from a meat hook and Robert Pickton standing beside it removing the skin. She later told Caldwell she didn't know human fatty tissue was yellow, an ominous indication she was telling the truth.

There was much more work to do, and obviously we needed to interview Ellingsen in person or, failing that, enlist an undercover operator to befriend her and hear the story firsthand. My mind spun with ideas, and I felt I had a sense of Ellingsen from the start. Why was so much time unaccounted for from when

Ellingsen left for the other room in the small trailer to when she saw the body? How much of what had happened might she have actually assisted with or taken part in?

Ellingsen's motivation would become clear: she told Caldwell she was using what she had seen to extort money from Pickton—blood money to buy her silence and ensure that she wouldn't go to the police. Clearly, she had been bothered enough by what she had seen—and possibly done—to tell someone. And that someone was Caldwell, who told Mark that she appeared genuinely disturbed by the incident—but not disturbed enough to mess up her cozy arrangement with Pickton. We later learned that she had told her story to others as well.

Caldwell appeared credible and forthright in his dealings with Mark and his partner, Ron Lepine. He had a history as an informant for the RCMP and had been paid for information in the past that turned out to be factual and useful; although later, during the Missing Women Commission of Inquiry, retired RCMP corporal Frank Henley referred to Caldwell as a "treacherous" informant, meaning he was not to be trusted. I did not know Caldwell; nor did I ever meet him. When Mark and Ron began dealing with him, he sounded not unlike Hiscox, trying to clean up from a substance abuse problem and get his life back on track.

On July 28, I met with Fred Biddlecombe, Geramy, Mark, and Ron after the two detectives' second meeting with Caldwell a couple of days before and asked them whether anyone found this source hand-off from Brown unusual. After my informant experiences in patrol and later with Hiscox, and seeing the proprietary way police officers protect their sources from other officers, I found this a little strange. My colleagues all commented that they'd never seen a Mountie offer to share a source, let alone actually pass one on so easily with no period of transition or introduction. Still, we had a hot new source and what seemed to be useful information, so we didn't sit around puzzling over our good fortune. I've certainly wondered since then what Brown's reasons were for effectively dropping Caldwell on our doorstep with no apparent further involvement.

Mark and Ron met with Caldwell several times from July 19 to 28, and more details emerged. Caldwell was able to get a vague physical description of the woman seen hanging from the hook—she was young, Caucasian, with short reddish hair—and we felt this could be Jacqueline McDonnell, a Vancouver woman last seen in January 1999 and the only 1999 case we had on our list at that time. Later, we would discover there were others missing that year of whom we were unaware. Again, because we were unaware of some of the victims, we couldn't see the full picture of our investigation.

In that July 28 meeting, Fred, Geramy, Mark, Ron, and I planned our next moves. We agreed that the Coquitlam RCMP had to take the lead, since the Pickton farm was in its jurisdiction, but Mark and Ron were the logical interviewers because they had the most knowledge of Ellingsen and the best relationship with Caldwell. Mark and Ron agreed to cancel their own vacation plans for that week and contact Mike Connor to set up a meeting. I was scheduled to fly to Washington, D.C., at the end of the week for the July 31 airing of an *America's Most Wanted* segment about the missing women and wanted nothing more than to cancel and stay in Vancouver to see how this would unfold. But I was already booked and had agreed to go.

The following day, Mark and Ron met in Coquitlam with several RCMP members, including Inspector Earl Moulton and Corporal Mike Connor. They discussed the new information and confirmed that two women and two men—Yelds, Ellingsen, Hiscox, and Caldwell—had come forward with similar information about Robert Pickton killing sex workers. When Mark returned to our office and relayed the details of the meeting to me, he was stunned that some officers were still raising doubts, questioning whether our sources were credible and whether Ellingsen had actually seen what she said she had.

I was dumbfounded. This was more than normal investigative second-guessing or devil's advocacy at play. There were some problems with Caldwell, without question, and the RCMP members seemed to equate drug dependency with lying, which we did not believe had to go hand in hand. Mark and Ron were working 24/7 to keep Caldwell on track; he wasn't unstable or mentally unwell at that point, merely feeling the pressure. For us, his substance abuse issues did not change the veracity of the information we believed he'd heard firsthand from Ellingsen, but it seemed to for some RCMP members.

While the RCMP determined its next move, we decided we would mobilize the VPD Strike Force to conduct surveillance on Pickton's property and his activities. This began on July 31, and after meeting again with Coquitlam, Mark and Ron were able to get the RCMP to commit Special O to assist with surveillance. I took off for two days in Washington, D.C., but all I really wanted was to be in the office following the surveillances and Mark and Ron's progress with Caldwell. Both mornings, I took long runs around the National Mall, but all I could think about was Pickton and how we could get onto that farm.

On August 3, we met with the RCMP in Coquitlam to discuss committing money and resources and forming an investigative team and an operational plan to pursue Pickton. Someone suggested that Crown counsel be consulted about how Ellingsen should be approached—as a witness or as a suspect—and a member was assigned to do this. The VPD agreed to supply Mark and Ron to assist the Coquitlam and Unsolved Homicide members. E Division—the name for the British Columbia division of the RCMP—was asked to review its commitment to the file.

On August 4, the newly formed investigative team met in Coquitlam. Coquitlam RCMP provided three members, including Mike Connor, and Unsolved Homicide supplied Detective Bruce Ballantyne, a VPD member seconded to that team. Mark and Ron were to continue working with Caldwell, who was becoming difficult to manage. He was living in a seedy hotel in Surrey and slipping deeper into heavy drinking and drug use. Mark and Ron met with Caldwell later that day, and he provided information that concerned them deeply. A man named Ron Menard worked on the farm and hung around with Ellingsen, Pickton, and the others. Menard told Caldwell that Pickton was tired of paying Ellingsen "extortion money." Menard had an abusive relationship with Ellingsen, and it was difficult to determine how all the players fit. It was then that Caldwell agreed to act as an agent for the police, and Mark and Ron provided him with a pager so that they could reach him anytime.

The next day, Caldwell attended an interview with the investigative team looking tired and worn. His mental state seemed precarious, and some suspected he was under the influence of drugs, alcohol, or both. The RCMP members, with the exception of Mike Connor, were increasingly sceptical about his credibility, to the frustration of Mark and Ron, who knew that Caldwell was feeling under pressure.

Ellingsen had told another friend, Leah Best, the story of the hanging body. Best was deeply upset by the information and was horrified when Ellingsen told her she was hoping to extort enough money to take a cruise—something she had never been able to afford because of her drug habit and poor

circumstances. Best thought Ellingsen was telling the truth—
she found the suggestion that anyone would make up such
a story ludicrous—and took the information to the Burnaby
RCMP.

The group agreed to locate Ellingsen and bring her in for
an interview, though Mark, Ron, and I questioned whether
interviewing her would serve our goal of getting onto the
Pickton farm and thought it would be better to make her the
target of an undercover operation. We were concerned that the
RCMP wanted to write her off as unreliable and stop pursuing
Pickton, but this was not our jurisdiction and we were forced
to do things their way. Our fears would turn out to be well
founded.

Lynn Ellingsen was first interviewed on August 10. I felt
this was poorly planned, because the RCMP had rebuffed Mike,
Mark, and Ron's suggestions that surveillance and wiretap be
put in place first. We had all thought that surveillance was
necessary so that Ellingsen could be followed afterward and
that an authorized wiretap should be set up to see and hear
whether she went straight to Pickton from the interview. I also
suggested that an undercover operator would be the best way
to get Ellingsen to retell this story so that we could judge its
truthfulness. Because she was a heavy drinker and drug user
and worked at a seedy bar, I thought a female undercover operator planted there working behind the bar or waiting tables
could befriend her easily, share a few beers, and engage her in
a conversation about what she had seen.

These ideas were rejected, and to this day, I don't know why,
though I suspect it was because Unsolved Homicide members
refused to believe our witness information and to believe that
anything sinister was going on at the Pickton farm. I later
heard Missing Women Commission of Inquiry testimony
from RCMP members that they feared an entire undercover

team would have to be called in, an operational plan would need to be created, and the safety of members would be in jeopardy because of so much drug use among the Pickton associates. In my experience, this did not sound much different from most undercover operations involving drug users that police embark upon every day.

It seemed no one wanted to go to the bother or expense because no one believed this was a murder investigation. I'd always worked on the premise that you rule things in until you can conclusively rule them out, so I failed to understand how the Unsolved Homicide members could so blithely discount our source information without any evidence to support dismissing it.

Mark and Ron were initially set to conduct the Ellingsen interview and were the most logical and prepared for the job. At the last moment, they were told they would not be doing the interview. VPD Detective Bruce Ballantyne and his Unsolved Homicide partner RCMP corporal Frank Henley would take over—with little preparation and even less confidence that Ellingsen had indeed seen a hanging body. Mark and Ron were understandably upset. They were relegated to watching from the observation room of the Whalley RCMP suboffice, where they observed an eighteen-minute-long discussion between Ellingsen, Ballantyne, and Henley.

The recording began with an acknowledgment that they had been speaking casually for a few minutes before recording. They asked Ellingsen some questions about her knowledge of Robert Pickton and her relationship with him. There were no questions about her extortion of Pickton for what she saw in the barn. The interview continued with Ellingsen alternately denying seeing a body hanging in the barn and defending her memory and asserting that being drunk doesn't make people forget something upsetting. Ellingsen's answers were one-word denials and short sentences, like "that's the truth," which many who study statement analysis believe are intended to slam the door on any further questioning but may not be indications of innocence. Unfortunately, the interviewer's questions were not open-ended, enabling Ellingsen to answer in the negative without the need for elaboration.

They didn't ask any behavioral observation questions—designed to gauge truthfulness—just old-school two-on-one interrogation with no plan. After eighteen recorded minutes of conversation, Ballantyne and Henley stepped out of that room and told Mark and Ron they believed Ellingsen—they believed she had not seen what Caldwell and Best said she told them she saw.

Mark called me from Coquitlam, his voice shaking with rage. As I listened, I had the sensation of air leaving me like a gigantic tire deflating. Ellingsen left the Coquitlam RCMP detachment without surveillance, without wiretap in place, without an undercover operation ready to launch, the object of no further plans to try to determine the veracity of her information. I was stunned and completely baffled at the apparent complete lack of a cohesive plan to rule Pickton in or out as a killer.

As Mark and I began to puzzle through the events, we wondered whether perhaps the Mounties knew something. *Maybe they have a plan and they just aren't telling us.* It had to be something like that, because it was inconceivable that they didn't see this the way we did. We both recalled instances where we'd dealt with the RCMP before in our careers—Mark more than me—and they'd habitually failed to share information or their plans with us lowly "munis." It certainly wouldn't be the first time, we reasoned.

We ended the call hopeful that maybe the RCMP were just doing their "Mountie thing" and preferred to pursue Pickton without our input. We agreed that would be fine by us, and Mark returned to the office. When he got back, Mark, Ron, Geramy, and I continued to puzzle over what could make the RCMP think they could flat out deny the credibility of this information without any proof to the contrary.

13

Another Opportunity
with Lynn Ellingsen

• • •

"I have discovered in life that there are ways of getting
almost anywhere you want to go, if you really want to go."
LANGSTON HUGHES, I WONDER AS I WANDER

MARK AND RON continued to pressure the Unsolved
Homicide Unit, and, amazingly, Ellingsen agreed to
return to the Coquitlam detachment for a second interview on August 26. To me, this was consistent with someone
who had a story to tell and only needed the right prompting and reassurance to tell it, and credit must go to Henley
for completing his assignment, which was to get her back in
the door. She certainly hadn't been shy about telling several
friends about her experience in Pickton's barn. In the meantime, Mike was promoted to sergeant, and we were told he
would no longer be working in the General Investigation Section of Coquitlam RCMP. The Pickton investigation had just
lost its best advocate in the RCMP. It was a huge loss, but we
had no idea just how huge.

The August 26 interview with Ellingsen proved little better than the first. Again, in light of their knowledge of the case and the information provided by Caldwell, Mark and Ron hoped to conduct it, but the RCMP pressed to have one of their members in the room. RCMP Constable Ruth Yurkiw and Ron began the interview together, only to have Ellingsen object to Ron's presence when he dared to press her on what she had witnessed in Pickton's barn. Ron voluntarily left the interview rather than compromise Ellingsen's information by making her more uncomfortable.

Henley then joined Yurkiw—who, by her own admission in the Missing Women Commission of Inquiry testimony and to Doug LePard during his interview with her for the VPD Missing Women Investigation Report, was inexperienced with murder files—and the interview proceeded. Again, Ron and Mark were incredulous that detectives with little preparation, no file review, and even less belief in the case would be entrusted with dealing with such a key witness.

Yurkiw tried to keep Ellingsen on track and in the room, and Henley attempted to salvage the interview and maintain some sort of rapport with Ellingsen, but little information was gained.

On the recording, the interview proceeded with back and forth about whether Ellingsen accompanied Pickton into Vancouver and whether she was with him when he picked up a sex worker. She went off on a tangent, ruminating on all the ways she could potentially prove her story was true. Finally, Henley refocused Ellingsen on the matter of the hanging body in the barn. He told her there was some trouble with her version of the story.

Henley went on to tell Ellingsen that there were Vancouver police officers who believed she had told others about seeing something in Pickton's barn. She indicated she understood that. Henley was clearly getting to her and suggested Ellingsen take a polygraph examination to prove she was telling the truth, and she agreed. Henley explained that the Vancouver police officers believed she helped Pickton pick up this sex worker and she saw him skinning her body in the barn. He warned her this story was not going away until it was either proven true or disproven as untrue. She said she understood. Henley emphasized that this was an important matter and Ellingsen agreed.

When Ellingsen left, however, there was no investigative plan in place to determine the extent of her involvement with Pickton other than to agree to let Henley set up a polygraph test.

As a result of these interviews, Ron and Mark had some discussion with Sergeant Bill Lean of the VPD Polygraph Unit about scheduling a time for Ellingsen to undergo a lie-detector examination in our polygraph suite in Vancouver. The RCMP also tried to have her come in, as their polygraph examiner, Sergeant Jim Hunter, felt she had to be tested. A time was arranged for August 31, but Ellingsen called at the last minute to cancel, saying that on the advice of her lawyer she would not be speaking to the police any further. We were dead in the water as far as Lynn Ellingsen was concerned.

During his May 15, 2012, Missing Women Commission of Inquiry testimony, retired corporal Frank Henley had the following exchange with Jason Gratl, the lawyer for Downtown Eastside interests. I listened intently as he confirmed what I had always suspected: despite Henley's considerable effort on the Ellingsen file, based on Caldwell's unreliable past performance as an informant, Henley—and by extension the PUHU—did not believe Ellingsen's story. Henley's opinions held considerable sway in the office.

Gratl: "Yes. So you weren't properly briefed?"

Henley: "I guess I wasn't. You're right."

Gratl: "You hadn't even taken steps to inquire whether there was other information important for an interview?"

Henley: "That's correct."

Gratl: "All right. So you understood going into your interview with Ellingsen that you weren't properly briefed then?"

Henley: "I can't agree with that."

Gratl: "All right. You don't have to agree. Now, did you know that Robert William Pickton was a suspect at the time of a sexual assault in New Westminster?"

Henley: "I don't believe I was aware of that, no."

Gratl: "Did you—were-were you aware that there was a profile of Robert William Pickton prepared by a profiler?"

Henley: "No."

This testimony left me shaking my head. I forced myself to listen to Henley explain why he didn't feel the need to consult RCMP corporal Russ Nash, who had been the source handler of Ross Caldwell on a previous file, about Caldwell's credibility.

Gratl: "He doesn't need to be your source in order for you to review the human source file, does he?"

Henley: "It would never be my practice to interview any human source file that wasn't my file without first notifying the source handler."

Gratl: "Sure. You can find the source handler, though, can't you?"

Henley: "And then getting permission from the source handler."

Gratl: "Fine. You can do that, can't you?"

Henley: "And then going to headquarters and reviewing the file."

Gratl: "Sure. That's how it's done. You ask the handler if it's okay to review the source file, correct?"

Henley: "That's right."

Henley: "You didn't do that in this case, did you?"

Henley: "No."

Gratl: "There's a way within the RCMP you can track down who the handler is, correct?"

Henley: "Yes."

Gratl: "For any given individual, correct?"

Henley: "Yes."

Gratl: "You didn't do that in this case?"

Henley: "No, I did not."

Gratl: "You took the position that Caldwell's information was unreliable, and you made that known within the group meetings that you attended, correct?"

Henley: "Mr. Caldwell's information was thirdhand, would not stand a test in court, was meaningless without some corroboration. That's the stand I took."

Gratl: "You also distributed information that Caldwell had on previous occasions distributed unreliable information, correct?"

Henley: "I was informed by then-corporal Nash."

Gratl: "Did you or did you not distribute that information?"

Henley: "To who?"

Gratl: "To the other people involved in the Port Coquitlam investigation of Pickton?"

Henley: "I'm sure it was discussed."

Gratl: "By you?"

Henley: "Amongst us."

Gratl: "By you?"

Henley: "Well, I'm sure I told somebody that I had information that he was unreliable, if that's the question you're asking."

Gratl: "All right then. You heard that information from Corporal Nash, correct?"

Henley: "That's correct."

Gratl: "And at that point you had an opportunity to go back to the source file and review the source file to check it out to see if it was accurate, correct?"

Henley: "Why would I doubt Corporal Nash's—pardon me—information to me?"

Gratl: "It's not a question of whether you doubt it. It's a question of confirming it."

Henley: "I did not confirm it."

Gratl: "And why was that?"

Henley: "I didn't-I didn't see the need to confirm it."

Those opportunities we had sitting face-to-face with Ellingsen had been squandered. Police would not speak to her about Pickton again until February 2002, after his arrest, when she would finally become a key witness, but even then, they had to be pressured to take her seriously to the point that I often wondered whether there wasn't some sort of concerted effort to keep her and her information buried. I've learned nothing since to lead me to understand this bizarre set of circumstances, and I stated in the Missing Women Commission of Inquiry that I hoped if the inquiry learned nothing more, we would hear testimony explaining the RCMP's rationale around their mishandling of the Ellingsen information.

14

Dead in the Water

• • •

"Three may keep a secret, if two of them are dead."
BENJAMIN FRANKLIN, POOR RICHARD'S ALMANACK

THE UNSOLVED HOMICIDE members told Mark and Ron they would continue with their attempts to interview Pickton, and indeed, Ruth Yurkiw tried to do so in early autumn of 1999.

From September 1999 on, very little was done about Pickton, but we weren't aware of just how little. At first, I called Mike Connor's old desk number almost daily after the second Ellingsen interview. I continued to call, thinking I would reach an officer who could direct me to the investigator handling the Pickton file. I finally learned that Ruth Yurkiw had custody of the file, and I was able to speak to her, but she said little was happening with the file and didn't mention that she had tried to interview Pickton. She expressed her frustration and her doubt that her superiors were giving the investigation the priority she felt they should. The Picktons had been selling parcels of their property to the City of Coquitlam, and I called her periodically throughout that fall to suggest the RCMP search that newly released land for evidence. The suggestion was always met with lukewarm enthusiasm at best. The file was dying before my eyes, and I didn't know what more to do.

No one from Coquitlam ever advised us about what changed for them. As VPD Deputy Chief Constable Doug LePard noted in his August 2010 report Missing Women Investigation Review, "Pickton was eventually excluded by DNA from being a suspect in the Agassiz Murders. (It appears no further investigation on the Coquitlam RCMP Pickton file occurred until November 2001, when Constable Yurkiw's replacement, Constable Sherstone, made several attempts to re-interview Ellingsen, but was unsuccessful.)"

In his research, LePard learned that Yurkiw visited the farm in an attempt to interview Pickton but was met by his brother, Dave, who asked her to "come back during the rainy season," because they were too busy working now. No interview took place until January 2000, when Yurkiw and RCMP Constable John Cater sat down with Robert.

The investigators were criticized for allowing Pickton's friend Gina Houston to sit in on the interview. In fairness to them, their hands had been tied because Pickton told them he wouldn't proceed without her present, and they tried to make the best of the situation. Again, it seemed that inexperienced or under-prepared people were placed in impossible positions because the file wasn't seen as important enough to assign top investigators or attract adequate resourcing. How familiar that theme would become to me over the years. It's difficult to blame these investigators who were only doing their jobs but with little or no guidance.

I pressed various RCMP members periodically that autumn and winter, asking what, if anything, was being done with respect to Pickton, including E Division Superintendent Gary

Bass, whom I saw at the October 1999 meeting to discuss POI 390. Every time, I was met with comments about how "interesting" Pickton was, along with vague mention of how "something" should be done, but it was "difficult" or so-and-so was "looking into it." I would check with the various so-and-sos, and they would have the same response: someone was "on it," but no one could tell me what was being done, and no one needed our help. No one seemed to be doing anything, yet no one could tell me that they had substantiated that Ellingsen's information was false. All I could hope was that if the super-intendent of E Division was aware of Pickton, someone in the RCMP must be assigned to follow this up.

But I didn't understand the politics within the RCMP. The Provincial Unsolved Homicide Unit investigators apparently had jurisdiction over members at the detachment—Coquitlam—level. In murder investigations, the investigative opinions of members such as Frank Henley of the PUHU took precedence, even over those of an experienced murder inves-tigator such as Mike Connor, who knew the players and the file far better than any member of the PUHU.

There seems to have been no police contact with Pickton after the January 19, 2000, interview, aside from RCMP corpo-ral Frank Henley's March 2001 one-man self-described "really, very much a social visit" to Pickton's farm to tell him the names of the two people talking to police about him: Ellingsen and Caldwell. Commissioner Oppal describes this visit in his report: "On March 30, 2001, Cpl. Henley of PUHU goes to the Pickton property to speak with Pickton. He tells Pickton that Ms. Ellingsen and Mr. Caldwell have been saying he killed a girl. Pickton admits to stabbing Ms. Anderson, but says that she stabbed him first. Cpl. Henley's meeting with Pickton is unexplained and done in total isolation from other police members."

That seemed to be the last police contact with Pickton until February 5, 2002.

SINCE MID-1999, PROJECT Amelia had worked closely with RCMP Behavioural Sciences Staff Sergeant Keith Davidson and his partner, Sergeant Scot Filer; Corporal Marg Kingsbury; and the criminal profiling staff. I maintained close contact with these officers over several months, and they shared my team's frustration that the Pickton investigation seemed to be going nowhere. This group of Mounties shared our conviction that Lynn Ellingsen's information needed to be more closely examined and that Pickton appeared to be a viable suspect in the missing women investigation. Certainly, no one had yet ruled out his involvement.

On February 10, 2000, Davidson called a meeting with VPD investigators Mark Chernoff and Ron Lepine; RCMP corporals Marg Kingsbury, Nicole St. Mars, and Grant Johnston; and Constable Paul McCarl and me. I was grateful that people in the RCMP still believed in Pickton as a suspect. This meeting was the follow-up to a January 13, 2000, meeting in which Geramy had asked Davidson and Filer to ask their unit to prepare a suspect profile on Robert Pickton.

At the February 10 meeting, I asked Davidson to use his influence to appeal to his RCMP superiors to create a joint forces operation with the VPD to investigate the missing women. We discussed pursuing Pickton, dealing with the Ellingsen information, and revisiting with Crown counsel the 1997 stay of proceedings in the Anderson attempted murder and forcible confinement case. Davidson and Filer supported the creation of a joint forces operation. We discussed an action plan, and Davidson stated his understanding that those of us from the VPD were there because we wanted a joint forces operation, and if the RCMP could not set one in motion, we were prepared to go to the provincial attorney general.

Unknown to me for years after that meeting, a second meeting took place on February 14, at Davidson's initiation. Davidson, RCMP corporals Filer, Kingsbury, St. Mars, and David McCartney, and Constable John Cater attended. As per Davidson's affidavit, "The purpose of the meeting was to discuss investigative strategies regarding Pickton as a suspect." At that meeting, McCartney was charged with obtaining "authorization to intercept communications and a search warrant for the property," and Cater was assigned to conduct a background investigation of Pickton, but for unknown reasons neither of these assignments was completed.

I struggled after the Ellingsen information seemingly died in late 1999, asking myself how I could have pushed this issue further. I don't believe I could have done any more than I did at that time and in early 2000. I passed on everything we knew to the RCMP Serious Crime members. Late 1999 and most of 2000 was a strange and bewildering time for me; I began to relate select portions of this situation to non-police friends when we'd meet socially, and their stares and exclamations of shock and disbelief that *something* couldn't be done to get on the Pickton farm both validated and deeply dismayed me. Regular citizens, normal civilian people, thought this was completely *messed up*.

More and more, I found myself telling this story to outsiders, relative strangers even; taking these minor risks of indiscretion was the first real indication I had aside from my nightmares that this case was really getting to me. I needed to do something to prevent the stalling of the Pickton file from dragging me deeper and deeper into despondency. How could my own colleagues and managers not question it, too? Or worse, why couldn't those of us who could see it overcome this toxic police bureaucracy to insist that the right thing be done?

I felt I had exhausted all acceptable avenues within the policing infrastructure, short of stepping way outside those informal but well-established codes of conduct known as "what's done" and jeopardizing my role—though ineffectual—on the case. As Deputy Chief Constable LePard would testify in the Missing Women Commission of Inquiry years later, circumventing the police department that held jurisdiction in an area just wasn't done, and to do so would be the police equivalent of anarchy. This prohibition wasn't written anywhere I was aware of; yet it existed, and I felt its restrictions powerfully. It was like the policing equivalent to a natural law.

It wasn't that I didn't feel prepared to fight for justice and break this ridiculous tradition, even if it meant risking my career; more than anything, I feared my actions would have little or no effect, would be witnessed by few, and I would be quietly shuffled off to the sidelines, a place very much like where I already was, and my advocacy, again ineffectual at best, would be lost to the victims and their families. I didn't even know what it would look like to try to circumvent the RCMP.

I knew how people were viewed who pushed too hard to make their views known. I would be written off as an overly passionate feminist crackpot, and whatever message I might be trying to communicate would be dismissed, much in the same way Lynn Ellingsen's information was dismissed. I felt trapped and frustrated and more bound by my duty and moral obligation to these families than by any sense of duty to the VPD.

I struggled professionally and personally through the early months of 2000, without any idea of what more I could do to further the Pickton investigation. No one offered any ideas. Nightmares tormented me, my stomach seemed unable to tolerate most food and drink, my head and body ached for no apparent reason, and I suffered from allergies I'd never had before. I found myself taking a sick day every few weeks when I couldn't deal with Fisk and Myers or sitting in that project room staring at the women's photos on the wall.

In March 2000, I attended a small memorial gathering at Crab Park, on the north edge of the Downtown Eastside, to commemorate the missing women. Perhaps twenty-five of us stood in a small circle, huddled under our umbrellas, weathering a typical Vancouver downpour. Dave Dickson and I were the only police officers there; standing beside us were Indigenous elders, family members, and women from the Downtown Eastside. People took turns holding the talking stick and speaking quietly to the group, and after about half of them had spoken, Dave passed me the stick. Barely peering out from under my umbrella, I opened my mouth, expecting my usual clear, well-projected voice to come out.

I began with "My name is Lori Shenher and I—" and I couldn't go on. My throat choked shut with emotion. I pulled the umbrella lower over my head as tears sprang to my eyes and big wracking sobs welled inside me and overflowed, forcing me to cover my mouth to muffle the noise. I wordlessly handed the talking stick to the next person, turned, and slowly walked away from the group toward the parking lot. Lindsay Kines of the *Vancouver Sun* followed me.

As I approached my Jeep, Lindsay called out to me.

"Detective Shenher?"

My first thought was *oh damn.* I felt sick, not myself in any way, and deeply embarrassed at my public breakdown. I'm sure I would have been mortified to learn this wouldn't be my last. I turned to see Lindsay standing behind me.

"Are you okay?"

Looking back, I think that's the split second I knew I would be able to trust Lindsay. He was kind and not mining me for a good quote or a scoop. I felt he actually cared whether I was okay. I think he knew I wasn't okay.

"I'm sorry, this just isn't a good time for me to talk. I hope you can understand," I said, still sniffling.

"I understand. Off the record, completely." He smiled sheep-ishly and I found myself joining him.

"I'm just incredibly frustrated. I can't say more than that, but this is really wearing on me."

"Is there anything you can say on the record?" He paused. "I understand if you can't."

"Only that this is so frustrating to not be able to give the families some closure." I sighed. "All I can tell them is where they aren't. As far as where they are, we haven't got there yet." I told him I just couldn't say any more. He told me if I ever wanted to talk, he was there, and I thanked him. And, with that, I walked away.

15

Finding Four Women

• • •

"Hope is the thing with feathers
That perches in the soul
And sings the tune without the words
And never stops at all."
EMILY DICKINSON

O ur team lacked hope. After we had trudged through
late 1999 and early 2000, there was little to be excited
about. The Project Amelia members had been working on
several avenues of investigation concurrent with the Ellingsen
tip investigation. We were deluged with useless tips from the
America's Most Wanted show and stuck in the tight confines of our
project room with Fisk and Myers, without much to call leadership. Chernoff and Lepine were busy working fresh homicides
and trying to shore up the Lynn Ellingsen information off the
side of their desks, while Alex and I were wading through the
mountains of paper that made up our investigation as we
moved from completing the obvious follow-ups to tackling
the more obscure, in addition to dealing with the RCMP.

In the midst of the Ellingsen investigation, we added two new women to our list—Lydia Chase* and Kendra Sparrow*. Lydia Chase was a young woman with a bachelor's degree in biology and a diagnosis of schizophrenia who had gone off her medication, winding up addicted to heroin and occasionally working the Downtown Eastside low track to pay the bills. She had been missing since 1994 but somehow hadn't been entered in our system. I later found letters written to our office by her mother, Pamela*, over the years, and it seemed a detective or Missing Persons clerk had investigated the case and determined it closed several years before. It was disconcerting how difficult it was to even try to analyze what went wrong with Lydia's investigation, so I focused my energies on finding out what happened to Lydia, and Alex set out to find Kendra.

Kendra Sparrow was a young Indigenous mother who had been missing for some time as well. Her family and friends thought she was in Edmonton, whereas others believed she was in Vancouver, and no one reported her missing. Her file was extremely frustrating. Progress was slow, as she was estranged from her family, and they didn't seem to believe that she was missing. We had very little information of value in her file, and, as with Lydia, little investigation seemed to have been done.

Throughout spring and summer of 1999, Alex and I were delving into the health care system, trying to obtain medical records of the missing women, with the help of Chief Coroner Larry Campbell. I had done some preliminary work on both Chase and Sparrow, but each seemed to be very cold trails. They both had boyfriends at the time of their disappearances, but our efforts to locate them proved difficult.

Lydia's mother, Pamela, was a fascinating woman with whom I greatly enjoyed working. She was in her sixties and lived alone in a small seaside community in Washington State nestled on the Canada/U.S. border about an hour south of Vancouver. She had been living in the southeastern U.S. when Lydia disappeared, which partially explained why the file had fallen by the wayside—often, without a family member to advocate and pressure our office, files gathered dust. Now that Pamela was closer to Vancouver, she felt better able to revisit what might have happened to Lydia.

Pamela was extremely helpful to us without ever becoming overbearing or frustrated by our lack of progress and the apparent previous mishandling of Lydia's case. She accepted that and we moved on. That was her way, to just carry on with what she had, accepting that the past is the past. She could have easily become bogged down in all the ways Lydia had been failed—by the health care system, by police, and by inadequate medication and support for the mentally ill. Yet she refused to lay blame, preferring instead to view it all with a wry cynicism honed by a lifetime of accepting that this was simply the way of the world sometimes.

Since 1998, I had been working closely with Chico Newell, identification specialist with the Forensic Identification Unit of the office of the chief coroner. Chico is a brilliant and driven man, highly committed to the identification of human remains found in the province. Through him and Sylvia Port of the RCMP's ViCLAS Section Missing Persons/Found Human Remains office, I learned a great deal about what happens to unidentifiable bodies and body parts found in B.C. In 1998, Sylvia was just beginning to set up a database of found human remains, complete with DNA profiles. There were—and still are—several hundred sets of unidentified remains, and the task of conducting DNA testing on all of them was monumental, but at least it had begun in earnest and would help future families find answers.

In March 1999, Chico provided me with a list of all the unidentified complete bodies of women who had died in B.C. It was easy to narrow the list even further to get only those closer in age to our group of missing women, including Chase and Sparrow. I found a 1994 overdose victim who I felt could have been Lydia Chase based on the physical description and on the fact that she had been found dead in a bowling alley washroom on Commercial Drive—a street where aging Old World immigrants, young artists, rich, poor, capitalists, anarchists, soccer fans, LGBTQ, straight, and everyone in between mixed and coexisted—just a short distance east of the Downtown Eastside and a popular destination for many of its inhabitants. The bowling alley was also a short walk down Commercial from the Kettle, a drop-in center for the mentally ill. I had a strong sense that this victim was Lydia, and Chico agreed to try to track down an autopsy photo for me to look at. In the meantime, I showed this list to the people in our office, and both Mark and Alex agreed there was a good chance that this was a match.

Autopsy photos are never ideal for identification because the face is often distorted or contorted, and there is usually bruising, either from an assault or lividity—the postmortem pooling of blood—or sometimes as a result of the autopsy itself. These photos often pose a dilemma for investigators: Do you show such a disturbing image to a loved one, knowing how dissimilar it may be to the living person? All we had for a photo of Lydia was a shot taken of her in a wedding party, but I thought the nose was the same, the hair color was close, and the ears were very similar. Alex concurred, and we agreed we had to show the autopsy photo to Pamela, certain that if anyone could handle something as difficult as this, she could. We had Pamela's DNA and could access Lydia's PAP smear DNA if necessary, but we felt if Pamela could make a positive ID, it would save her several more weeks of not knowing and save us the cost of the lab work.

Pamela had told me that Lydia had had a greenstick fracture to an arm as a child, possessed an extra rib, and sustained a broken nose later on that Pamela suspected was the work of a violent boyfriend. With the assistance of Larry Campbell, I was able to obtain a coroner's order to seize—a document with seemingly sweeping applications and fewer limitations than any search warrant I had ever seen. After some digging, I found several sets of X-rays taken of Lydia over her years in Vancouver and the number of visits to the emergency room that unfortunately all too frequently come with a life of addiction and poor mental health on the Downtown Eastside.

Chico provided me with the autopsy X-rays, and I asked each radiologist to compare them with those of the unidentified dead woman. Three hospitals and several radiologists later, no one was willing to sign off with absolute certainty that they were the same person, though there were several points of comparison that perfectly matched up. It's fascinating that a profession that is so seldom successfully sued for malpractice has developed such a deep-seated fear of lawsuits, but I found very few people willing to go on the record with a finding. That is not to say they weren't helpful—most medical people I dealt with speculated freely and were often able to give us opinions with certainties of 80 or 90 percent. But no one would commit to those opinions on paper. They all strongly encouraged us to find someone else to concur or back up their findings with some other proof of identity so that theirs wouldn't have to stand alone. Regardless, we were still faced with having to show Pamela the photos.

Alex and I made the drive to the U.S. one sunny morning in July 1999. Pamela met us at her home, a newly built, tiny bungalow on a small acreage. It was an odd meeting; it felt social, but each of us knew we were engaged in a task of deadly seriousness. It was quite possible that Pamela would discover for certain that Lydia was dead. I explained what we had found to date and that we believed the woman in the photograph was quite possibly Lydia. I told Pamela we were going to show her an autopsy photo, and she assured us she was able to view it.

She looked at it long and hard, commenting that the hair didn't look like quite the same color, which Alex and I agreed with. Pamela said she knew Lydia changed her hair color often, so it could be her. It was obvious Pamela had the same struggle we did—it was close, but without seeing the eyes and with the distortion around the mouth, it was impossible to say for sure. I explained that there was no pressure to make the ID, that we still had the DNA testing to fall back on, but it would take a couple of weeks. Pamela apologized and said she just couldn't be 100 percent certain. Both Alex and I reassured her that we felt exactly the same way about the photo, that we wanted to give it a shot, but regardless, we would have an answer soon. We stayed for quite a while, chatting while Pamela showed us around her home and garden. We left, assuring her that we would initiate the DNA testing immediately.

Several weeks later, we had our answer—Lydia was a match for the unidentified woman. The testing gave astronomical odds against it being anyone other than Lydia, and the PAP smear sample was the clincher. I told Pamela of our findings with very mixed feelings—elation at having solved a mystery and provided some closure but also a deep sadness, knowing we had to tell a mother she had outlived her own child. There was also a feeling of disappointment at no longer having a reason to speak with Pamela. Both Alex and I felt that loss and would speak of her often in the coming months. Finally, something we had done felt like it had gone the way it was supposed to—leads led to more leads, trails went somewhere instead of to dead ends, and science had provided the confirmation of what we had strongly suspected. Finding Lydia had seemed so simple a process, so straightforward in comparison with the others. Where were they? Could we find twenty-seven more women this way? It didn't seem likely.

As part of our effort to expand our search to areas of the country we hadn't previously had access to, I began doing a province-by-province driver's license check on each of the missing women. I had done this for the newer files, but it had not been done on many of the older files, perhaps because of the erroneous assumption these women were not capable of driving or could not afford a vehicle. Regardless, it was important to run this check, if only to be able to say we had done it and were unable to find them this way. I planned to run the names through every six months in case there were any new entries.

As all of this was going on, I was also working closely with Larry Campbell to search the coroners' and medical examiners' databases for each province, including their departments of Vital Statistics, to ascertain whether any of the women had died, used health care services, or given birth in another province. Surprisingly, two of the names on our list showed up in the Ontario medical records—Lily Jones*, missing since October 1991, and Paulette Adamson*, missing since 1978.

Finding Lily Jones was embarrassingly simple. From her medical records, I was able to contact a physician who had seen her and explain my predicament. He agreed to look at a faxed photo and confirmed that this was the same woman that he had seen only a short time ago. I asked him if he would phone her and have her contact me, and he agreed to do so. He called me back a short while later and said that Lily was indeed alive and well but that she didn't want to speak with me, since she had left her life in Vancouver behind and did not wish to be reminded of it. I conferred with Geramy, and we agreed this was more than enough to satisfy us that Lily Jones was fine and should be taken off our list.

From what I could gather, the people who reported Lily Jones missing in the first place were not family, and I believe they thought they could get some money if they could locate her. Lily's appearance had changed radically since her Vancouver days, which is probably why no one who knew her had ever recognized her from our poster or *America's Most Wanted*. I had never been able to reach the two people who reported her missing; nor did I have any information about her family. The more I looked at it, the more obvious it became that Lily was never really "missing" to any of the important people in her life, only to these two clowns who reported her missing in the hope that they would be the first to know if we located her.

Paulette Adamson's story is one I wish belonged to more of these women—the kind of *Pretty Woman* boy-meets-girl, boy-saves-girl-from-a-life-on-the-street story I know many people like to think happens to sex workers all the time but sadly does not. She had never entirely fit our profile. She ran with a more upscale, affluent crowd, preferring clubs like the Penthouse to the Downtown Eastside beer parlors. Her drug use was not prolific, and I had a difficult time proving that she was using anything more than recreationally. What had always troubled me about Paulette was that she left behind family—including a young son—without a word. As with our other victims, this factor led me to believe she had not left the area of her own free will.

Paulette had been missing since 1978—the longest of any of the women on our list at that time—making the simplicity of her discovery all the more embarrassing and somewhat humbling. As part of my nationwide driver's license search, Paulette's name was run through each province's motor vehicle

licensing bureau, but we hadn't known her new last name at
the time. Out of all of our missing women, Paulette's was the
only name that showed up—Adamson showing as a previous
surname replaced by what appeared to be a married name—
with an associated address and telephone number. Again, I
couldn't believe it could be this easy after all these years—was
this all we had to do? Check medical records? Rerun a driver's
license check? Check the damn phone book? Why had this not
been done when the file was first opened? Why hadn't I done
it when I reviewed the file?

With a trembling hand, I dialed the number as Alex sat
excitedly beside me, also unable to believe that we'd found
her. A woman answered, and I identified myself and asked if
she was Paulette Adamson. Clearly, she was not comfortable
at having been found, but she politely answered my questions
and simply said she had changed her life, married, and now had
a new family and did not want her birth family to know where
she was or what her new name was.

I should have felt on top of the world that we had found
her, but my heart was heavy with dread as I called her family member on the file and said we had found her. Naturally,
she was upset to learn Paulette did not want contact with the
family, but she understood Paulette's position and thanked
me for my efforts. Unfortunately, the rest of the family did not
seem to share this person's gratitude—I received several nasty
phone calls and messages from one person berating me for not
providing contact information for Paulette and questioning
my obligation to protect Paulette's privacy. I was beginning
to think Paulette may have had good reason to run away and
not look back.

Kendra Sparrow remained a mystery. At the same time
we were working on identifying Lydia Chase, Alex was busy
delving into Kendra's background, trying to track her down.

We had information that she could be in Vancouver or Edmonton or on a reserve in Saskatchewan, but no one could say for certain. Alex had been in contact with Detective Keith Kilshaw of the Edmonton Police Service's Project KARE, their task force formed to look into several unsolved Edmonton-area sex worker homicides in the late '90s and early 2000s. Keith was a great resource for us and was helping Alex with contacts on his end but had encountered the same dead ends locating Kendra.

A woman contacted me who claimed she had seen the photos of the missing women on *America's Most Wanted* and felt she could assist our investigation. She was a psychic and provided me with several references from within the law enforcement community in both Canada and the U.S. During the missing women investigation, four or five psychics had reached me on the phone through the VPD switchboard and I'd indulge them for a few minutes before it became obvious they had little to offer the investigation. This woman was different. She told me she had specific feelings about a few of the women in particular, and I felt I could at least spare an hour to hear what she had to say. One thing about our conversation that struck me as interesting was that she asked me to provide a separate photo of each woman so that she could view them one at a time rather than all together on the poster, which she said muddled her perceptions and caused her to be unclear about whom she was sensing. I told her we could do this, and she agreed to come in one morning to meet with Alex and me.

This same week, Alex obtained some information that indicated Kendra Sparrow had possibly died in an Edmonton hospital. She was still working hard to confirm this with the Alberta branch of Vital Statistics, and there were some issues regarding the possibility that Kendra had died under a different surname. Keith Kilshaw was also trying to find her ex-boyfriend on the reserve in Saskatchewan, where he was apparently raising their son.

Alex and I didn't exactly broadcast it around the office that we had a psychic coming in that morning—Fisk and Myers would have laughed themselves hoarse, and we didn't need to hear any more of their old boy cynicism and true crime paperback policing theories. They were incredibly closed-minded, and it was easier to keep them out of the loop than listen to them mock us for entertaining someone they would surely have branded a quack.

The psychic was not what we had expected. She was very professional and unassuming and said all she could promise was if she didn't sense anything, she would tell us that. We gave her a binder of the photos—one per page, with no names. We had inserted Lydia Chase's photo as a test, even though at this time we were awaiting the DNA results and were almost certain that she was the deceased woman from the Commercial Drive heroin overdose. Paulette Adamson's photo was also included as a test because we'd found her and closed her case.

Slowly, the psychic looked closely at each photo. With some, she admitted to feeling nothing. With others, she had a vision of where she saw the particular woman last in her mind. One woman was seen near a gravel pit—we had no idea if the woman had been near a gravel pit but made a note of each observation. Another was pictured on Vancouver Island, where we had never heard of that woman being, so we were sceptical. As the psychic continued, many of her observations were interesting but disappointingly vague and virtually impossible to follow up on because she couldn't identify any of the locations.

Then she looked at Lydia Chase's photo. She said this woman made her feel cold, and she feared she was dead. Alex and I looked at one another, practically gulping.

She continued without much to say about the remaining women until she came to Paulette Adamson. She told us she saw this woman in a city—she told us the name, but I am omitting it here out of respect for Paulette's privacy—which was very close geographically to where we knew Paulette was living. This location had never been mentioned in the press or to anyone outside our office. The psychic said she was alive. Alex and I were encouraged—now we needed to hear something we didn't already know.

When she came to Kendra Sparrow's photo, she was visibly shaken. She said she was very cold and she saw her laid out on a stone, perhaps a marble slab or something in a mortuary—she couldn't say for sure. She told us this woman was dead and very much alone. Chills ran up and down my spine. I watched the color drain from Alex's face. Shortly after this July 1999 meeting, Alex determined that Kendra Sparrow had died in an Edmonton hospital of complications arising from her drug use. There is absolutely no way the psychic could have known that.

The psychic finished, and we talked briefly. We didn't mention whether any of her observations had been close, only that she had been of help and we appreciated her time. She apologized for not being able to do more but said she would let us know if she thought of anything else. After she left, Alex and I just stared at each other, unable to get over those observations we knew to be accurate. Unfortunately, there were the others that were off base enough to keep us from getting too excited, but still, it left us both with a new appreciation of people with this sort of gift and reinforced for us the importance of maintaining an open mind. We felt we had done the right thing in not dismissing anyone who claimed they had had visions of any of the missing women. Unfortunately, those others we spoke with were not of the caliber of this woman.

In the space of a few weeks, we had gone from thirty-one missing women back down to twenty-seven, and this hint of success was both inspirational and daunting. The relative ease with which we had found Adamson and Jones—alive, no less—caused me to rethink the entire investigation to ensure that we weren't missing any other obvious sources of information or making assumptions about the victims that had prevented us from pursuing avenues that might be fruitful. This was a healthy fear and provided a much-needed infusion of enthusiasm and motivation at a time when I sorely needed a boost.

16

Investigating Person of Interest (POI) 390

• • •

*"If two men on the same job agree all the time, then one is
useless. If they disagree all the time, both are useless."*
DARRYL F. ZANUCK

WAYNE MYERS AND Gary Fisk joined Project Amelia in
July 1999 utterly convinced Person of Interest (POI)
390 was responsible for killing these women. Although
their conviction and tenacity were admirable, this certainty
was based on nothing more than the hair on Myers's neck. I
wondered if I wasn't the same in my interest in Pickton. I felt
we had more solid evidence that indicated Pickton could be
our guy, but on bad days I wondered if I wasn't just like them,
hanging my hat on nothing more than my gut feeling.

Repeatedly, they would tell anyone who would listen about
the time Myers and his patrol partner pulled POI 390 over in a
Downtown Eastside traffic stop, about the sick feeling Myers
got from the man, and about how that made him their number
one suspect in the missing women investigation. There was

no other evidence that elevated POI 390 to this status or made him any different from the hundreds of other men who used and abused the women on the low track on any given day. Still, Fisk and Myers would ride POI 390's considerable back into this investigation and bring what semblance of a team we had to its knees.

POI 390 was an interesting subject, no question. The adopted son of recently deceased elderly parents from Lethbridge, Alberta, he led a strangely nomadic life, driving exotic sports cars often fifteen or twenty hours nonstop between Lethbridge, Calgary, and Vancouver, selling contraband cigarettes and picking up sex workers. He was an extremely large man—almost a giant—with a rock star hairstyle and piercing eyes. He had a huge crack habit and would flash a bag full of rocks or a wad of money at the girls on the street, enticing them to come along for the ride. He was a regular on the bad date sheets—regular newsletters published and distributed by the Downtown Eastside Youth Activities Society (DEYAS) to warn sex workers of known bad dates—more often for bad driving and not paying for dates than for violence.

The rest of us on Project Amelia tried to maintain open minds where suspects were concerned. We were desperate for someone to pursue. I was growing so tired of dead ends and leads that went nowhere. Still, POI 390 remained nothing more than a sex offender with no evidence to suggest he had killed anyone, and Fisk and Myers were assigned to find out whether he could be responsible for more. POI 390 dated the same sex workers repeatedly and had a long-term relationship with a woman outside of the sex trade. His DNA would later match that found in the sexual assault examination of a North Vancouver sex worker who had since died of AIDS. Still, there seemed to be nothing to link him to any of our victims.

Constable Paul McCarl was an RCMP Serious Crime investigator generally assigned to homicide cases outside the major urban centers of the Lower Mainland, such as the Fraser Valley. He and I attended many of the same information-sharing meetings over the years, and we spoke often because the three Agassiz homicides—Tracy Olajide, Tammy Pipe, and Victoria Younker—were Paul's cases. Paul worked extremely hard with us while maintaining a great sense of humor and a compassionate attitude toward the victims. He was invaluable to me and opened his files to Project Amelia whenever we asked.

Fisk and Myers pressed McCarl to allow them to present POI 390 to the RCMP as a viable suspect in the missing women investigation and the Agassiz homicides and to ask for the RCMP's help with surveillance. I felt this meeting was premature and that the VPD stood to be embarrassed for requesting it. I expressed the feeling, both to the team and to Geramy, that POI 390 was no more a suspect in these missing women files than any of the hundreds of other men we had in our database who were sex offenders, violent to sex workers, and the like. I explained that we needed more information about POI 390 beyond Myers's gut feeling. Geramy and I agreed that if this surveillance gave us more information, we could hope to rule POI 390 in or out as a suspect, and we would just have to risk the possibility of embarrassment.

A meeting was arranged for October 27, 1999, at the RCMP E Division Surrey satellite office and Geramy, Fisk, Myers, and I attended to represent the VPD. The RCMP had several members there, including Superintendent Gary Bass, Corporal Marg Kingsbury, Constable Paul McCarl, Sergeant Bob Paulson, Corporal Nicole St. Mars, Sergeant Bill Thordarson, and Norm Libel, representing the B.C. Coroners Service.

Initially, the air was full of expectation—obviously, because of whatever Fisk and Myers had told McCarl, the Mounties were expecting to hear some solid evidence against POI 390 and to be asked for their assistance. Instead, Fisk told a rambling account of what a terrible person POI 390 was and how his poor personal hygiene somehow translated into his being a serial killer of prostitutes. Slowly, eyebrows around the table rose.

There was no evidence of anything beyond the fact that POI 390 was a sex offender who didn't like to let his dates leave his condo when the party slowed down or the coke ran out. But when asked whether they were aware of anyone who hadn't got away from POI 390, the answer was a sheepish no. McCarl asked what else they had on POI 390, and Myers raised his voice and asked, "What more do you want?"

He launched into his now-tired reenactment of the vehicle stop and the hair on his neck standing on end at meeting POI 390—as though he had some kind of follicular barometer to register the propensity to kill. He appeared incensed that the others couldn't see what he and Fisk could. Glances were exchanged around the table. *So? And?* I looked to Geramy as if to say *See? This is why I didn't think this was a good idea.* She just nodded slowly. Bad idea to come here.

Myers stuck his finger accusingly in McCarl's face and demanded to know why it was taking so long for McCarl to compare the DNA on the Agassiz homicides against that found in the North Vancouver sex worker assault case to determine whether it came from the same suspect. To his credit, McCarl maintained his composure and simply replied that these things took time and it was happening as quickly as it could. Myers was livid, convinced this would prove POI 390 killed those women—and the Vancouver missing women, the victims of Green River, and presumably every other unsolved sex worker homicide in the Pacific Northwest. Finally, Bob Paulson, who would go on to become the commissioner of the RCMP, asked them a question.

"Hair on your neck notwithstanding, what *evidence* do you guys have?"

Paulson was a highly respected investigator known for his expertise on outlaw motorcycle gang files, and he supervised the RCMP Special O surveillance team. The final decision to grant us their support rested with him. Fisk and Myers hemmed and hawed, referred to the bad feeling they had for POI 390, until Paulson relented and agreed to give them a few days of surveillance in the Lethbridge area. Arrangements were made to conduct surveillance on POI 390 to obtain a discard DNA sample. This sample would then be tested and, if it was a match, it would further the North Vancouver sexual assault case against POI 390 and enable Fisk and Myers to request a DNA sample by warrant.

On the positive side, we all agreed that POI 390's DNA sample should be obtained and tested against the samples we had from our North Van sex assault victim and the Agassiz homicides. But the disappointment in the air was palpable, and we felt we had lost credibility in the eyes of the RCMP as a result of this poorly conceived meeting. Fisk and Myers pushed their way wordlessly out of the meeting, while the rest of us stayed behind, Geramy and I apologizing to McCarl for Myers's questioning his work and yelling at him in front of everyone. Good-natured to the end, Paul laughed it off, saying, "We've all been under that kind of pressure, I guess."

The next two weeks were very difficult in the Project Amelia room. Fisk and Myers barked orders to Bob Paulson over the telephone, referring to POI 390 as the "only suspect worth a damn," oblivious to the rest of us continuing to work on the list of other more compelling potential suspects we had information about, including Pickton. Despite my desire to support the entire team, I found myself for the first time in this investigation wishing that the DNA sample would not match a single thing. Then maybe they would finally see the value in pursuing the only decent potential suspect we had—Pickton. At the same time, I didn't want to behave like them and dismiss a good suspect, and I desperately hoped something would link POI 390 to the missing women so that maybe we could tie this thing up for these poor families and move on. I realized I didn't care who our killer was; I just hoped we would catch him and put these cases to bed, finally.

On November 16, 1999, POI 390's DNA sample came back from the lab. It did not match any of the DNA found on Agassiz victims Tammy Pipe and Tracy Olajide. It did match with matter collected in the North Van victim's rape kit, enabling Fisk and Myers to proceed with charges in her case, so the effort was not a total loss.

This information didn't appear to register with Fisk and Myers in any way. Myers immediately said he wanted to begin dealing directly with Mission Institution, a prison in the Fraser Valley. He wanted to obtain DNA samples from all the men incarcerated there for comparison with the Agassiz homicides. Clearly, that was not Myers's investigation; it was McCarl's, and the discard DNA proved it had nothing to do with POI 390. There was no indication that McCarl was dragging his heels or was incompetent in any way—quite the contrary. Clearly, these were not Vancouver cases. Myers's understanding of federal DNA legislation was severely lacking, but I was no longer shocked by his and Fisk's lack of investigative knowledge and acumen. I expressed my concerns to Geramy, who agreed she would speak to them.

Over the next two weeks, I tried without success to assign several new tips to Fisk and Myers for follow-up. They continued to do their own haphazard assessment of potential suspects and work on only what they found interesting, ignoring the mountain of tips related to the missing women we still had sitting untouched in the Project Amelia office. This all occurred in the same time frame as the aftermath of the

Ellingsen/Pickton debacle of late summer 1999, and I was already disheartened and discouraged. I would have welcomed a new direction had I truly believed we had exhausted the Pickton information and ruled him out as a suspect, but we hadn't.

My frustration grew from my inability to direct Fisk and Myers in any way, from their apparent unwillingness to take direction from Geramy, and from Geramy's inability to find the time to direct and manage them. The futility of my position wore on me. As the file coordinator, I was supposed to have largely administrative duties—reviewing files, assessing new information, liaising with other agencies, ensuring that everything each investigator was doing was properly documented, conferring with Geramy, and assigning tips where appropriate.

Daily, I vacillated between running to Geramy with every little concern and trying to deal with problems myself, problems that included the management of two people with their own agenda. Geramy's investigative skills were in high demand during a violent gang war and her role as a homicide supervisor consumed all of her time. I was not given the title of a supervisor—acting sergeant—yet here I was, coordinating the largest serial killer file in Canadian history, and I couldn't motivate my investigators to do what needed to be done. I didn't want to wield power through rank, but clearly these guys weren't going to listen to a woman with eight years on the job. Something had to change.

In early December 1999, I made a formal written request that either I be assigned as an acting sergeant on the case or that management assign a senior man such as Ron Lepine to that role—someone who would be in that room full time and could see Fisk's and Myers's apparent incompetence and unwillingness to cooperate with the others, someone who had the power and authority to deal with them. It was clear Fisk and Myers had little respect for anyone, but women and junior members seemed to rank lowest on their totem pole. Assign a senior man, I asserted, someone who could direct them and hold them accountable should they choose to not complete their assignments. Making Ron that man was my first choice of possible outcomes.

I compared Project Amelia with the Home Invasion Task Force, which represented a who's who of investigative talent in the VPD; there wasn't a weak link among the ten detectives assigned at the height of that case. Apparently, victimized homeowners warranted the big guns—missing drug-addicted sex workers did not.

My request was turned down. *Lori needs to understand this thing won't be going on much longer.* That was the verbal response Major Crime acting inspector Dan Dureau gave Geramy. I don't believe I ever received a written reply. This stunned me. How could anyone say this case would not be continuing? Had someone found the victims and neglected to tell me? I failed to understand how anyone thought this could simply be swept under a rug. Who truly believed we could go to these families and say, "Sorry, we couldn't find them, investigation closed"? Not only did I not get my first choice—Ron as acting sergeant—I wasn't assigned to the position either, and the status quo remained. *There is no problem here.*

The next few months contained more of the same. Each week, Fisk and Myers seemed to have some new Best Suspect Ever, but they kept their information close to the vest, afraid the rest of the Project Amelia team would steal their information, make an arrest, and receive all the glory they were certain would be waiting. They didn't seem to realize that there would be no glory in confirming someone had murdered thirty women—the number we were dealing with at the time. The rest of our team wasn't interested in glory. They failed to understand that the rest of us had work to do. They also didn't seem to understand that their suspects held little interest to the rest of us in the absence of solid evidence to link them to the case.

During Missing Women Commission of Inquiry testimony, I found it exasperating that Jason Gratl, the lawyer for the Downtown Eastside interests, continued to portray Fisk and Myers as the only detectives who subscribed to the "serial killer theory" and were seriously concerned with finding a serial killer, while the rest of us supposedly poured cold water on their efforts to solve the murders. The truth was that these two officers took valuable time and energy from the team and our efforts to find the killer of the missing women. They also withheld vital witness photo identification of Pickton that would have spurred a renewed attempt to press the RCMP to ramp up its investigation of Pickton.

In April 2000, Fisk and Myers showed a pile of photos to women on the Downtown Eastside, including photos of POI 390 and Pickton. I expressed my concerns to them at the time that this was not a proper photo lineup and, as such, would not be admissible in court if they used the photos to make identifications and they later became evidence to support criminal charges. Fisk and Myers laughed off my concerns as well as my offers—and the offers of our administrative assistant, Dorothy—to make them a proper photo lineup they could use on their rounds that would be admissible in court. I was afraid that Pickton would end up being our killer and the identifications would be inadmissible, and I told them so.

They later testified at the Missing Women Commission of Inquiry that I didn't want Pickton's photo shown, which was never my intent at all. What I wanted was for Pickton's photo to be shown on the street in a proper photo lineup. It had to be done correctly. I wanted women in the Downtown

Eastside to identify Pickton, and we needed that ID so that we could take it to our supervisors and fight for more resources by showing we had proof he was frequenting the Downtown Eastside. At this stage, we had little recent evidence that Pickton was spending time in the Downtown Eastside, yet I felt certain he was. Still, I would later learn that Fisk and Myers continued to include Pickton's photo in their pile of photos, and women picked him out.

In 2002, when a public inquiry was likely to be pending, Doug LePard was tasked with investigating and documenting the VPD side of this investigation. I met with him in late November, and he interviewed me over two days. At one point, I was reviewing my experience with the work of Fisk and Myers.

"You know women ID'd Pickton from the photo they [Fisk and Myers] showed in their street interviews." It was more a statement than a question. I didn't understand what he was saying to me. It was inconceivable to me that women could have picked Pickton out without my knowing, without Fisk and Myers telling me.

"What?"

LePard went on to tell me that Fisk admitted in his interview with LePard that women on the Downtown Eastside had recognized Pickton from the photo they had shown them. I couldn't process this shock for several moments. *Why? Why hadn't they shared this with the team?* When I regained my ability to speak, I told LePard they had never made the rest of the team or me aware of this identification. LePard said he knew that.

"He said he told you and put it in his notes, but admitted he might not have," LePard said.

"He never told me that! Never!" I could barely control my rage.

"I know. He allowed that he might not have told you." He sounded sympathetic to my position.

"Why wouldn't they tell me that? I just don't get it."

"I don't know."

"That would've been a game changer," I whispered.

"I know," LePard answered.

"Why?"

"I don't know."

"I was alive to anything, *anything*, that would link him to the Downtown Eastside and get us on that farm." I felt my throat closing. I swallowed hard, determined not to cry.

"I know you were."

I sat there, thinking how, especially after the bitter disappointment of the Ellingsen interviews, we were desperate for more information we could use to reinvigorate the Pickton investigation. I was completely stunned that Fisk and Myers apparently kept this information from the team.

Again, my gut feelings had been valid and my sense that Fisk and Myers were secretive and withholding valuable investigative information from the rest of the team appeared accurate. Once again, I felt deep dismay that I couldn't have pressed harder at the time to bring these two guys in line with the rest of the team, because I do believe they had energy we could have harnessed for the good of the investigation. Unfortunately, they didn't trust us, and in turn, we didn't trust them—and their actions turned out to be unworthy of our trust.

I also believe the VPD of the time bears some of the responsibility for this. Fisk and Myers should never have been assigned to our team, when everyone up to our inspector and in the Internal Investigation Section knew of their shortcomings and history. Or, given the knowledge of their alleged past actions, they should have come to us under close supervision so that they could be managed and their energy directed properly.

Secrecy and questionable tactics were how these two rolled, in my view, and no one was surprised when they quickly became a cancer in our investigation. I tried so hard to give them the benefit of the doubt, but they just couldn't seem to work with the team.

I also had reason to believe they were offering to test other jurisdictions' DNA samples on the VPD budget, but I refused to spend my time investigating my own supposed teammates rather than continuing to search for the women. I advised Geramy of my concerns about the DNA testing, and she said she couldn't deal with them at that time. The role of Office Tattletale was wearing on me, and I began ignoring Fisk and Myers's behavior as best I could and stopped going to Geramy with my concerns until the POI 390 debacle made that impossible.

My stomach problems and nightmares continued to worsen, and I took a week off in the middle of April 2000 in an effort to get some time away. When I returned on April 18, I was surprised to discover that Fisk and Myers were not in the office. I was alone and ventured out to Geramy's desk in Homicide to find out where they were. She told me they had gone to Lethbridge to arrest POI 390 on sexual assault charges—the charges they had taken nearly a year to prepare. I was surprised. They had made no previous mention of their plans to me, but she said they had approached her late the previous week—the week I was away and unable to comment or make suggestions to them—and she thought I had known, so she approved the travel.

There had been no team meeting, no discussion of interview strategy, and—what would normally be done prior to the arrest—no discussion of a media strategy. Although I couldn't prove it, I felt certain that they had intentionally waited until

I was away to avoid any such conversation or planning. In allowing them to handle this arrest, Geramy had made the assumption that they were competent, but the errors they made exposed the extent of their incompetence.

POI 390 was arrested a couple of days later. Fisk and Myers were difficult to reach via phone, and Geramy received little information from them on their progress. On April 21, they called the office and I spoke to Myers, who could barely contain his excitement. He told me how he was certain that POI 390 had killed the missing women and how fabulous the taped interviews were. As desperately as I wanted to believe this, I couldn't help feeling sceptical. They would be back the following week.

On April 25, they bounced into the office and presented me with eight videotapes—some fourteen hours long—of their interviews with POI 390 in a Lethbridge jail interview room. I found it hard to believe they had the right man, but I knew I had to keep an open mind, and I felt a stir of excitement that we may have found our answer.

POI 390 was still in Lethbridge, awaiting remand and transport to the Vancouver Pretrial Centre. Fisk and Myers were insistent that I watch the interview tapes—which I had every intention of doing—because they insisted that POI 390 "practically confesses" in the interview. I could not imagine what they could contain that would last fourteen hours. I took the tapes to the RCMP headquarters to be copied, then returned to the office. That afternoon, I began to watch, hoping my fears would be unfounded, hoping he was indeed our man and the search was over. Maybe we had our guy. Maybe we could forget the disappointment of Pickton and be certain we had our serial killer.

17

Salvaging Project Amelia

• • •

"The supreme quality for leadership is unquestionably integrity.
Without it, no real success is possible, no matter whether it is on
a section gang, a football field, in an army, or in an office."
DWIGHT D. EISENHOWER

I HAVE NEVER BEEN as ashamed to be a police officer as I was
that day. The first tape began with both Fisk and Myers sitting in the Lethbridge interview room with POI 390, telling
him how certain they were that he was the killer and demanding to know where the bodies were.

There was no recorded or documented reading of POI 390's
charter rights, and there was no recorded or documented explanation of the difference between the sexual assault charges and
the disappearances of the missing women—which is a very
important legal distinction. An investigator cannot piggyback
a charge onto another arrest or criminal charge and use that
to interview a suspect on a different case without very clearly
defining that for the subject and explaining to him that he is
well within his rights to refuse to take part in such questioning.

If they had done this, it wasn't on the tape, and that would be a problem for us in court. This wasn't an interview; it was an inquisition. Fisk and Myers spoke over each other and over POI 390 and lacked any sort of plan or direction, and when they did allow POI 390 to speak, they wouldn't let him finish.

Within the first few minutes, Myers told POI 390 that a first degree murder charge could probably be dropped to second degree if POI 390 would just tell them where the bodies were. This was a blatant inducement, which is entirely the domain of the prosecution—it is not within a police officer's power to make any such promises in return for a confession. I cringed at this exchange. *Here we go.*

When POI 390 didn't immediately confess, as Myers expected him to, Myers then said he doubted POI 390 would be charged with anything at all if he gave up the location of the bodies, because all anyone was really interested in was finding them. *Oh my God.* It was worse than I could have ever possibly imagined. *Oh my God.* My mind reeled—how were we going to recover from this if he was the killer? I left the room to find Geramy and Al Boyd.

I explained to them what I had seen, and they agreed that this was not good. I asked them to view the tapes also. Neither one was able to view them at that time, so Geramy asked me to take them home and watch them in their entirety and report to her on the contents. I bumped into Myers in the hallway, who hollered an excited *Whadya think?* at me. I just walked past him; I could not deal with him after what I'd seen.

I took the tapes home the night of April 28 and watched them from start to finish. It was at times shocking and at other times tedious; always, it was excruciating. POI 390 was not an easy interview, and Fisk and Myers became convinced that the way to get a confession from him was to have him hypnotized. POI 390 was so tired after hours of "interrogation" that he began saying he didn't remember killing anyone, but he agreed with the idea that they could hypnotize him to be sure.

They had somehow secured a Lethbridge psychologist and his young assistant to carry out the hypnosis, calling them out in the late hours of the night. The following several hours were a bizarre combination of amateur interrogation, quasi-psychotherapy, and hypnosis attempts. POI 390 kept telling them he could not be hypnotized and tried to convince the psychologist he was trying, but somehow it just didn't work on him, as though he were some sort of rare subject. It didn't "work" because he was exhausted. I don't know if anyone in the room knew what it might look like if he was hypnotized. I know I kept waiting to see some Amazing Kreskin-esque behavior, but nothing happened—hardly surprising.

For a week, the arrest of POI 390 was all over the news, and the day he was returned to Vancouver, his photo spanned the cover of the *Vancouver Province*. As I read the papers, it became clear that they contained a level of detail about his activities and personal information that I found unusual, given he had merely been arrested and was not yet before the court. I feared the worst—that Fisk and Myers had not taken the standard step investigators always take in such cases—that they had not sealed their information to obtain a search warrant in Lethbridge, an administrative step taken by police to keep such information private until it reaches court. If not sealed, a warrant application can be accessed by members of the media and anyone else who looks into the matters on the local police arrest records and court docket.

I had two questions for Fisk and Myers that morning: Why had they not video- or audiotaped the reading of POI 390's charter rights, and had they sealed their warrant? The first question elicited a blank look from them both. They told me they hadn't taped the first three hours of the interview because they "didn't want to go that route." I asked whether they had chartered him—read him his rights, including the right to counsel, under the Charter of Rights and Freedoms. They answered no, they hadn't wanted to "spook" him.

The situation grew worse. All of the taped interviews were going to be inadmissible based on these crucial errors, and if POI 390 was the killer of the missing women—we still couldn't rule that out—we were in serious trouble. I felt I was in some strange vortex, spinning around with these two guys who had absolutely no idea how to investigate anything of this magnitude and having to explain to my supervisors something I could not understand myself. How could people of this level of incompetence be allowed to handle such a serious file? Did no one else think this was serious?

So we had three hours of an interrogation apparently unaccounted for—defense counsel would have a field day with this. They could allege everything from beatings to inducements—in addition to the *taped inducements* we had on video—and they would be right to suggest it all, because in the absence of tape, *who knows what they said or did to him?* I knew the answer to the second question before I asked it, but I still had to. Did they seal their warrant in Lethbridge? Two fifteen-year veterans of the VPD stared at me as though I'd just asked whether they'd been to the moon yesterday. *Oh my God.* Clearly, they didn't know you could and should seal warrant applications. I suspected that before this investigation, all they had ever applied for were drug warrants and *who cared about those people and that stuff getting into the press?* They didn't know about sealing warrants, because, like everything Fisk and Myers had worked on under an alleged veil of paranoia and secrecy, fearing someone would steal their thunder, they were convinced they knew everything and hadn't bothered to ask.

Now we had an even greater problem. There was so much information in the news, and it would be impossible for us to test the credibility of any new victims of POI 390 who came forward as a result of hearing of his arrest. There was so much detail out there—where he lived, what kind of vehicle he drove, what his sexual proclivities were, the fact that he had a drug habit—that we would not know whether a new victim knew these things through her own experiences with POI 390 or as a result of reading it in the paper or seeing it on the news.

Still, there were no apologies from Fisk and Myers, no acknowledgment they had made serious errors in both practice and judgment and perhaps needed to start to defer to some of the more experienced and competent investigators sitting mere feet from our office. No sign that they would be asking for advice before undertaking something they were not familiar with. No indication that in the future they would clarify to ensure things they had been doing the same way for years were now being done correctly. No sense that they would begin to check to see if criminal case law might have changed in the past twenty years. For them, it was business as usual. They arrested POI 390. They were heroes.

This was a watershed moment for me. Somehow, I felt strangely galvanized to protect the integrity of Project Amelia. My worst suspicions had been realized, and my instincts had been confirmed. I saw how easily things could go very wrong and how very few people in the organization seemed to care or really understand the gravity of the situation, how truly lacking in direction this investigation was. I again expressed my concerns to Geramy, and she suggested I watch the tapes with Sergeant Bill Lean and Sergeant Dennis Paulsen of our Polygraph Section. They were expert interviewers and interrogators and would be able to assess the interviews for Geramy and Al Boyd.

Lean and Paulsen were as horrified as I was. We watched the tapes together over two days on the weekend of April 29, and they agreed—Fisk and Myers could not be within a hundred miles of POI 390 as we prepared this thing for court, and even then, the damage was probably irreparable. We could probably salvage the sexual assault cases, but anything to do with the missing women would be inadmissible.

We discussed strategy for an interview of POI 390 to be conducted by Lean and Paulsen and began to prepare for that. They spoke to Geramy and echoed my concerns, which I had hoped would provide the push she needed to overcome her own inertia in dealing with Fisk and Myers. Geramy's heart was with Project Amelia, but it had always been a second job; her plate was piled high with homicide responsibilities. Throughout this crisis, she had seemed frozen, unable to comprehend what they had done and—to an even greater degree—what she should do in response. I began to pressure her to remove Fisk and Myers from Project Amelia.

The interview was planned for May 1, 2000, at eleven in the morning. Lean, Paulsen, Fisk, Myers, and I were present, as well as Lepine; Chernoff; Gord Spencer, my new Major Crime inspector; Geramy; and Staff Sergeant Keith Davidson of the RCMP Criminal Profiling Unit, visiting English profiler Sergeant Neil Trainor, and their protégée, an Australian policewoman.

The tension in the air was unmistakable as Lean and Paulsen told Fisk and Myers they were tainted and no longer to be involved in the POI 390 investigation or to interact with him in any way. They were dumbfounded. As we continued to discuss strategy for the pending interview, the tension in the polygraph suite mounted. Fisk and Myers were defensive and belligerent, unable to understand how they could be criticized for their flawless arrest and investigation.

Lean did not back down, telling them directly that they had screwed up and would be lucky if we had any investigation at all at the end of the day. Lepine and Chernoff were sent to collect POI 390 from pretrial and escort him back to the VPD polygraph suite. When they returned empty-handed, our worst fears had been realized. POI 390 was so befuddled by the Lethbridge interviews, he refused to be interviewed again. On the advice of his lawyer, he would not be taking part in any interviews with any of us.

I wrote a very pointed memo to Geramy outlining my concerns about the POI 390 investigation and requesting that the case be immediately transferred to the VPD Sexual Offence Squad for follow-up and completion. I requested a meeting with her for the following day and demanded that Fisk and Myers be removed—not only from the case but also from Project Amelia, as I believed their actions would greatly undermine the credibility of the team and our ability to investigate the missing women files.

Geramy met with me the following day, and I told her the only thing to do was move the file to SOS and get Fisk and Myers out of Project Amelia. She felt trapped, helpless because the former deputy chief constable—Brian McGuinness—had placed them in Project Amelia. I told her that didn't matter to me, because either they had to go or I would. Her choice. But I would not further threaten my own professional integrity and reputation by working alongside those two people. I hated pushing her like this, but I was done.

We met again the next day, and Geramy asked whether it would be acceptable to me that Fisk and Myers be allowed to remain in Project Amelia until they had completed the POI 390 investigation. I looked at her as though she'd lost her mind. Had she not heard a thing Sergeant Lean had said? No, that would not be acceptable. I reiterated all of the points on my memo of the previous day—the problems with their integrity, their lack of information sharing, and their demonstrated incompetence. She nodded her head. She knew it was a bad idea for them to remain on this file. This was challenging for Geramy, because she had only ever supervised competent and self-sufficient people.

Geramy agreed to speak with Inspector Barb Morris of the Sexual Offence Squad and have the file transferred to an experienced detective there. In the meantime, I sent a fax to the officer in charge of Vancouver pretrial, asking that no one be allowed to interview POI 390 without first clearing it with me and to advise me if anyone tried. I feared Fisk and Myers would try to talk to POI 390 again.

On May 4, Geramy drafted a memo to Fisk and Myers explaining that it was anticipated that Project Amelia would be winding down, that the POI 390 file was now assigned to Detective Constable Sean Trowski of SOS, and that their services would no longer be required. They reacted strongly to this news, and I tended to agree that the idea that we were winding down was hard to fathom. Again, I met with Geramy and suggested that this half-truth, probably designed to spare their feelings, was misguided. She met with them and told them there were concerns with their handling of the POI 390 arrest and that was the reason they were being transferred out. They argued, saying this was the result of persecution by jealous members of Project Amelia. They asked for time to complete their notes and wrap up their tip files, and Geramy complied with this request, against my wishes.

A date for their leaving was never set. On May 9, they said they would leave at the end of the week and proceeded to spend that entire week locked in a Homicide interview room, with one telephone and a piece of paper taped over the peephole, coming out only to photocopy the volumes of files they had taken from the Project Amelia office.

When I told Al Boyd they were photocopying files, he shrugged, saying there was little he could do. I asked him what they could possibly need Project Amelia files for if they were leaving the team and had been ordered to stop work on this investigation. He shared my sense of bewilderment but did nothing. I suspected they were planning to continue investigating POI 390—this was their style and reputation at the VPD—and I advised Gord Spencer of my concerns. He warned the two in writing that they were to cease and desist working on the POI 390 investigation.

The remaining days were tense; the Project Amelia office small enough when people were cordial was much smaller when the mood was hostile. Fisk and Myers drafted a long-winded and bizarre letter to Chief Constable Blythe complaining of their dismissal and asserting that without them this investigation was destined to failure. They cited the myriad suspects they were pursuing—many I had never heard of. They criticized Project Amelia members for everything from lack of work ethic to lack of arrests.

They showed a complete lack of understanding of this investigation and the various roles of the people on Project Amelia. Their memo to the chief included a page of footnoted references to various true crime novels and amateur criminal profiler paperbacks in an effort to bolster their self-professed expertise in the investigation of serial killers.

It was bizarre and amateurish, and the chief did not respond other than to criticize them for circumventing the chain of command. He asked me to respond to their allegations, and I did so gratefully, welcoming the opportunity to address their criticisms point by point and outline all of the ways they had ruined the POI 390 file and poisoned the work environment through their incompetence and ignorance. Sadly, this was probably the best report I would write in my time working on this case.

They left the team without providing me with proper notes of their activities or time spent on behalf of the team, including their admitted procurement of sex workers' identifications of the Pickton photo. The POI 390 case was delayed because the Crown counsel report they had written on his arrest had to be rewritten almost completely. It was unacceptable for Crown counsel in the state Detective Constable Trowski, who took over the file and rewrote the report, received it. They failed to provide Project Amelia investigators with many of the contact names or numbers of the investigators they had supposedly dealt with in Calgary, Edmonton, and Lethbridge.

I would come to learn that Fisk and Myers continued to be in contact with these investigators even after being directed to stop and turn these contacts over to Project Amelia. Myers pressured one of Project Amelia's admin staff to give him bad date sheet information contained on floppy disks, but she managed to put him off and report the incident to me. I notified Boyd, but nothing further was done. Obviously, under normal circumstances, having more people working on our case was preferable to fewer, but not people who worked at cross-purposes to the team, failed to disclose information, employed unsound methods, and failed to acknowledge their mistakes. These actions often formed the basis for mistrials, and we couldn't afford one if we finally caught our killer.

POI 390 went on to be convicted on some of the sexual assault charges against him and served significant prison time. I believe that if the charges against him had been handled correctly, two things would have resulted. One, we could have had more victims who would testify against him, potentially giving us more charges. Two, I believe that a proper interview conducted by skilled interrogators would have given us a far better indication of whether POI 390 had ever killed and of whether he had any involvement in the disappearances of any of the sex workers.

I will say this in Fisk and Myers's defense: the VPD of that era was not strong on training and mentorship. They were the products of a time and culture in which young patrol constables were encouraged to run with their own investigations and in which innovation and creativity were applauded. These are all good things, and perhaps the current era could use more of this energy. However, constables of Fisk and Myers's vintage quickly went from junior constables to those guys the junior constables looked to for guidance.

Fisk and Myers joined the VPD just as or shortly after the new Charter of Rights and Freedoms was passed into law, in 1982, and they were trained by many of the old-school cowboys who still held fast to abusive tactics and a Wild West mentality, eschewing the virtues of or need for a new charter that addressed things such as human rights, even for bad guys. Indeed, Myers's father was a VPD constable before him, and young Wayne learned how things were done in those days at his father's knee and later regaled us with many of these stories in the Project Amelia office.

Through a perfect storm of untrained partners and inadequate supervision, they both quickly reached a point where it would have been embarrassing to admit they didn't know many of the most basic investigative procedures or were unaware of current case law and rules of evidence. The police culture being what it is, it certainly wouldn't have been easy for two big, tough, experienced policemen to admit they didn't know how to prepare a photo lineup or seal a search warrant.

I'm sympathetic to this set of circumstances, but it doesn't excuse them. Not telling us that our prime suspect had been identified by our victim group was hugely detrimental to a very important investigation. I was willing to help my team-mates learn new skills and become better investigators, if only they had asked or taken the help when it was offered to them without judgment. A large part of my bitterness toward Fisk and Myers lies in that they couldn't admit their shortcomings and their insecurity took so much valuable time and energy away from catching the killer.

18

The Creation of
Project Evenhanded

• • •

*"I am somewhat exhausted; I wonder how a battery
feels when it pours electricity into a non-conductor?"*
ARTHUR CONAN DOYLE, THE ADVENTURE
OF THE DYING DETECTIVE

OVER THE SPRING of 2000, our few remaining team members found their way back to their previous assignments.
Only Geramy and I remained on Project Amelia. Gord
Spencer asked the RCMP to review our files to ensure we had
done all we could to find the women from our end. There was
no sense of urgency around this review; Geramy and I tied
up those loose ends we could, closed tip files that had gone
nowhere, and completed interviews Fisk and Myers had
failed to. We met with the leaders of the RCMP Provincial
Unsolved Homicide Unit a few times in anticipation of their
file review.

This review would eventually morph into RCMP Project
Evenhanded, a task force formed in January 2001 dedicated

to reexamining B.C.'s cold missing and murdered sex worker
files. Project Evenhanded would operate under one very mistaken belief: that women had ceased going missing from the
Downtown Eastside. Based on this assumption, Evenhanded
functioned mainly as a file review—of old RCMP files and our
Project Amelia cases. Evenhanded retained the capacity to
shift its focus to more active investigation, but from January
2001 until the Pickton farm search began on February 5, 2002,
they operated with little apparent urgency and a huge pool of
potential suspects. In this project, Pickton became merely one
of more than three hundred men of interest.

Retired RCMP inspector and former Evenhanded leader
Don Adam testified before the Missing Women Commission of Inquiry in 2012 that he did not believe the reason for
not pursuing Pickton was related to resources. He suggested
there were so many potential predatory suspects, to focus on
one—even one so clearly linked to our victim demographic
and geographic area, and with compelling source information—would be potential disaster for the investigation. I
failed to understand what the risk was, but I listened to the
testimony of a man I'd come to idolize as an investigator and
interviewer, hoping I'd learn something. Adam's lawyer, Janet
Winteringham, asked him, "Did you have a number of different priorities?"

Adam replied, "Yes, we did. We-we felt that we needed to
have a Priority 1. Those would be the worst of the worst and
those would be the people that we would-we needed to figure
out how many there were of them and then-then assess them
for which ones would we go on first. But you couldn't do one
without the other. Like, if I described it to you this way: If you
walked into a room that was full of files, you-if you reached out
and looked at a file and said, 'Wow, this is a horrible person,'
say Mr. Pickton, you go, 'This is a horrible person. I'll go work

him." But if you haven't looked, how do you know that the fifth file down isn't worse? How do you know that the tenth isn't? So you take all of your monsters and you try and put them together and then assess them. And I know that Mr. Pickton has entered this room.

"He's-he's really the only monster who has come in here and his crimes have been fleshed out, but I can assure you that the people we are looking at are evil people. And if-if you think of Mr. Pickton as a, like a bright red ball that you've brought into this room, you can move that ball anywhere in this room and none of us will ever miss where it is. But if you open those doors and you brought in 30 red balls suddenly and you start moving them around, it's not so easy. You keep those doors open. By February there are 60 of them. There were right now when Evenhanded has fully assessed everyone, of people that have murdered, attempted murder, brutalized women, at that number one category there are 374 of those balls. And if those balls are in this room, there's a very different feel to what we were facing. We hadn't read the end of the book. We were at the beginning and we couldn't make mistakes."

Perhaps my experience in Homicide was too limited, but I fail to understand how you solve a serial killer investigation with compelling source information pointing to an excellent suspect by introducing as many less-compelling suspects as possible and then claim that looking more closely at your original suspect will taint the investigation. Pickton wasn't merely one of many horrible people, he was someone we possessed credible information could be killing our victims. I appreciate that Adam's task was huge. I am in no way suggesting they should have gone after Pickton as though he were the only one, to the exclusion of all other valid suspects. I simply fail to understand why Project Evenhanded did not treat Pickton as a top priority when it began.

I LEFT MAJOR Crime at the end of 2000 and struggled to find work within the VPD that might re-ignite my passion, and I continued to suffer from nightmares and all the other physical and emotional symptoms I'd had since 1999. Eventually, I settled in as a detective in the Financial Crime Unit (FCU).

Lindsay Kines of the *Vancouver Sun* called me in the summer of 2001. He told me he was doing a series on the missing women and sensed I had some things I might want to talk about. I agreed to meet with him one sunny afternoon on Granville Island, a small idyllic tourist spot on the downtown Vancouver waterfront known as False Creek. I had not decided how much to tell him prior to our meeting, but as we spoke, I found myself telling him the story of Pickton. It was the right thing for me to do personally, but I placed him in an awful position, knowing he wouldn't be able to use any of it, but feeling someone needed to know this—*the public needed to know this.* Professionally, I was breaking all sorts of VPD policy and codes of conduct, but I didn't care. How could I responsibly share this information knowing it could jeopardize an investigation? *Because by then there was no investigation.*

I placed my trust in him—something I would not grow to regret—and found Lindsay to be a rarity: an incredibly ethical and discreet reporter and person. I told him of the setup of Project Amelia, of the shell game that was the VPD's and the RCMP's response to these women's disappearances, of the couple of incompetent people we were forced to work with on both sides of the house. I told him of my fears surrounding the bungling of the POI 390 investigation. Perhaps if Lindsay's stories could reawaken the public consciousness to this file and the plight of these women, the RCMP would respond to the pressure and revisit the Pickton investigation. Another aspect of my motivation was my own conscience—I needed someone outside of my own family and close friends to know my frustrations at strongly suspecting Pickton was a serial killer and not having the support and tools to prove it.

Lindsay's *Vancouver Sun* series definitely helped to bring more public awareness to the missing women, and he was able to interview several of my teammates, many on the record, but he kept mum on the Pickton information, because none of us could go on the record with it. His stories won him well-deserved awards and accolades. We all—Lindsay included—held out hope that the RCMP's Project Evenhanded might be working on Pickton at that very time. Sadly, it was not.

ON FEBRUARY 5, 2002, a young Coquitlam RCMP constable named Nathan Wells would execute a search warrant on the Pickton farm for a weapons offense unrelated to the missing women. He would uncover an inhaler belonging to Sereena Abotsway, one of Vancouver's missing women, last seen in July 2001. He immediately contacted Project Evenhanded to tell them of his discovery. Within hours, the largest crime scene search in Canadian history was underway, and police discovered forensic evidence indicating many of the missing women were killed on that farm in the months and years the Pickton investigation languished.

Robert William Pickton was arrested on February 22, 2002, initially charged with the first degree murders of Sereena Abotsway and Mona Wilson. Over the next months, he was charged with the additional murders of Andrea Joesbury, Brenda Wolfe, Marnie Frey, and Georgina Papin. As DNA evidence uncovered through the exhaustive search of the farm trickled in over the ensuing months, the Crown charged Pickton with first degree murder in the deaths of Jacqueline McDonell, Dianne Rock, Heather Bottomley, Jennifer Furminger, Helen Hallmark, Patricia Johnson, Heather Chinook, Tanya Holyk, Sherry Irving, Inga Hall, Tiffany Drew,

Sarah de Vries, Cynthia Feliks AKA Mongovius, Angela Jardine, Diana Melnick, Debra Jones, Wendy Crawford, Kerry Koski, Angela Borhaven, and Cara Ellis. They'd been there all along.

19

Post–February 5, 2002

• • •

*"I do not speak as I think, I do not think as
I should and so it all goes on in helpless darkness."*
FRANZ KAFKA, THE METAMORPHOSIS

THAT DAY IN February 2002 when Mark paged me and told
me the Pickton farm search had begun, my back immediately seized up and I could barely get around, let alone run
or work out. In a few days, it improved, but my overall health
had been declining from as far back as the POI 390 investigation. I couldn't sleep deeply, and when I did, nightmares
tormented me. My digestive system was constantly upset,
I wasn't eating much, and even my workouts and running,
which had always given me so much solace, were lethargic
and uninspired.

In early February, I was putting the finishing touches on
a huge investigation I'd been working on, and the report was
nearly a hundred pages long. I'd booked off sick from work for
a couple of days after Mark told me about the search, because

my back was so frozen and I was in shock, but I had to come back and get the work done, no matter how terrible I felt.

I dragged myself out of the office for a run the day I returned to work, hoping the exercise would clear my head and loosen up my back. Normally, I could run six or eight miles with ease, but I ran a couple of miles along the ocean and my chest squeezed tightly around my ribs and my legs felt dead. I stopped, fighting for breath. *What the hell is the matter with me? You haven't even done anything. Get moving!* The thought of running again seemed impossible; walking was all I could manage, and I slowly trudged back to the office, berating myself because I didn't even need a shower, so little had I perspired. I went back to my desk.

Crown counsel required several copies of the report, and I'd been editing and proofing to get it just right. There was one large Xerox machine outside the FCU office on the fourth floor and another on the third floor outside Homicide/Robbery, where my old Project Amelia office was. Neither machine offered reliable photocopying, and completing even a small job without a jam was a rarity. Copier malfunctions were reported, but technicians took weeks to respond.

I took small sections of my report to the copy machine outside the FCU, but after months of jams, I decided to venture down to the Homicide/Robbery machine. I slid the first stack of twenty or so pages through the document feeder and listened to the satisfying *click, click, click* of each page sliding nicely through, until the inevitable *clunk* when everything stopped and the readout told me a jam had occurred. My blood pressed hard against the walls of my chest. I felt seething rage. I opened the lid and stared at the glass for several moments. *This fucking chickenshit place. Nothing works. Nothing.*

I wore my gun most places throughout my workday; I'd been executing search warrants daily and couldn't go out without it. I imagined how it might feel to fire a bullet into the glass. I walked through the entire scenario in my mind. I imagined the feeling of unholstering my weapon, the click as I undid the snap, the feel of pulling cool metal out of the leather holster. It felt *so good* to picture it. Like the best sex or food fantasy, multiplied by ten. I visualized myself pointing the gun at the glass. Slowly squeezing the trigger, the glass shattering, the machine emitting a low whine as it quivered and died in front of me. *I want to do this so bad.*

   What the hell is wrong with me?

   Images of the bullet and glass ricocheting back at me entered my mind, and I felt like an idiot. *What if I inadvertently shot myself trying to kill the photocopier? What a moron.* I envisioned winning a Darwin Award. I imagined *not* being hit by the bullet or fragments but standing there as my colleagues ran to see what happened. Would they tackle me to the ground? Would someone shoot me as I stood there, .40 cal in my hand, Xerox machine bleeding out in front of me?

   The most frightening aspect of this fantasy was this: even after intellectually understanding it was a bad idea, I still wanted to do it. *This will help me feel better.* Sanity prevailed to some degree. I did not rule out shooting the copier in the future, but I decided that today wasn't the day. I ripped my jammed papers from the feeder, knowing kicking the machine would not come close to satisfying my frustration and anger.

   For the next three days, I tried to photocopy my report on the Homicide/Robbery machine, only to have it jam each time after a few precious seconds. Before venturing down the hall, I considered leaving my gun in my desk, but somehow carrying it made me feel powerful, as though *I could shoot it if I wanted to.* The choice was mine. I also had the choice to try the Financial Crime machine again, but it was no better, and something about the Homicide/Robbery copier drew me to it. I could not shake this desire to put a cap in the glass.

On the fourth day, I decided shooting the copier was a sound idea. *It would make a statement, a pivotal moment for detectives at the VPD. Maybe my colleagues will wish they had been the ones to shoot the Xerox machine. I'll be the Howard Beale of the VPD, mad as hell and not going to take it anymore. The Norma Rae of detectives.*

As I gazed at the machine, in that pregnant moment before something life-changing happens, I saw an old friend walking down the hall smiling at me. I hadn't seen her in a long time and couldn't help but smile back at her despite my diabolical plot. I knew then I didn't want to shoot the photocopier in front of her or hurt her in the process.

"How *are* you?" she called out from a few yards away. I set my report down and stepped away from the Xerox machine.

"Good," I said. "I'm good." I managed to conceal my mania from her. After we chatted for several minutes, I walked back to my office and immediately booked off on stress leave.

Rennie Hoffman, my sergeant, was supportive and suggested I complete a Workers' Compensation Board (WCB) claim form, which I did. The full gravity of my Xerox plot terrified me, and I fought to make sense of my thoughts.

Within days of the beginning of the Pickton farm search, the VPD Human Resources Section decided to arrange for a critical incident debriefing for those of us who had worked on Project Amelia. Normally, these are held a day or two after a serious incident, such as a police shooting or the death of a child. Members are encouraged to share their feelings about what they saw and how it affected them.

I later learned that several former Project Amelia members had booked off on stress leave at the same time, leading Human Resources to fear that they had a problem on their hands. When one of my Project Amelia teammates told me about the plan, I became incensed. Carol Tarnowsky, an acting sergeant in Human Resources at the time, called me at home, excited to be organizing the debriefing. I tore into her, telling her this was "a day late and a dollar short," alternately venting my rage and frustration and apologizing for shooting her, the messenger, when this wasn't her fault or decision and she had no idea about the lack of support from the VPD for those of us working on Project Amelia.

I had no intention of attending a critical incident debriefing, even if I was ordered to do so. I failed to see how it would benefit any of us. I knew all I would do was rail against the VPD, and that wouldn't be helpful to my colleagues. I conferred with a therapist I knew, and she supported my choice. She told me that critical incident debriefings had been in vogue a few years earlier, but that the latest research, in 2002, found that they did more harm than good and the workplace culture did not facilitate open sharing of people's true emotions. I had no intention of sharing my feelings, and I did not attend, even though Geramy and Alex implored me to come. I felt guilty, but I knew I was too bitter to be among the others.

I was at home on sick leave on February 12, when VPD Homicide Detective Steve Pranzl paged me. Steve and I were friends and had worked together on the Forensic Interview Team (FIT), where he was known for his high level of skill as an interviewer and interrogator. His assignment on the Pickton file was to interview several of the higher priority witnesses—many of whom had not yet been ruled out as potential suspects—and help develop interview strategies.

Steve began to tell me about his interview with Lisa Yelds the day before and how he had gone in cold, knowing nothing about her, and she had basically stonewalled him about Pickton. He said he discovered afterward that I had done extensive research on her, but no one could find it before the interview.

I felt terrible, knowing he hated to conduct an interview unprepared and he had wasted a golden opportunity for an interview with a key player.

He asked me to reconsider joining the team, because my knowledge of Pickton was sorely needed, if only to find the vast information about him we had accumulated over the years. I felt torn, but ultimately this request changed things for me. I reasoned it was one thing for me to sit at home, shell-shocked, bitter, and useless but quite another if my being there could help the investigators in their quest to find our women. If I could save everyone a step here and there, I had to suck it up and pitch in. I couldn't let my depression stand in the way of helping the families get answers more quickly. I agreed and asked him to arrange it for two weeks, no longer. He said he'd take care of everything and get back to me.

Geramy called me immediately; she was thrilled I was join-ing the team. I agreed to start on February 15—a Friday—and work until March 1. I made demands—a car, no overtime—and I would remain in the office as a resource person, nothing more. No fieldwork, though I had no idea why I didn't feel I could do it. I wouldn't carry my gun for fear I'd do something insane in the office.

How much things had changed since my first day in Homi-cide/Missing Persons in 1998, when I was like a kid on the first day of school with the big boys, eager to begin a new life. Now I was simply terrified—of changing my routine, which included riding my bicycle to work at 5:00 AM and coming home at 3:00 PM; of seeing less of my young family, which formed the center of my life; of coming face-to-face with the reality that these women were really, truly dead, and we could have stopped the killing sooner. Although I had loudly voiced my belief that the women were dead, I had somehow harbored a faint hope that we would find them the way we had found Paulette Adamson.

That was another thing I had to come to terms with. They were at that farm.

As I embarked on my new role, I felt a familiar mixture of excitement and dread. It was gratifying to know that after all the work and thought that had gone into Pickton when I was in Project Amelia and before that, something was finally happening. It was also sickening to know how many women had disappeared since the summer of 1999, and I dreaded finding those bodies the most. Every victim on that farm would represent a waste, a failure of someone, somewhere—but each woman from 1999 onward represented a complete travesty, and I felt we were responsible—all of us.

Mark Chernoff and his partner, VPD Detective Bruce Wahl, picked me up and we drove to the Project Evenhanded offices in Surrey. We arrived a couple of minutes late for the morning meeting. Detectives and higher ranks filled the room, and several people spilled out into the doorway and the adjoining lunchroom, straining to hear Staff Sergeant Don Adam, head of the project, speak from the head table. The sheer number of people involved struck me—at least forty-five by my estimate—as did the progress they were reporting. Every single person had something interesting and relevant to add to the case, and each update provided information the others could use and act upon. *Things were happening.*

I felt a stab of regret as I scanned the room, looking at all of these keen, committed faces. Many were people I recognized. *Where were they when we needed them? Where was all this money, where were all these resources when we had none? Why had this taken so long?* Everyone was to report on their progress in that afternoon's meeting, scheduled for five o'clock, and with that, Adam sent the team off to see what the day would bring.

After the meeting, several of us went for coffee, as would become our custom, and it was there I would learn the little tidbits of what was really going on and what kind of evidence we had on the farm. Part of Adam's strategy to limit information leaks was to keep forensic investigators on the farm separate from those who were out running around doing interviews and chasing down tips.

During the first few days after the warrant had been executed, Adam read the riot act to the team, concerned that leaks to the media would be the case's undoing, and no one was to talk to the press or each other about any discoveries. Only the senior managers were privy to knowledge of what the searchers found, and they would then decide what and how much information would be disseminated to the team. It was an excellent strategy and a necessary one—cops love to talk, and it only takes one person to tell the wrong person before information ends up in the wrong hands and evidence is ruined or a family ends up hurt. I thought back to my call to Lindsay the night of the search with a pang of guilt, but I knew I hadn't spilled any secret beans.

I met informally with investigators and began to assess the management and accessibility of the information from Project Amelia that Geramy and I had sent out to Surrey for the "review" months ago. Very little of it was on computer, and much of the original information about our thirty-plus victims remained solely in our hard files. SIUSS data entry was still incomplete—the same old problems persisted, despite my efforts to make them known. I was concerned that a name or person from the past would come up in the Pickton investigation and no one would know the relevance. We could miss linking it to something relevant, which could be crucial. Much of Project Amelia's information was inaccessible, and I would never set eyes on many of the tip files I had created. In late 2011 and early 2012, as I prepared for my Missing Women Commission of Inquiry testimony, it would become clear that so much of our work had been lost or misplaced. I knew what we had and what had been lost, because everything had passed through my hands as the file coordinator.

Again, we were dealing with conflicting and incompatible information systems. All of the new Pickton information was going into E&R, the RCMP evidence and reports database, which did not speak to SIUSS. The administrative staff was working hard to enter everything into one system, but with all the new Pickton data to be entered daily, it would be months until the staff would be able to go back and enter the old information and make it accessible in an automated format.

I was dismayed that so little of what we had done in the past was easily accessible to investigators, and I tried to impress on the senior managers the need to improve this situation. They agreed, though I don't believe they truly understood the problem. I questioned how much of the work we had done had even been reviewed by Project Evenhanded investigators, and I worried that they had begun Evenhanded determined to start fresh from where we had left off. My feeling had always been that knowledge was power, and the more you knew about your file, the better prepared you were to assess the relevance of new information coming in.

I resigned myself to the fact that I probably held the most information about Pickton in my own head, and although it was duplicated in the files, no one was going to bother looking at it, aside from someone like Steve Pranzl as he prepared for an interview. All I could do was keep my ears open and hope to guide someone to those files if they needed something.

I alternated between feeling that no one knew who I was and how far back I went with this file to feeling everyone was looking at me and whispering behind my back about my being the one who "quit," the one who refused Don Adam's offer to work on Project Evenhanded back in 2001, "the one who couldn't handle it." I knew how irrational and egocentric this was, but I had felt so much ownership for Project Amelia. I couldn't help feeling judged for its inadequacy and for the failure of the vpd to devote the proper time and resources to these women. I struggled with whether that made it my failure.

Don Adam made a point of greeting me that morning, saying he was glad I had reconsidered and joined them, but my insecurity made me ask myself, *Really? Was he just saying that? Did he think I was crazy for refusing to work on such a great investigation?* I wasn't normally given to such strong and sustained periods of self-doubt, but this investigation and my feeling of failure overwhelmed me.

At the end of that first day, Geramy and I made our way to the afternoon meeting early to ensure a place at the large square of tables that accommodated forty people. Again, it was standing room only. As we made our way around the table and each investigator summed up the day's events, I sat gobsmacked, unable to believe the progress that had been made from eight o'clock in the morning until now, a mere nine hours later. So many people working so hard, solely on Pickton. In Project Amelia, we didn't make this kind of headway in six months. I thought of Fisk and Myers and all of the assignments I had given them that sat untouched and uninvestigated for months on end, still sitting there when they were forced to leave the team.

At seven thirty, when the meeting was over, I sat in my car and cried.

Hundreds of tips flowed in daily and the team followed up on several leads. The most pressing one involved Dinah Taylor, a Downtown Eastside sex worker, drug addict, and longtime associate of Robert Pickton's. She had lived in the Roosevelt Hotel on Hastings Street—an address that would become synonymous with betrayal and death. Taylor's name continued to come up in connection to Pickton, and she had lived on the farm at various times over the past seven years.

She was alleged to have steered women out to the farm, and according to sources, Pickton would pay her for this service at the rate of $100 per woman. By all accounts, she was mean, violent, and self-serving. Dan Roy, a French-Canadian sergeant on loan from the RCMP in Quebec, was assigned to manage Taylor and set her up for an introduction to an undercover operator. She was typically unreliable, and instead of meeting with Roy at the prearranged times, Taylor would be out allegedly threatening potential witnesses on the Downtown Eastside, warning them not to talk about Pickton to the police or they would end up beaten or worse.

Taylor personified a major problem that would recur throughout this investigation. So much of the anecdotal "buzz" around many of the players in this case seemed to indicate that others beyond Robert Pickton had knowledge of and participated in the murderous activities on that farm. Pickton himself would indicate many times throughout his February 23, 2002, interrogation that there were several others involved, yet no one else was ever charged. At what point should "witnesses" be treated as suspects and arrested and charged? Would the RCMP offer immunity from prosecution to potential co-accused persons to secure statements implicating Pickton?

I have no inside knowledge of the strategic plans—if any existed—made by investigators around these questions, but it appears that these matters were under-considered early in the investigation. I believe if these issues had been explored more carefully, the jury's uncertainty about whether Pickton had acted alone and therefore could be found guilty of first degree murder—and the jury's ultimate finding that he was guilty on six second degree murder charges might have been avoided. Can someone kill six people at six different times and say these killings were not premeditated acts? Can someone really kill six people on six different dates and say each occurred without planning or forethought? It is a difficult legal question, certainly, and one that investigators may not have known how to navigate early in the investigation.

In spring 2001, Dinah Taylor had been struck by a vehicle as she crossed a Downtown Eastside street and received very serious injuries. She had spent much of her convalescence at Pickton's trailer, where her physical therapists would come to treat her. She was expecting a settlement from the Insurance Corporation of British Columbia (ICBC) any day, and we learned her plan was to fly to her parents' reserve in Ontario. It was hoped that the undercover operator could reel her in before then. Unfortunately, she refused to confide in the operator or spend any time with him.

Taylor left Vancouver in late February 2002. Steve Pranzl and his partner, RCMP corporal Lee Bergerman, followed her, tracking her down to her parents' home, where they interviewed her at length. They told her she was being considered as an accessory to the murders of these women, and it would be in her best interest to tell them what she had seen on the farm and testify against Pickton to spare herself. But Taylor remained steadfast, refusing to roll over on this man whom she considered her boyfriend. Her family urged her to do the right thing, both for herself and for the missing women and their families. She refused, saying Pickton was innocent. This line of investigation remained open, but other issues would arise.

All sorts of names from the past arose in the tip files I read—Lisa Yelds, Gina Houston, Scott Chubb, Ross Contois, Ron Menard—all part of the cast of rounders and hangers-on that formed the Picktons' social circle. And few were cooperating in any way, perhaps knowing how little evidence we were likely

to find on the farm and the even smaller likelihood we would
be able to charge any of them with a crime. Whatever any of
them knew, they weren't saying. As I read through the tips, I
kept asking myself: Where is Lynn Ellingsen?

In the meantime, Robert Pickton was not under arrest and
carried on with his daily activities under the glare of international media attention. Each day, he would drive to work at a
jobsite in Richmond and try to pretend his life hadn't been
turned upside down. A plan was made to introduce a female
RCMP officer—a highly skilled member of the Forensic Interview Team—to Pickton and see if he might talk to her. Dana
Lillies, a striking redheaded constable, was assigned to act as
a uniform patrol officer. Her role would be to pretend to be
assigned to the jobsite to keep an eye on Pickton and look
for any problems that might arise from the media. In reality,
Pickton was under additional surveillance, but Lillies's assignment had the potential to make him believe she was the only
member actually watching him. For several days, she sat in her
marked patrol car wired for recording, and soon they began
to talk.

I was never privy to the specifics of what they discussed,
but it was clear he was quite taken with Lillies and believed
she was wrongly characterized as a loose cannon. Mark Chernoff and Bruce Wahl were to plant the seed with Dave Pickton
that Lillies was unreliable and not a particularly good police
officer, and he, in turn, passed this to Robert, who felt that
this characterization was undeserved. The plan worked beau-
tifully. To Lillies, Pickton portrayed himself as a sensitive and
simple man, a poor pig farmer caught up in the middle of this
machine that he didn't understand. He played on her sympa-
thies and at one point actually cried in the car as they talked
together, remorseful that things had gotten to this point—not
quite a confession but another piece of the puzzle. Later, when

Pickton was interviewed, Lillies's presence would serve to highlight just how skilled and chameleonlike he was.

Over the next few days, I listened intently as Lynn Ellingsen's name arose in the daily meetings. At one point, Don Adam said we needed to determine whether we were going to pursue her as a witness, and it was clear her credibility remained a question for the RCMP members. Mark and I exchanged looks. I'm sure my face said it all. I was shocked that anyone would continue to doubt the veracity of her information and her motivation for not coming forward with it. *What was the matter with these people?* Did they expect a witness like Ellingsen to come to them on a silver platter? *Hello? Yes, I've just seen a murder—several, actually—and I'd like to speak to someone, please.*

I approached Steve Pranzl, and we discussed her at length after the meeting. He had much more influence with the senior managers than I did and was highly respected for his experience and instinct. I implored him to push to ensure that her evidence was thoroughly explored and not ignored for a third time. He believed she had seen what she said she had, and he agreed she could no longer be ignored.

There was a buzz in the office the week of February 19 that led me to suspect Pickton's arrest was imminent. We were told at the evening meeting on the 21st that the next day would be the day, and we were sworn to secrecy for obvious reasons, the most important being that the families were to be notified before the media. There was no danger that Pickton would flee, as he remained under surveillance. The morning of February 22, Don Adam laid out the plan. Pickton would be arrested at noon at the Richmond jobsite, and as soon as he was arrested, a team of investigators would contact the families by phone.

Before the arrest, four investigators in teams of two would visit the families of Sereena Abotsway and Mona Wilson and make the grim notification that their daughters had been the victims of murder—the first two murders Robert Pickton would be charged with. Although these investigators had been in close contact with these two families over the past two weeks, explaining what evidence was being found and preparing them for what was to come, the task of notifying them would not be easy or gratifying in any way.

I asked to be assigned to the team that was to do the telephone notifications, and Don Adam allowed me to select those I wished to speak to because of my history with the families. I was afraid, questioning my ability to hold myself together while I made these calls. In the past, I had been able to make such calls with the armor of detachment, knowing this was not my life or my reality. But I had changed so drastically over the last four years. I now felt things deeply, and a profound well of sadness would rise inside me that I was unable to suppress.

The entire day had a surreal quality, and I continued to struggle with my emotions. In the middle of it all, Bill Hiscox paged me. I called him back and we spoke at length, each of us frustrated that our work years earlier hadn't resulted in a search warrant. After we hung up, I mentioned to another investigator that Hiscox and I had talked but that he didn't have any new information about Pickton. Somehow, this officer misunderstood me, because a couple of hours later I received an angry voice message on my pager from Hiscox, furious I had set my "bodyguards on him." I later spoke to the officer who had misinterpreted my earlier words as my saying that Hiscox was harassing me, which was never the case. I felt terrible, but I was in the middle of my calls to families, so I forgot about it. Years later, during the Missing Women Commission of Inquiry, Hiscox and I had the opportunity to clear the air, and I felt he bore no hard feelings.

I found myself bursting into tears at the slightest provocation. Commercials, frustration, anger, beautiful music, or visuals arts—it didn't matter what it was; I felt I couldn't hold myself together. On some level, I understood this had something to do with trauma, but I had no education about trauma reactions, so I suffered, not knowing what was happening to me. I felt making these calls was something I had to do, and I missed these people who had shared so much with me over hours and hours on the phone during the months of Project Amelia.

Their questions were my questions; their confusion was my confusion. These people, these families—they were the ones I had consoled, counseled, and commiserated with those two years I worked to try to find their daughters, their sisters. These were the people I felt I had worked for, and I resented not being able to tell them the truth about the unwillingness to commit resources and manpower to finding their loved ones. We're still plugging away. That had been my standard line to them, but there were only ever a small, ineffectual, half-time handful of us plugging away. To tell of this real progress now was bittersweet. An arrest meant death, probably unnecessary death, avoidable waste—and we would be accountable.

I finished my calls, not wanting any of these people to hear about the arrest on the news or through the grapevine. After I hung up, I sat in that small RCMP office for what felt like a long time, not wanting to come out. Each of the people I had spoken to sent me the same unspoken message: Was our loved one there? When—if ever—would we know? Each was filled with compassion for the two grieving families, but I also sensed a touch of envy, for now they knew and their long search was over. The mixture of overwhelming pain and welcome relief was what they all craved, preferring the knowing over not knowing.

I wanted answers for all of these families. I wanted so much to be able to give them that closure they needed so desperately to begin to move forward and rebuild their lives. I hated the word "closure," because so many people misconstrued it as an ending to the pain. The best closure we could ever give these families was a start to some semblance of healing.

I asked Geramy to request that I be allowed to sit in on the interview of Pickton as an observer, suggesting that I might be of some help if he mentioned anything from the past about the victims with which the other investigators might not be familiar. The interview was planned for the following morning, and Don Adam agreed to allow me to observe.

A Letter to Sereena Abotsway

● ● ●

DEAR SEREENA,

You did all you could.

Yet, you still fell victim to this man, this predator, this place.

You did all you could. You used to run up to me on the street or at the WISH, pull out your well-thumbed copy of that week's bad date sheet, and thrust it in my face saying, "See? I'm bein' careful." It became a bit of a routine for us, a far cry from the days I would pick you up for outstanding warrants and you'd cry and beg me to let you go, calling me "hard-ass." You were right—I was a bit of a hard-ass back in those days, when, like you, I was trying to get by, to prove myself, to not be seen as a pushover on the street.

We go back a while—to around 1992. I always had a soft spot for you, and our first meeting was unusual. I was out driving around, driving the wagon that morning. I heard another police officer on the radio saying she was checking a female down at Alexander and Gore and figured I'd swing by and cover her. I didn't bother telling radio I was going. I rounded the corner and there you were, up against the wall of a business, the police officer's hands around your throat, your feet barely touching the ground. I got out of my car and asked to speak to her. She wasn't impressed—*Didn't I know I was interrupting her? That she was in the middle of something?* I looked at you and said, "You aren't going anywhere, are you?" You gulped hard and shook your head. No. Where would you go?

The officer quickly explained how you had failed to appear in court on a prostitution charge and she was arresting you on the warrant and you had resisted. "This little bitch," she said. You—all of five foot three or four and a hundred pounds—resisting this officer nearly six feet tall and easily outweighing you by sixty or seventy pounds. I listened, knowing this was entirely possible and that the prospect of going to jail and being without drugs is enough to make any addict fight, but her explanation was too hurried, too forced, and you didn't look like much of a threat to her. I told her that since I was there with the wagon, I would drive you to jail and she could go. She quickly got back into her car—not bothering to stay to cover me against you, the oh-so-dangerous warrant arrest.

I searched you and asked you if I needed to handcuff you. "No, I'm not much trouble." I guided you into the back of the wagon. Once at the jail, I opened the door to the wagon and we talked for several minutes. You thanked me for treating you decently, and I told you it was no problem. I offered you a business card, in case you ever heard of something on the street I might want to know, but you declined. "I don't want anyone to see it in there." Right, of course. You looked at the card for several moments. "Constable Lori." You said it five or six times as though to commit it to memory. You handed it back to me. "Thanks, Constable Lori." We went inside.

That was before our hard-ass days—days when I'd catch you in a fight or trying to kick in a window of some business that didn't treat you well—typical of someone who suffered from fetal alcohol syndrome, as you did—and have to haul you off to jail. You'd implore me, "Don't be such a hard-ass. Can't you just let me go?" I took my job seriously and couldn't deal with the lack of gray, the lack of discretion in matters like that. You committed a crime; you had to go to jail. If only life could be that simple.

I went on to do other things and didn't see you for several years. I heard about your bad date—when some john picked you up, beat you beyond recognition, and left you for dead beneath one of the downtown viaducts. Much of your face had been shattered, but you survived weeks in the hospital. Your face was changed, now etched with more prominent cheekbones and faint scarring. Our paths crossed again because of your new face.

Angela Jardine's disappearance affected you deeply. I still don't know if you were ever actually close, but it really doesn't matter, does it? Angela was a fixture on the Downtown Eastside, and it was her disappearance in November 1998 that convinced me something terrible was happening to the women of this poor community. You and Angela hung out in the same area just east of the police station at 312 Main Street. She used to stand on Cordova, often lifting her shirt or dress to show potential customers what she was selling. When she was gone, people—many of them police officers—would see you on the street and call me, relieved, convinced you were Angela and that she was not missing, that she was all right. The first time, I ran out of my office and searched the area, finding you and—seeing your cheekbones and reconstructed face—knowing that it was you they saw and not Angela. *Knowing* Angela was long gone. Still, we would repeat this scene several times in the coming months, wouldn't we? After a few times, I stopped running and walked out to see you.

"Hey, Constable Lori." We caught up: you told me again how your face came to be this way and how little you recalled about the assault. You were so lucky to live, and you assured me you were more careful now, only seeing regulars, always checking the bad date sheets. But I knew those promises were only as good as your dope supply on any given day, and if she was desperate enough, a girl would get into any vehicle with anyone—despite warnings, press releases, or bad vibes. I hated that it was always up to the women to protect themselves. Who told the men to stop attacking them? I stressed how important it was for you to let people know where you were, and you explained how you called your foster family almost every day, how you had been with them since you were four. The only family you had ever known, other than your street sisters.

You began telling everyone Angela was your sister, you sought out her family to share the pain of seeing so many of the girls on the street vanishing. You became an adopted daughter of sorts. You stood up at First United Church and gave a moving tribute to Angela—your sister—and pleaded that justice be done so that these women wouldn't have died in vain. You knew they hadn't just taken off to cool their heels somewhere for a while. You knew.

We talked about that from time to time. *Where were they?* You would rack your brain, trying to conjure up some tip, some tidbit that might help me. You shook your head at the photo of Robert Pickton I showed you on the street in 1999, and your newest companion—a pet rat—poked his head out from underneath your jacket. "Nope, never seen him." Was that true? Had you really never been out to that filthy, overgrown plot of land from which few women returned? Were you protecting that place, that mecca of addiction and depravity, saving it for yourself and others so that the cops would never know and never shut it down? "The cops always fuck up my deal. You guys are no fun."

Among your stuff at the farm, they found a worn copy of the bad date sheet, dated the same week you picked up your last welfare check and prescription asthma inhalers. Being careful. Taking precautions, because *you never know.*

The last time I saw you, it was the summer of 2000 at the WISH. You hollered to me, "Hey, sister," and we laughed, comfortable with the familiarity of knowing someone through years of bizarre coincidence and shared experience. I marveled at your longevity on the Downtown Eastside, realizing you were one of the few women from my early days who weren't dead.

We talked for a while, then you bounced off down the street. "Catch you later, Constable Lori."

20

Interrogating Robert Pickton

• • •

*"I have a theory that the truth is never told
during the nine-to-five hours."*

HUNTER S. THOMPSON, KINGDOM OF FEAR

ON FEBRUARY 22, 2002, Robert Pickton slept on a cold mattress in a Surrey detachment jail cell. His cellmate was an undercover RCMP officer. When I arrived at the detachment early that morning, I sat down in a video room with Sergeant John Woodlock, an RCMP member and the undercover officer's handler. We stared at the video monitor showing Pickton asleep in his cell. It felt surreal sitting there looking at him, this object of my thoughts for so many months. John and I had ski-raced together twenty years earlier in Calgary, and he shared his disgust with me. Pickton had masturbated almost immediately upon entering the cell the previous night and, to the horror of his poor cellmate, would do so several times throughout the night.

Eventually, the members of the RCMP Forensic Interview Team arrived and began preparation for the long day of interviewing ahead. The mood was high and expectant of success—these were the best and brightest interviewers in the province, and they were not accustomed to failure: the goal was a confession. I was joined by VPD Homicide Detective Phil Little and RCMP sergeant Randy Hundt, a forensics expert, and we were taken to a larger meeting room outfitted with a large projection screen so that we could watch the interview from there. Throughout the day, several high-ranking RCMP members would come and go, but the three of us remained throughout.

Sergeant Bill Fordy was first in the room, and he spoke to the monitor before Pickton came in. He had the most difficult job—to lay out the groundwork of the investigation for Pickton so that he could understand the case facing him. The first interviewer is much like a starting pitcher—often the confession isn't given to the starter; it is the closer who hears it. As the first interviewer, you are in a thankless, often frustrating position and are frequently left wondering whether the person has even heard or grasped what you've said. Not until the person confesses do you see that you've done your job.

Fordy apologized for the way he might have to speak about the women, suggesting that this would be a tactic and in no way represented his own feelings or judgments about the victims. I found this to be a sensitive and compassionate preamble that would be likely to put family members and loved ones at ease when the time came for the tape to be viewed in court. This statement moved me unexpectedly, and I had to fight to hide my emotions from the others in the room. My objective was to observe and try to understand as much as I could about this man who stood accused of such unimaginable crimes.

For this reason, I made no notes during the interview. I would have had to provide them to the court, and that was not my function. My description of this interview is, therefore, based on my recollection of what was said and the spirit in which it was said. When I paraphrase, it is in my language, not Pickton's—unless I specify otherwise—because his language was at times incomprehensible and so lacking in focus that it was often impossible to fully decipher.

Fordy brought Pickton into the interview room just after ten o'clock, and the two sat down. The room was furnished with a few upholstered chairs, a video monitor and VCR, a table, and an easel. Pickton looked haggard, his hair unkempt and scraggly, and he had several days' growth of beard. He was the personification of Charles M. Schultz's Pig-Pen, all grown up and accused of horrific crimes. Fordy explained the two murder charges to Pickton and reiterated his right to speak to counsel, confirming that Pickton had spoken to a lawyer that morning. Pickton looked at the floor, and often his answers were incoherent mumblings, difficult for us to understand over the monitor.

Fordy assured Pickton that he would treat him with dignity and respect and that he expected the same in return from Pickton. The two shook hands on this, and Pickton appeared taken aback at Fordy's earnest attempt to treat him like a person; it seemed to throw off his plan to appear uninterested. It also seemed that Pickton was only half-listening; he would grunt or chuckle slightly when Fordy told him he was being investigated in the disappearances of fifty women and had so far been charged with the murders of two. Hearing that number shocked me, as it first had when I began looking at the Project Evenhanded material on my first day. I assumed these were women who had gone missing from outside of Vancouver or after my time on the case. Pickton made some halfhearted assertions that he wasn't guilty but was the victim of some sort of conspiracy or setup.

As is often done in the rapport-building phase of an interview, Fordy spoke about himself in an effort to bond with and create empathy in Pickton. The goal is to allow the accused to see the interviewer as a human being, not merely a police officer in a position of authority. Throughout this portion of the interview, Pickton appeared to be almost slow or mentally deficient, referring to himself at various times as "just a pig man" and a simple, hardworking guy. He sat hunched over in his chair, turned slightly away from the table holding the TV monitor, his feet tucked up underneath his legs on the chair.

Fordy told Pickton a story of the worst thing that had happened in his life, about how a hockey injury cut short his career and ended his dream of playing professionally. Fordy asked Pickton what the worst thing was that had happened to him, and Pickton talked about being stabbed in 1997. He referred to himself as being "nailed to a cross" by that event, though it was unclear what he meant by this. Pickton's answers to Fordy's questions were bizarre and almost ridiculously simple and inappropriate, considering the gravity of his situation.

Eventually, the conversation led to Pickton's mother, who died of cancer in 1979, and Pickton quoted the exact date. He told Fordy how close the two of them were, how he got his work ethic from his mother, what a strong person she had been, and how he had always tried to emulate this strength and work as hard as she had. He said he respected her strong mind and her willpower. Fordy went on to talk about the best thing that had happened in his life—having his children—and asked Pickton to tell him what the best thing in his life was. Pickton said it was hard work—work was the best thing in his life.

After some reflection, Pickton offered that he had gone on a holiday once. I leaned in close to the monitor, expecting to hear him tell of some trip to Hawaii or Mexico to lie in the sun. Pickton said he went to Kansas City, Missouri, in 1974—

his one holiday away from Port Coquitlam and the farm that both sustained and trapped him. He was twenty-four years old and had money in his pocket and friends to visit, and within a week of being there, he met a woman named Connie and they fell in love.

They became engaged and spent the next five weeks together, hanging out, traveling around the area, and meeting people. He told of free cherry pie being given away in the streets with a hint of disdain, as though this waste was offensive to him. He said several times he figured Connie was probably married with kids by now. It was an odd thing to say—as though he still thought about her often and wondered whether she would be available today. He said he had to return to the farm, and she had a job she couldn't leave in Pontiac, Michigan, so they went their separate ways. His resentment toward the farm was obvious as he spoke. He continued to speak in his mumbling, rambling manner.

He and Fordy talked briefly about Pickton's siblings, Dave and Linda, and he was clear that he and Linda weren't close and had never spent much time together, as she had left the farm at a young age to attend Catholic school and go on to university. Pickton seemed uncertain whether she had become a lawyer or a realtor. When talking about Dave, Pickton seemed almost indifferent, as though he tolerated Dave and merely allowed him to control and dominate him. I got the sense that he enjoyed making Dave believe that he controlled him, but that, in reality, it might have been the other way around.

Several times during the conversation, Pickton would go off on a rambling explanation of his life philosophy in connection with a particular question. He portrayed himself as having a live-and-let-live attitude and of accepting other people's faults. He expressed the belief that we're here today, gone tomorrow, and that's all it's really about—and that the best die first.

He had a very casual attitude about death and several times said that someday you won't wake up and life will go on. He wouldn't commit to naming anyone as his best friend but preferred to explain how he helped anyone who asked for it without judging. He said he didn't care whether people were honest but then said he disrespected people who stole.

Pickton told a story about being injured trying to break up a fight between two boars on his farm. He dragged himself to the hospital for treatment, but the staff couldn't do anything for him other than wrap up his wounds. He was told to rest, but it was the height of summer and there was much work to be done. He described how he climbed up on his tractor in the midday heat and worked, puss streaming down his injured leg, heat blisters forming and breaking on his back. He told Fordy he stayed on that tractor and worked, despite his pain, despite the heat, and it was clear he took a great deal of pride in this.

He told another story about being injured by the hogs on the farm when he was younger, and from these two stories, it seemed there arose a respect bordering on hatred for these beasts. My sense was these events galvanized Pickton. He made a decision to never be conquered by these animals again and turned into the slaughtering machine he would become locally famous for, killing up to 150 pigs a week. He had been close to other animals—a calf he raised as a young boy and a horse he would later have to put down because of injury—but they had disappointed him, causing him a great deal of sadness, and it seemed he decided not to go through the pain of losing a loved one again.

The story of his horse was bizarre. Fordy asked him about it because the head of a horse was mounted on the wall of the trailer on Pickton's property. Again, Pickton quoted the dates and times of the horse's birth and death as though they were yesterday, even though both events had taken place more than twenty years ago. His command of dates was almost savant-like, and I suspected that if he had killed these women, he would probably be able to recite every detail surrounding the events. I wasn't at all certain I was prepared to hear that.

He had to put the horse down because another of the horses kicked his horse in the leg and the damage was irreparable. He put it down, then loaded it into his truck to take to a taxidermist for mounting, but there was some problem with the truck and Pickton ended up hauling the head—blood leaking from the burlap sack he carried it in—onto a city bus. The people on the bus stared at him, but no one spoke to him, and he just sat there, stunned in his grief. Thinking back, he said, they must have thought he was crazy.

He also told a story about the calf he had raised, which was another pivotal event in his life. Pickton wasn't more than ten years old and played with the calf like a pet. He came home from school one day and couldn't see the animal anywhere in the yard, so he set out to find it. Because he had trained the calf to stay away from the barn, where the slaughtering was done, he didn't think to look there first, telling himself his calf wouldn't go there after being told not to. Finally, after exhausting all other options, he went to look in the barn and found his calf—his special friend—hanging upside down, butchered. He was clearly devastated, though he seemed to try to downplay the event's effect on him in front of Fordy. He said he had never spent time in the barn before that incident. He didn't like the killing.

Fordy asked Pickton how he got into butchering pigs, and Pickton explained the process to him, stressing the need to do it cleanly and not rush, because the meat is for the public's consumption. He was obviously proud of this work and became quite self-deprecating when Fordy suggested that Pickton was the best butcher around—he said that everyone has their own way of doing things and they all butcher animals. He was unable to estimate how many pigs he had killed but allowed it could have been more than ten thousand over the years.

Fordy began to introduce the evidence against Pickton and to explain DNA profiling and blood spatter evidence. Pickton appeared to become lost and uninterested almost immediately, asking Fordy more than once what this had to do with him. Eventually, Fordy and Pickton agreed that for DNA to be at a scene a person must have been there physically. I sat watching, wondering if this man had any clue what was happening or if he really was the stunned, slow hayseed he was making himself out to be.

Fordy left the room for a moment and brought in a large poster board displaying photos of the fifty missing women and set it off to the side. I couldn't see whether their names were beneath their photos; nor could I make out each woman's identity. But the board was a looming and ominous presence in the room, and I knew it bore many of those same images I had stared up at for long hours in our project room. Pickton would not look directly at it until Fordy began to point to various photos and ask questions about the women.

Fordy asked Pickton to tell him which of these women had been out to his farm. Fordy began with number one, and Pickton said she had been out to the farm "lots." For some of the other photos, Pickton said he didn't know the woman; others he commented were pretty. When shown number twenty-six, he said she looked like Lynn. I leaned forward, thinking he must be referring to Lynn Ellingsen. Fordy asked Pickton whether he would want that to be Lynn in the picture, and Pickton didn't respond. Pickton then asked Fordy to show him which ones he was charged with murdering, and Fordy pointed to Sereena Abotsway and Mona Wilson. Pickton exclaimed, "Who the hell is she?" to one of their pictures, and it came out sounding phony and rehearsed. This was the first indication I saw that perhaps the dumb pig farmer persona really was an act.

The conversation turned to sex, and Fordy asked Pickton to explain what he meant by sex. Pickton seemed particularly obtuse on this point, ignoring Fordy's questions. Pickton asserted that he hadn't had sex in more than a year and that had been with a woman named Roxanne. Fordy asked questions about Roxanne's sexual skills, and Pickton replied that she was a very, very nice person. He was indifferent about his first sexual experience, first saying there wasn't much to tell about it, then saying he couldn't remember. He couldn't remember his first sex worker experience. He said he hadn't had sex with Connie, his fiancée from Michigan. Pickton's responses to this whole line of questioning seemed to be deliberately obtuse and out of place for someone who demonstrated such a solid memory in so many other areas.

Fordy played a videotape for Pickton. It was difficult to hear the tape, but it contained an interview with a man named Scott Chubb, a Pickton associate and frequent visitor to the farm, who would later testify in the criminal trial. The gist of the tape seemed to be that Chubb had seen Pickton do things to women, including injecting them with antifreeze. Pickton seemed shocked by this tape, stunned that someone would actually come to the police and say these things. He shook his head over and over saying, "What? What? Is that Scott Chubb? Is that Scott Chubb?" He told Fordy he had spoken to Chubb on the telephone just a couple of nights earlier. Fordy told him Chubb would be giving evidence against him, and Pickton responded by asking, "He's going to give evidence? After everything I helped him with?" He seemed to imply that Chubb was involved in the same type of behavior as he was, but he refused to elaborate. Later in the interview, Pickton repeated his disbelief at Chubb's involvement.

At this point in the interview, Dana Lillies—the female RCMP constable who had been talking with Pickton at the jobsite before his arrest—arrived and brought lunch for Pickton and Fordy. Fordy left, and Lillies offered to sit with Pickton and keep him company. Pickton seemed pleased to see her, and she acted as though she was genuinely concerned about his well-being. As they talked, we saw another, very different side of Robert Pickton.

He was very quiet and non-confrontational and said several times that he didn't deserve to live, didn't deserve Lillies's kindness, didn't deserve to eat and that he should be on death row. It was like watching a child try to elicit sympathy from his mother, saying demeaning things about himself so that she would respond that he was wrong and that he did deserve all those things and so much more.

Lillies played the role well and managed to portray a level of caring I know she did not truly feel. She told Pickton she had seen a side of him others hadn't and she cared about him as a human being. He seemed to lap this up, and it was obvious he wanted nothing more than to believe that this professional, attractive, bright woman could actually be interested in him. Lillies tried to steer the conversation toward the investigation, but Pickton seemed wary and said little about the specifics of the case. Still, her mere presence served to illuminate the complexity of Pickton's personality—seeing him with Fordy and then with Lillies was like watching two different people.

Pickton repeatedly told Lillies he was finished, that his life was over, that he was "nailed to the cross." She made some bold attempts to get him talking, asking questions about a dildo that was found on the end of a handgun and wondering aloud how Pickton's DNA and Mona Wilson's DNA could both have been found on the end of that dildo. He said he sometimes used the dildo as a silencer for the gun because of the new subdivision beside his property. She said that didn't explain how DNA ended up there, and he didn't respond.

He kept going back to Scott Chubb, shaking his head incredulously and saying, "Of all guys, Scott Chubb." Lillies asked Pickton whether he had some dirt on Chubb, and Pickton answered that was neither here nor there. But the implication was that perhaps Chubb had a few skeletons—proverbial or real—of his own in his closet.

Lillies played a videotaped compilation of all the local media coverage since the search began on the Pickton farm on February 5. He watched for a few moments but then asked Lillies to stop the tape and asked to go back to his cell.

Lillies left, and Fordy resumed his task of laying out the evidence against Pickton. This was a particularly difficult job, because all of the evidence at this point was purely circumstantial. Pickton had a contract with the City of Vancouver to buy abandoned vehicles that were headed for the junkyard, and they began to talk about this. Pickton seemed to believe that he could explain some of the evidence—such as Abotsway's asthma inhalers—as actually having come to his property in one of these vehicles. He seemed to focus on some black gym bag and told Fordy that Dinah Taylor would straighten the whole thing out and that the bag belonged to Nancy, Pickton's girlfriend.

Pickton went off on a long diatribe about how he helped people and, unfortunately, it often got him into trouble. He said Fordy would have to take him as he was, that he would be there to help the next person and repeated that he was just a poor, plain little farm boy, nailed to the cross. He said "I'm sorry" several times, but it was unclear what he was apologizing for other than who he was. All he tried to do was help people, he said.

Pickton spoke about the guns on his property, for which the original search warrant had been obtained. He told Fordy his lawyer would be angry with him for talking, but he didn't care about being open. He said he used the Hilti gun and a .22 to kill the pigs before slaughter, that it would often require three or four shots from the Hilti to do the job. He told Fordy how he put plastic on the end of one of the guns to quiet it. Then, this speech ended as suddenly as it had begun.

One of the very few funny moments I had when working on this case was listening to the wire room monitors tell everyone in the morning meeting about how Pickton likened his own notoriety to that of "Bill Laden"—Pickton's reference to Osama bin Laden. It had been clear from February 5 that Pickton was pretending to hate the publicity but obviously relished the attention the case was garnering in the international media. He would often tell whomever he was speaking to that his life was over and the attention would never end, but it was evident that this was an act and that he was getting off on the spotlight.

Fordy seized on this and began to tell Pickton how truly large this case was. He told Pickton he was bigger than the Pope, Princess Di, and bin Laden. He said Pickton was on the front page of the paper that morning, and Pickton seemed to fixate on this. Several times in the interview, just as it seemed Fordy was getting into some very deep and emotional territory, Pickton would look up and say, "Am I really in the paper?" or "Today's paper? Really?" or "Front page, huh?" It must have been incredibly frustrating for Fordy to waste his time going over evidence, but his hard work would come to fruition later on.

Fordy narrowed in on the incriminating facts of the case and told Pickton he knew that he had killed these girls and that he was going to prison; the decision to talk was his. Fordy explained that investigators had found Mona Wilson's blood in the Dodge motor home parked behind Pickton's trailer— enough blood to be called a bloodletting, enough to at least have rendered her unconscious. From here, Fordy began to minimize the degree to which he viewed Pickton as a monster, to show Pickton that the world might see what he had done as horrific but that he, Bill Fordy, understood the real reasons behind the killings. He told Pickton he didn't hate him; he merely wanted to understand him and understand his story.

Fordy slowly began to turn up the heat. He explained to Pickton that this was not going away, and the only matter left to deal with was stopping the lies—lies that were like a cancer that only Pickton had the power to cut out. Pickton made some weak denials at this point, saying two or three times, "I didn't do anything." But then he told Fordy that if he could show him how the evidence meant he did it, he would admit to the killings. Clearly, Fordy was getting to him. Fordy tried to give him palatable reasons for committing these murders, saying some people felt these women were the masters of their own destinies, out shooting drugs and selling their bodies. He told Pickton that he understood why he must be afraid right now, and he understood Pickton's need to hang onto a lie—that it was normal.

Fordy played another videotape for Pickton, this one featuring a man unknown to me in an interview with police. Again, the tape was unintelligible, but Pickton was clearly bothered by it. Fordy told Pickton that several of his friends and associates were coming forward and filling in facts of the case. Did Pickton want to stick to his story that he hadn't killed anyone when so many people had said he had? Did he want to look stupid, sticking to a lie when others were proving it to be untrue? Pickton said they were telling stories, and Fordy asked if they could all be telling stories. Could everyone be lying and he, Robert Pickton, be the only one telling the truth? No response.

They spoke at length about the mingling of Pickton's and Wilson's DNA on the end of the dildo and in the motor home.

By now, it was after six in the evening; they had been talking for more than eight hours, and Fordy was understandably running out of gas. Pickton, however, seemed to be gaining energy and strength as the interrogation wore on, something I had never seen before.

And then, something even more extraordinary happened. Staff Sergeant Don Adam, the lead investigator of the entire case, stepped into the interview room. Phil, Randy, and I all jumped into the air, since we had been standing close to the monitor, straining to hear Pickton's every word. Like Gretzky the coach suddenly lacing on skates and taking to the ice in overtime, Adam the star interrogator could no longer watch from the sidelines. In what could have been the ultimate in self-indulgence and arrogance, Adam came in for the kill, and it would prove to be the perfect decision at the perfect time. Fordy remained for a few minutes, but, clearly, Adam was now in control.

Adam explained who he was and said that he was there to clear up some misunderstandings Pickton may have picked up over the past eight hours. This is where Adam shone, cutting to the chase and distilling the entire case into one succinct point—that Pickton was done, plain and simple. Even more fascinating than this turn of events was Pickton's change in demeanor the moment Adam entered and began speaking,

Pickton metamorphosed, puffing up in his chair and turning to face Adam squarely, feet firmly planted on the floor, as if to say, *Finally, you've brought me my equal.* It was chilling. As Pickton hunkered down to go toe-to-toe with Adam, I realized that Pickton had heard every single word that had been said in those eight hours, that he recalled everything, and that he most definitely was not the thick hayseed he had tried to portray. He was a calculating and cagey manipulator and a hard-nosed negotiator. His ego was almost visible.

Adam reviewed each piece of evidence and each lie that Pickton had been caught in, delivering them like staccato blows from a machine gun. *Blam blam blam*: Abotsway's inhalers found in layers in Pickton's garbage; her blood on needles, not in some scrapped car as Pickton tried to explain; the black tote bag with Sereena's clothing in it that Pickton and Dinah Taylor tried to say had come from the Cobalt Hotel; Mona Wilson's blood on the mattress and the bloody drag marks on the floor, showing how she was carried out after the murder; the dildo on the end of the gun with Mona and Pickton's DNA on it, Heather Bottomley's identification found on the farm; the syringes of windshield washing fluid found in Pickton's trailer.

Adam went on to talk about the women in Pickton's life—Dinah Taylor, Lisa Yelds, Lynn Ellingsen. He took the approach that Pickton should tell the truth so that none of them could hurt or blackmail Pickton anymore. Adam told Pickton he knew these women steered many of the girls out to the farm and quite possibly took part in the killings. He portrayed Pickton as someone who had been used and blackmailed by these women for so long that now was the time for him to fight back, to take away their power over him by telling the truth. But Pickton wouldn't budge other than to say he needed to talk with Dinah before saying anything. Adam went on to say that deals were being made with Ellingsen and Yelds, that they were preparing through lawyers to give up this information, and if Pickton told the truth, those deals would be off.

Pickton insisted he couldn't say anything without speaking with Taylor first, and Adam told him that would not be possible—what kind of police officer would let two witnesses or two suspects talk to each other. Adam continued, telling Pickton about how large scale the investigation was, how many investigators he had out there right now, taking statements from people, how long they would be on the farm, digging, because Dave Pickton had told them there were bodies to be found. Then Adam changed his tack slightly and began to work on the reasons Pickton had killed these women: he blamed them for giving him hepatitis C, for stealing from him, and for taking advantage of his generosity. This line of discussion didn't seem to move Pickton, so Adam changed course.

Clearly, Pickton had some type of psychiatric diagnosis. He was not entirely devoid of emotion, but he'd gone off the rails emotionally a long time ago. Adam began to play to Pickton's ego, which was exactly what was needed to bring Pickton out. He talked about Gary Ridgway, the Green River Killer, and told Pickton he didn't know which of the two of them was the bigger serial killer. Pickton laughed at this, clearly enjoying Adam's acknowledgment of his abilities. Adam asked Pickton how many he had killed, if he knew the number. Pickton said he didn't know. Adam asked whether we should keep looking for other killers or was it all him, and Pickton nodded, then said he shouldn't say anything more without his lawyer present.

Adam began to thank Pickton for some of the good things he had done, such as not killing children and letting many of the women who had visited the farm return to the Downtown Eastside after their dates. There was a tone of admiration in Adam's voice and Pickton reveled in the attention of this man who was overseeing the entire investigation. Adam spoke of the people who had told investigators how Pickton could slaughter pigs all day long, longer than any other man in the area. He told Pickton he thought there was a part of him that liked killing and that because he felt trapped by the farm, anger and sex had become mixed up with killing and disease, and the whole thing caused Pickton to slip, to cross that line from slaughtering pigs to killing women.

Adam sensed Pickton was closer to a confession than at any other time in the interrogation, and he began giving him alternatives—two reasons for committing a heinous act where one is particularly distasteful and the other is less so and, therefore, more understandable or palatable to the accused. Agreeing to either the greater or lesser offense is an admission of guilt. Anything short of a strong denial of either is a good indication of guilt. An innocent person would vigorously deny either alternative. Adam began peppering Pickton with such alternatives.

Was there any killing before the attack on Ms. Anderson, or was she the first one? Pickton said there "shouldn't be" any women killed before her. Did the killings start by accident or were they planned? I don't know. Do you really not know or do you just not want to say? Don't know. Did you catch some of the first ones stealing? Was that it, or was it purely rage and anger? I don't know. Did it start out hard and get easier for you? Did you feel bad after? I don't know. Pickton's "I don't knows" were barely audible, and he looked down at the floor as he spoke. Were you angry that they had infected your body, given you hep C? You felt anger, didn't you? Pickton nodded silently. How come you spared some of them? They were nice people. Was anger all it was? I shouldn't be talking to you. It doesn't matter what I say. It's all over for me, anyways.

Phil and Randy and I stood stunned, two feet from the huge video monitor, mouths agape. We had each witnessed dozens of interrogations, and this was textbook—rarely does anyone sit there and say, "This is what I did and this is how I did it." They are prompted and encouraged to let little bits of the truth sneak out through nods and uh-huhs, but that requires a great deal of trust and a feeling of safety with the interviewer, because often what they are admitting to is horrific, and they know the world will view them as a monster. This will be the safest place they encounter for the rest of their lives, and they know it.

Adam began to talk about the numbers, and Pickton said he wasn't the only guy, but he was the "head honcho." Repeatedly throughout the interview he directly referred to other people's involvement in the killings—Dinah Taylor, Lynn Ellingsen, and at least one man. For reasons unknown to me, Adam did not pursue this line, preferring to focus only on Pickton's role. Adam asked him how many murders we could put him to, would it be twenty? I don't know. Fifteen? Thirty? I don't know. Adam told Pickton he could put him to twelve right now, and Pickton silently nodded his head again. Adam pressed him again on numbers until Pickton asked, "What's in it for me?" Hardly the question an innocent man would ask.

Watching the two of them sitting across from each other, sizing each other up, assessing and appraising each other was like observing a pair of tigers slowly pacing around a cage, stopping, changing direction, pacing again. Pickton had swung one leg up on the table beside him, assuming a very open and almost defiant posture—proud, cocksure, arrogant.

And then Pickton played his hand, asking Adam whether he would pull fences down on the property—presumably so that Dave Pickton could access the machinery and continue working—if he told him what Adam wanted to hear. Pickton wanted to deal. His confession in exchange for his family getting their livelihood back. Adam said no, no deals. Pickton told him to take his offer to the higher-ups. Adam said he was as high as it got and the answer was no. No deals. If Adam made a deal, everything in the statement to this point would be inadmissible, and Adam wasn't prepared to take that chance when he hadn't been able to test Pickton's truthfulness. He wanted Pickton to tell him something Adam could send investigators out to confirm, but Pickton refused, saying again he was already nailed to the cross.

As cool and calculating as Pickton appeared, I got the impression that he wanted Adam's people off his property more than he was trying to let on and not only to save his family's money. He asked Adam again if his people would pull out if he told everything, and again, Adam refused to deal. Adam asked Pickton if he had ever killed and felt regret afterward, and Pickton asked Adam what he wanted him to say. Adam said all he wanted was the truth.

Adam switched directions again, telling Pickton he didn't think that Dave was involved, and Pickton agreed, saying he'd swear to that, that Dave was protecting him. Adam asked Pickton if he was protecting Dinah in the same way, and Pickton said yes. Adam asked Pickton if it was true she helped him kill, and Pickton said he had to speak with her before saying anything more. He would bring everything out in the open, but he needed to speak to her first.

Adam pressed him, saying that if Dinah had killed, the police couldn't let her go. Pickton said "No comment." When Adam asked him if he was prepared to take the fall for all of them—Dinah Taylor, Lynn Ellingsen, this other unidentified man—Pickton just kept repeating that he had to talk to Dinah. Adam reiterated that if Pickton didn't tell his side of the story, someone like Dinah or Lynn would, and they would get the reward money. Once again, Pickton would be the victim of their betrayal. All Pickton could say was he had to talk to Dinah. When Adam asked him whether Dinah was involved in the killing or steering women to the farm, Pickton answered "No comment" over and over again.

When Adam took Pickton out of the interview to allow him to use the washroom, he walked him through the large atrium of the Surrey RCMP detachment, past the room where Phil, Randy, and I were watching. We had the windows papered so that no one could see in, but the three of us peered through the cracks in the paper to watch this man, the focus of so much attention, walk by on his way to urinate. He seemed tiny, frail, and pathetic—hardly like the frightening serial killer we were learning he was. He shuffled like someone who had fallen off a horse one too many times. He was the personification of brown—a drab, dusty brown, a mixture of dirt and hopelessness and misery.

As he walked through the atrium, he seemed almost child-like, looking up at the architecture, mouth slightly open. It was clear he hadn't seen much outside the farm. Many times in my career, I have been face-to-face with people accused of horrible things, and I am continually struck by the ordinariness of these people, by their lack of any remarkable feature or characteristic. As Pickton walked past us, unaware that he was being watched, he could have been just a small ineffectual man, who became so horribly misguided in his attempts to avoid living a small ineffectual life. He did not conjure up fear in any of us, merely pity and regret. What do monsters really look like?

Adam brought him back to the interview room, and Adam began to talk about other people who were involved in the murders, specifically one other man. Adam focused on Pickton's carelessness throughout the time he was killing women. Adam asked Pickton whether he thought they'd be charging Lynn Ellingsen. Pickton nodded yes. Adam asked him whether there would be aspects of torture in the killings and Pickton smiled slightly, shook his head, and said no. Adam asked whether he knew why he killed, if he understood that about himself, and Pickton said no, then quickly said he meant no comment, he had to speak to Dinah first. He reiterated that he was the "head honcho" several times but that he needed to speak with her before saying anything more.

They spoke for several more minutes along these lines.

Then Adam tossed out a throwaway line, saying he thought Pickton didn't do a very good job cleaning up the blood in the trailer in light of how much was found. Pickton quietly replied, "I was sloppy." Adam seized on this, asking several more specific questions about what Pickton did to try to hide the blood of Ms. Anderson and Sereena Abotsway, but Pickton would say little more other than it was merely bad policing that made it possible for this investigation to go on for so long.

Adam agreed and asked whether Pickton had ever thought of quitting the killing. Pickton said "Yeah." Was it anger that motivated him? Pickton wouldn't say, but then he told Adam he had one more killing planned; that was going to be the last one, but he never got that far. Adam peppered him with questions about why he didn't clean up better, why he hadn't disposed of the bloody mattress after killing Mona Wilson, and Pickton kept repeating sloppiness, he was sloppy. A few moments later, Pickton laughed and told Adam he was making him out to be a much worse murderer than he really was.

They continued in this way: Adam asking specific questions and Pickton making vague admissions. Clearly, Pickton was enjoying the cat-and-mouse game with Adam and was well aware of what a direct confession would mean to the investigation. He took obvious pleasure in being in control, and I felt certain that he had lorded this sort of control over his victims, probably forcing them to do all sorts of depraved things for his own enjoyment. I tried to block these images from my mind, but they were streaming in, pictures of all the women I knew begging for their lives, for a chance to go home, and Pickton just laughing at them, telling them that would be impossible because he was the "head honcho."

Pickton sat there and pointed his finger at Adam, telling him to go home and think about it and come back to him in the morning when he was ready to make a deal after talking with Dinah. Adam again refused to deal. Pickton told Adam they wouldn't find anything if they dug on the property, but Adam wasn't buying it, and neither was I. There was something in Pickton's tone and manner that suggested he was trying to appear nonchalant about the digging but didn't want it to happen—perhaps because it would disrupt his family's business, but I felt there was more. Adam told him the police had spoken to several people who had told them Pickton had often said if the police started digging, he'd be finished. Pickton said nothing.

Adam ended the interview by telling Pickton they would talk again tomorrow, and Pickton repeated that Adam should think about it, think hard—and it was clear he was talking about his original proposal that he give information to Adam in exchange for the tearing down of the search of the property.

Pickton was returned to his cell, and we all met for a debriefing of the interview. It was well past ten o'clock, yet the air was electric with excitement. Although there had been no outright confession, the mood among the team members said the day had been a success. There was much discussion about how to approach Pickton the following day and who would do that interview. Members of the team approached Lynn Ellingsen again that day and she finally began painfully retelling her story, but it was slow going, as she was extremely emotional and became distraught as she spoke about the difficult things she had seen in that barn.

She would be interviewed further the following day, and then investigators hoped to have more information with which to go at Pickton. All in all, it seemed as though the pieces of the puzzle were finally falling into place. I said little in the meeting, I was a guest and preferred to listen and absorb the incredible events of the day. By the time I got in my car at one o'clock, I was mentally exhausted.

When I arrived back at the Surrey detachment later that same morning, the interview team members were meeting and I joined them. Pickton had apparently bragged to his cellmate—another RCMP undercover officer—that he was *the* pig farmer, that he had killed forty-eight women, and that he was giving the interviewers' heads a rap.

The eventual consensus of the team was that Pickton was a psychopath and had enjoyed the feeling of control he felt when talking with Don Adam. To now deny Pickton his anticipated second meeting with Adam would be an insult to his huge ego. I quietly disagreed with this strategy. I didn't think that insulting Pickton would serve any purpose other than to close a door. This wasn't the time to get into a pissing contest with this man. I believed we should pander to his massive ego in strategic ways if that was what it would take to get to the bottom of this case. There was always the chance that he had used the night in his cell to strengthen his resolve to say nothing and the interview would be short, but I felt this weekend would be our only chance to talk with him like this. What did we have to lose?

The decision was made to let Pickton cool his heels in the cell and stew, indignant that his friend Adam was not dying to talk with him again. The team discussed Lynn Ellingsen and how they had approached her for questioning on the weekend. Finally, people were beginning to believe she played a significant role in this case. I listened to the discussion, filled with both disgust and relief. I held my emotions in check as the team was told that when Ellingsen sat down with interviewers and began to tell the story of what she had seen in the barn that night in 1999, she became overwhelmed by emotion and vomited at the recollection. *Finally.*

Plans were being made for an undercover operation involving her boyfriend, Ron Menard, as investigators had gathered some information that he had been the driving force behind Ellingsen's extortion of Pickton. Supposedly, Menard would send Ellingsen to Pickton for money, and if she did not return with it, he would beat her and forcibly confine her for extended periods of time. Again, I hoped this was in aid of determining who else had taken part in the killing. The interview team would continue to interview Ellingsen and determine how to protect her and keep her on track for a trial down the road.

This day signified an end point for me, an end to my investing so much hope and effort into forcing this investigation in the right direction. I was suddenly faced with my own limits. I knew that I could not continue to be close to this *thing*, that it was destroying me to have such strong feelings about the way the investigation should move forward and no power to make those things happen. I decided to finish out the week and then return to the VPD. The week was sadly anticlimactic. Pickton was not interviewed again. The forensic search team working on the farm was deliberately kept separate from the detectives, so I received no information about what evidence they were finding. I could only hope it was significant enough to warrant forgoing further interviews with Pickton.

I took three weeks of sick leave in March to try to regroup after all that had happened and to reduce my stress levels and anxiety. Nightmares and soaking sweats terrorized me nightly, and I awoke stiff and sore, as though I'd had an intense workout. Diarrhea, indigestion, lack of appetite, and fatigue dogged me every day. I snapped at everyone, from my partner at home to friends, colleagues, supervisors, and total strangers. I'd always been someone who'd cry at sad movies, but now I found myself breaking down in tears at the most inappropriate and bizarre moments. I worried irrationally about my toddler son's safety and well-being, terrified that even the most benign activity would cause him injury or death. I began to shout and swear at other drivers whenever I was behind the wheel. Everything irritated and annoyed me. Whereas I had always possessed a strong attention span and ability to concentrate, now I could barely sit still for any period of time. I began to clean my home and office obsessively.

I had no idea what was going on with me, but I would come to learn it was a post-traumatic stress injury. When I finally sought out therapy for the intrusive thoughts and violent dreams that had plagued me for these past years, I wasn't prepared for the diagnosis of post-traumatic stress disorder (PTSD). I thought it was something for wimps, sucks, and malingerers, and I quickly dismissed the doctor's finding, though I felt that she was an excellent therapist and that she had helped me. I wanted to understand my anger and feelings of helplessness and find some ways to let myself off the hook for the futility of our investigation. I hoped I would recover quickly.

My time working at Project Evenhanded proved to be a double-edged sword. It fulfilled my need to see the Pickton file finally taken seriously with adequate resources dedicated to investigating his crimes, but it drove home over and over again how much more should have been done far earlier. Like Geramy, I questioned daily whether I had done all I could to portray this case to the RCMP as the priority it was. Intellectually, I knew I had. Emotionally, doubts remained.

For the second time in this investigation, it was time for me to go—and I experienced all of the same guilt I had the first time. I struggled, believing if I stayed, perhaps in some small way I could help the other investigators. But all I felt compelled to do was collect material for this book, and I knew I couldn't misrepresent myself in that way, especially to those few people working on the file—Geramy Field, Steve Pranzl, Linda Malcolm, Mark Chernoff, Alex Clarke—whom I considered friends. It was time to go, and this time it was clearer to me that I had to do this for my sanity and for my family. My level of anxiety and agitation was higher than ever, the cumulative effects of which I wouldn't fully understand for years.

PART
TWO

21

Soldiering On

• • •

"Tell 'em to God. Don' go burdenin' other people
with your sins. That ain't decent."
JOHN STEINBECK, THE GRAPES OF WRATH

I BOOKED OFF ON stress leave in May 2002 and returned
to my job in Financial Crime in September. I didn't seek
any treatment during that time and naïvely hoped that all
I needed was a break. I began to consider a career away from
policing, but I lacked the energy and clear thinking to explore
that in any way. I was pregnant with our second child and continued to work on my book about the Pickton investigation. I
hoped to take my maternity leave and then resign from the
VPD when it was over. I became convinced that the truth of
the Ellingsen tip would never come out in evidence, and my
need to be a truth teller bordered on the obsessive.

All of the physical and psychological symptoms I was experiencing led me to seek counseling in the fall of 2002. I had
never felt so down and hopeless and suffered from so many
physical ailments. I had never before had trouble sleeping

or falling asleep. As a previously active, upbeat, positive person engaged with the world, I no longer recognized myself. I avoided people, preferring isolation to social activity. The VPD maintained a list of psychologists who had passed a security screening, presumably in case we confided in them about difficult cases we had worked on. I'd seen a psychologist a few years earlier, after a difficult breakup, so I made an appointment with her.

After a couple of sessions, it was clear to me that talk therapy was not going to fix whatever was wrong with me. My psychologist informed me that this was all she did and that she had no other trauma treatments to offer. I asked her if she practiced any of the newer trauma treatments I had learned of in my own research, and she said no. I thanked her and told her I had no hard feelings, but I'd be seeking a therapist better versed in the latest trauma treatments. She wished me well. No one else on the very short VPD psychologist list had such training, so I found my own therapist.

Margo Weston, my new psychologist, diagnosed me with PTSD after several sessions. This was 2002, and I had never heard of PTSD, much less imagined I would ever suffer from such a thing. I received Eye Movement Desensitization and Reprocessing (EMDR) treatment to try to improve my sleep and reduce my night sweats and nightmares.

I worked with Margo for a few months and then decided I was "better" and stopped going, despite my continuing symptoms and her skill and kindness as a therapist. Looking back, I see now we had barely scratched the surface of the work I needed to do. Margo politely suggested I might not be done with treatment, but I tried to move on, convincing myself that my PTSD was gone and I was fine. This would be the first of several times I'd walk away from treatment when it became too difficult, another hallmark of PTSD I had yet to understand.

Little in policing had lived up to my expectations, but I had enjoyed many aspects of investigative work well enough until then. The salary, benefits, and job security all beckoned me to stay so that I could support my family and maintain the comfort of my lifestyle. I had chosen policing in large part because it afforded me the time off and subject matter to enable me to pursue my writing as a hobby, yet I felt duty-bound to not share a large portion of what I'd seen and done. All my life, I'd assumed I would pursue fiction as a writer, but the truth was far more compelling.

Ultimately, circumstances took the decision about publishing this story out of my hands. The first Pickton trial publication ban came into effect January 15, 2003. In late 2002, I had secured an agreement with McClelland and Stewart to tell my story. We naïvely hoped the ban would be lifted by the time we published, but it became clear over time that this was only the beginning. I started my maternity leave and continued writing. In May of 2003, Doug LePard contacted me to let me know I was receiving a Chief Constable's Commendation for my work on the missing women file.

Later that month, he invited me to attend the ceremony at the Roundhouse Community Centre. My feelings were mixed. On the one hand, it felt good to have people at my workplace recognize all I had tried to do with very few resources. On the other hand, my grief remained raw and jagged, and I didn't trust myself to talk about the case or anything surrounding it in public without breaking down. I told Doug I didn't see myself coming back to work for the VPD after my leave. He said he understood but hoped I would attend.

Around the same time as the ceremony, Jane Armstrong of the *Globe and Mail* wrote a story about my agent, Michael Levine—whom she referred to as "Mister Conflict of Interest" in the world of literary and media representation. Her story mentioned that Michael also represented Stevie Cameron, author of the Pickton true crime book *On the Farm*. This effectively announced my book to the country and, more importantly, to the victims' families, and many were hurt and angry that I would publish a book about their loved ones. They assumed the worst about the content and my intentions, which some of the families felt certain were monetary.

I attended the awards ceremony and received my Chief Constable's Commendation from Doug LePard. In some ways, I felt better afterward. So few of our colleagues knew the story of what my team and I had tried to do, and it was gratifying to have Doug tell a small part of that story to the crowd of coworkers, family, and friends. It could never make up for the lack of support for the investigation, but it was something, and I did appreciate it. I spoke to a few people, shook some hands, and turned to leave.

A large camera lens obstructed my vision of anything else, and I heard a female voice asking me about my book. How did I feel knowing the victims' families felt betrayed? I felt totally unprepared and handled myself abysmally, mumbling something about needing to get home to my newborn son. I sounded more like a La Leche League spokesperson than a police officer. I heard a question thrown at me, asking me whether there was going to be a book. I paused.

"No, there is no book."

And I meant it. My decision came out of months of anxiety and concern about whether publishing would be the right thing to do, assuming publication bans would even allow it. There would be no book published as long as I didn't have the blessing of the families or the green light of the courts. I drove straight home and emailed Michael to see whether I could get out of the contract. I spoke to Anne Drennan of the VPD media office and told her I had indeed written a book but had decided not to publish it. I apologized for not making her—and the vpd, by extension—aware of it, but this was my own doing, and I would take responsibility. She was gracious and sympathetic. Fortunately, so were Michael Levine and Douglas Gibson, my publisher, who let me out of the contract with no legal ramifications and wished me the best. I think they were happy to see the last of me; I was nervous, insistent, and panicked—not an ideal client or author to deal with in that state.

Several publication bans relating to evidence, witnesses, and undercover operations were issued from 2005 until Pickton lost his final appeal in 2010. There was no way I was risking Pickton's probable conviction by publishing anything, and I hoped the story would come out in its entirety during the trial. Working on the book forced me back into that investigation and a world that stirred up the old trauma over and over again. I had no idea how toxic that was for me until I stopped working on it. There would be no book, but now its existence was known.

22

Salvaging a Career

. . .

"I have no spur to prick the sides of my intent, but only
vaulting ambition, which o'erleaps itself and falls on the other."
WILLIAM SHAKESPEARE, MACBETH

ATTEMPTED TO COMPETE for sergeant in 2005, after several
members of the VPD executive and Chief Constable Jamie
Graham implored me to consider it in spite of my uncertainty. I decided to go for it but unceremoniously flamed out
after a heated argument with the sergeant in charge of the
assessment center when I disagreed with my poor mark and
told him I felt the entire promotional process was "a crock of
shit." I'd had even less sleep than usual all week because I was
executing a number of search warrants on a complex financial
crime case, and I told myself I never should have sat for the
assessment center that day.

In truth, lack of sleep was the least of my problems; agitation, anxiety, explosive anger, and a short attention span
dogged me and everything I tried to do. I sent angry emails
and deliberately ignored and circumvented the chain of

command, pissing off my supervisors and managers, many of whom were trying to keep me on track and out of trouble.

Word got around that I wouldn't be carrying on in the competition. No one suggested to me that I change my mind. No one asked me if I might need some help, and I certainly wasn't asking for any. I blamed everything on the VPD and the people running the place. *They created me. Now they can deal with the result.* Everyone else moved forward. I remained stuck.

My PTSD continued to manifest itself in my explosive interpersonal communication at work and at home and in my poor physical and mental health. I avoided drinking because it terrified me: whenever I did, a wave of relief so comforting and enticing washed over me that I feared I might never stop. If I had two glasses of wine one night, I'd have three the next, four the next, until I realized I had to stop or it would kill me.

After that, whenever anyone asked me whether I wanted to be promoted, I said "I'd rather stick needles in my eyes," and I meant it. It felt better to me to be on the outside, isolated from everything in the VPD that had let me—and the missing women—down. Everything about the VPD stank to me. I wanted no part of it, but I was too damaged to go anywhere else.

I threw myself into my position in the Threat Assessment Unit, working long hours, evenings, and weekends in addition to my normal shift. It felt easier to be away from home than watch myself snap at my partner and my poor kids, who got so excited when I did get home and only wanted to play with me. It seemed impossible to shift gears from work to family life. *If only I could unwind, just for a few minutes,* I'd tell myself. But I never unwound. At work, my targets were anyone who crossed me and angered me, my rallying cry always *That guy is so stupid* or *That girl is such an idiot.* Incompetence of any kind sent me over the edge and reminded me of the kind of incompetence I had encountered on the Pickton file. My own mistakes angered me, too. For years, I walked around agitated and volatile.

One rare Saturday when I wasn't working, I decided to play my guitar in an attempt to relax. I set it down while I went to the kitchen to brew a cup of tea and when I returned, I found my three-year-old daughter holding the guitar. She turned to me and accidentally banged the neck on the corner of the wall. Nothing was damaged, but I glared at her.

"Never, EVER bang my guitar like that again," I growled. For the first time ever, I saw fear in her eyes. *My beautiful little girl was afraid of me. I was a monster. I had let a stupid $200 guitar come before my relationship with my child.*

She handed me the guitar and hugged me.

"I'm sorry, Mommy," she said. "I didn't mean to make you mad." I held her for a few moments and looked into her eyes. I felt like the biggest ass, someone I could barely recognize. This was a rare occasion when I could actually step outside my anger and see it.

"You haven't done anything wrong, baby. I'm the one who's sorry," I touched her face. "You touch my guitar anytime you want, okay? I want you to play it if you want to."

"Okay, Mommy," she skipped off to find her brothers, leaving me ruminating over whether I'd ruined her forever.

I rarely sat down at home. I always saw something that needed dusting or cleaning or fixing or moving—it didn't matter what. Watching an entire movie at home without getting up was unheard of for me in those years. I was overly critical of my partner's attempts to reassure me that the cleaning and cooking could wait, could be done less perfectly, that I could be less hard on myself.

"You don't understand," I said. "These things need to be maintained, they need to be kept up or they have to be replaced." I pointed to the furnace or the siding on the house or the bath drain. It didn't matter what it was; I was crazy with worry.

"You can leave it," my partner would say. "It's okay."

"No, it isn't okay! Don't you get it? It is not okay!" I can't count the number of times I'd snapped at my partner and she called me on it, which merely reinforced my self-justification and determination to see myself as a victim. I was abusive and nasty, but I couldn't see it. Time and time again, I would be convinced she was somehow thwarting me, and I'd speak to her in ways that made her see she lived with a crazy person who spoke to her harshly. I wondered how much longer my family would put up with me. I coped by being home less and less, pouring myself into my intelligence job. My office drawers overflowed with boxes of green tea and dark chocolate. I drank tea all day to soothe myself and ate chocolate and avocados brought from home so that I wouldn't have to leave my office for lunch. Hardly a balanced diet, but the routine seemed to comfort me on some level.

In December 2006, my work partner, Malcolm, and I spent a week on a course at the RCMP Pacific Region Training Center. Working among RCMP officers reminded me of my time working on Pickton, and my symptoms intensified. We had little homework on our course, and each evening after a workout and some dinner, Malcolm and I found ourselves in the lounge drinking beer and watching hockey on a big screen. Each night, I pressed him to drink more with me. Malcolm was six feet four and weighed two hundred pounds. I weigh one hundred and thirty. On our third night there, we finished our fourth beer, and he told me he'd had enough.

"C'mon," I said, "one more. It's not like you're driving anywhere." I held my credit card out to him enticingly. "I'll buy."

"Okay, but that's it for me. I am done." He laughed, hands held up in a gesture of surrender. I made my way to the bar to buy our fifth round. I returned with the beers, splashing them on the table.

"Oops, sorry." I laughed.

"I had no idea you were such a party animal," he said.

"Yeah, I really probably shouldn't drink at all." We finished our beers and called it a night when he refused to let me buy us another.

Back in my room, I called my partner on the phone for our nightly chat and to say goodnight.

"I don't think drinking's good for me," I told her. "For a bit, I feel so great, then I get totally depressed. I feel like crap and tomorrow's going to suck." What I didn't tell her was I felt despondent, worthless, and hopeless, and if Malcolm had joined me, I would have had five more.

"Well, just don't drink so much next time," she told me, ever the cheerful, sensible one. She always spoke to me with patience and reason.

"No, I think I have an actual problem. I've never been able to stop. I'm done with drinking."

"Okay, whatever you think, love." And with that, I never drank again. I vowed to face my problems head on, without self-medicating.

WHEN THE PICKTON trial finally ended in December 2007, after nearly two years, I felt some relief that maybe this awful chapter in my career was ending. I didn't feel better about the organization or about policing, but I did about my place and myself as a police officer. I *knew* I was a good cop. I knew people like me were needed more than ever. I began to hope I could climb back out of the hole I'd be in for almost ten years. It wasn't a recovery, but I felt I could throw myself back into policing in a meaningful way and perhaps use my bad experiences for good. I thought this would heal my PTSD, and I hoped the symptoms I'd been coping with would magically lessen.

In 2009, I was given the opportunity to read Deputy Chief Constable Doug LePard's report on the role of the Vancouver Police in the missing women investigation when it went to print. This was a year before the report's 2010 release. Each copy was held under tight guard, and I could only view one in

Doug's office, under the watch of Superintendent Andy Hobbs because Doug was out of town. I devoted an entire workday to the four-hundred-page document, and it took me a little over four hours to read it. When Andy poked his head in the door to see how I was making out, I had just finished it.

I realized he was not there to ensure that I wouldn't run away with the copy but rather to safeguard me from whatever emotional reaction they feared I might have. I'm not sure what they expected, but I felt mainly vindication at Doug's treatment of me and the hard work and passion I'd devoted to the file for more than two years. I found his analysis and conclusions accurate and fair, and I was pleased to see the VPD fall on its sword in admitting the organization's shortcomings. There were a few small points here and there where I held differing views, but I felt on the whole the report echoed my experience and most of my sense of what went wrong on our end. Having the story on paper—much of it *my story*—filled me with relief and comforted me.

When I finished reading, I sat alone in Doug's office, overcome with equal parts grief and relief. By then, I'd relied heavily on my various coping mechanisms—all based on strict routines—and I avoided everyone aside from my immediate coworkers and functioned at a high level of anxiety that allowed me to keep myself wound tight and pushing forward. Every time I read about this investigation, I was struck anew by how those long depressing days in that windowless Project Amelia room held me in their grip, continually ripping the scar wide open again, pressing my coping mechanisms into service. I fought back tears of relief that I'd been spared any undue criticism. I had been sensitive to any possible criticism for years. *It wasn't my fault, but I share blame with everyone who touched this disastrous investigation.*

I stared at an entry discussing the photo identification Fisk and Myers hadn't shared with the team: "April 5 and

12, 2000—Myers and Fisk showed several suspect photos—
including Pickton's—to several sex trade workers and their
notes indicate three different sex trade workers selected Pickton's photo. Myers and Fisk did not report on this information
to Shenher or anyone else in the MWRT."

My anger was as raw as the first time I'd discovered this,
eight years earlier.

"How're you doing?" Andy asked, sitting down beside me at
the table where I'd been reading.

"Good," I lied. "I'm good."

ON SEPTEMBER 27, 2010, the Missing Women Commission of
Inquiry was formally announced, and the year that followed
proved challenging. Even after the many years of investigation,
the painstaking search of the farm, the intermittent discovery
of new victim DNA over months and months, and the long
Pickton trial and appeal process—it still wasn't over. *When
would it ever truly be over?*

I hoped I could survive the inquiry and triumph over
this nightmare, but my doubts remained. In 2010, I'd eagerly
awaited the release of Doug LePard's report—released to coin-
cide with the government's expected announcement of an
inquiry—hoping that finally people would begin to see what a
serious tragedy this investigation had been and to understand
why a public inquiry was so sorely needed. As it was, the report
was leaked mere weeks before the announcement of the Missing Women Commission of Inquiry, but it didn't matter. At
least it was out, and the inquiry would finally take place.

My anxiety level reached new heights as I anticipated the
announcement of the inquiry, and when I learned that former
B.C. attorney general Wally Oppal would be the commissioner,
I was overwhelmed by mixed feelings. That evening, I sat at
my computer and composed a letter to Fazil Milhar, editorial
page editor of the *Vancouver Sun*. I detailed my concerns about

Mr. Oppal as commissioner, given his past roles as the provincial attorney general who once announced there would be no public inquiry into the missing women and as previous head of the B.C. Criminal Justice Branch when the 1997 charges against Pickton in the Anderson matter were stayed. I explained that I felt no animosity toward Mr. Oppal; on the contrary, I knew him a little from playing basketball at the police station and liked him personally and professionally. I merely felt he was the wrong choice, encumbered by too many conflicting roles in this case over the years.

I copied the email containing the letter to Deputy Chief Constable LePard and Paul Patterson of the VPD Public Affairs Section, because I didn't want them completely blindsided in the morning press briefing. I hit Send and then went straight to bed. I fell straight to sleep for the first time in years.

My partner roused me from a rare deep sleep, holding the telephone out to me. My mind was blissfully blank for several seconds. Then I remembered.

"It's Doug LePard," she whispered. I took the phone.

"Hello?"

"Hi, Lori, it's Doug LePard." I cringed as I noted the gentle tone of his voice, as though he were talking an unstable person off a ledge. "I got your email."

"Uh-huh," I answered. "I thought you might be calling. I'm sorry."

"It's okay. Listen, I can understand why you feel the way you do and why you wrote it, but would there be any way for you to ask them to pull it?" He paused. "Have they said it's going in?"

"I dunno. No one has answered, but I haven't checked my email since I wrote it." I began to feel pinpricks of regret.

"Okay. I'm not *ordering* you to pull it, but if there was any way you could, I would appreciate it. The chief and I are meeting with people from the provincial government about this tomorrow, and this would put us in a difficult position and set a bad tone going forward." His patience, kindness, and lack of insistence made me feel even worse. *Was I just paranoid? Were my feelings and this letter unwarranted? Would everything ever really be fine? Was I losing it?*

"I can try. I'll ask them to pull it," I said, suddenly understanding how little I wanted to bring this attention to myself both within the VPD and across the province. *What was happening to me?*

"Tell them you're under a doctor's care and you've reconsidered." He hesitated. "That's true, isn't it?" This suggestion opened up a whole new field of embarrassment and shame. My attendance at therapy was sporadic at best, though I needed it badly.

"Yeah, unfortunately." I said, laughing for the first time in the conversation. He joined me. "Doug, I'm really sorry to cause you grief. This thing is really getting to me."

"I know. Hang in there. You will get your chance to speak, and it'll mean so much more in the inquiry than in the newspaper. You want your opinions to count, trust me. Just hang in there and it'll happen."

"Okay. I know you're right. At times I just lose it."

"I know. Let me know how you make out with Fazil, okay?"

"Okay. Thanks, and I am really sorry for causing you so much grief."

I managed to get the *Sun* to pull the piece, but not before the editorial staff had read my little manifesto. I worried whether I could hold it together and keep my mouth shut throughout the inquiry. I told the story to my friend Lindsay Kines, now a reporter for the *Victoria Times Colonist*, who made me promise to duct-tape oven mitts to my hands whenever I was at the computer and wanted to send something like that again. Or if I was determined to hit Send, he suggested I address the email to him and he promised to put it straight into his trash. I felt better knowing that others were able to laugh my behavior off, but it continued to worry me because I knew it was serious.

I decided then to compete again for promotion to sergeant. I hoped my career could survive.

As I began the preparation for the inquiry in the summer of 2011, my old doubts about whether I could become part of the policing world again returned, but I pushed them aside, determined that I would find a way to feel better as time went on. My lengthy interview with Peel Regional Police Deputy Chief Constable Jennifer Evans—engaged by the Missing Women Commission of Inquiry to chronicle and prepare an independent report on the entire police investigation—reopened many of my old wounds and brought me back to those long days I wanted so much to forget. I'd set my manuscript aside over all those years; it was simply too upsetting for me to revisit, so this return to the investigation hit me hard.

I appreciated Evans's sensitivity and obvious investigative knowledge, and she clearly had worked extremely hard to grasp the nuances of this very complex file in short order. Retelling my story brought me to tears, and I hated myself for my weakness in front of a successful police officer who had risen through the ranks and knew the game.

I retook the sergeant promotional assessment a few months later and scored a very high mark. I remained committed to forging on with plans for my promotion, despite my growing doubts that I could handle it emotionally. I believed the way to triumph was to remain in the policing world and make a difference.

In September 2011, I returned to the Downtown Eastside to fulfill a uniformed patrol requirement for the promotional competition. Returning to the heart of skid row was the oddest sort of homecoming. Nearly nineteen years to the day since I'd last been there, in that place, in my uniform—now wearing the current VPD black uniform and not my old pale-blue one from a bygone era—I stood among the people, doing this bizarrely janitorial work cleaning up after the city's most needy people. As with most homecomings, much had changed, but so much had also stayed the same. Hurting, hungry, toothless, drunken, disheveled, disabled, discarded, dispossessed human beings staggered from bar to bar along East Hastings Street, which was littered with garbage and items stolen from Vancouver's more fortunate inhabitants. I suspect that I was not alone in imagining that I would never end up back down here after so much time. Yet here I was again, back where it all began.

When I said I never imagined being back there, I wasn't being overly dramatic. The doctor who performs the health assessments of police officers every five years had advised the VPD Human Resources Section that moving me from my current intelligence job in Threat Assessment—a position I'd held since 2005—was not in my best interests or the VPD's. I was in no emotional shape to take on a more visible role in the VPD. I drifted in and out of therapy but had no real idea how to get better and received no guidance from anyone in the VPD. All I knew was that I had to try to make this horrible experience count for something, and I believed promotion was the way to do that.

My short time back in uniform on the Downtown East-side proved unsettling. Accompanied by Toby Hinton, a very capable sergeant, I moved from call to call supervising the Beat Enforcement Team officers, ensuring that procedures were followed and that the team members had sufficient backup and support to do their jobs. I was stunned by my inability to focus. In my past assignments as a patrol officer, I was highly competent and my senses were attuned to my surroundings and the potential danger of each situation. I noticed everything and easily remembered license plate numbers, names, dates of birth, and wanted persons.

Now I felt numb and struggled to make sense of events happening around us. We attended several violent scenes: bar fights, people savagely slashed by broken beer bottles or knives, noses and skulls crushed by lengths of rebar, domestic violence cases in which women and men nursed a range of wounds as well as shattered expectations and dreams. The smell of blood had never bothered me in the past, but now it hung thick and metallic in the air all around me, reminding me of all matters Pickton. I found entering the meat sections of large grocery stores more and more disturbing and began avoiding them.

I worried about everything all the time. I felt less "safe" as a police officer on the street—too empathetic to both criminals and victims, too aware of the gray area in between the necessary black and white that serves police so well in helping them assign blame and meaning when doing their work. My boundaries—in place to keep me safe to some extent—were gone. I stood out there hugging people, kissing babies, and high-fiving old acquaintances. I hoped I could survive these three weeks in uniform and do what I needed to in order to get promoted and go to a plainclothes supervisory job.

On my last day shift, I saw large blotches on the computer screen in front of me. I sat there for several minutes, thinking that I'd stared too long at a fluorescent light and that the spots would fade, but they didn't. Within fifteen minutes, Toby—fearing a repeat of a brain tumor that had killed a colleague of ours a few years back—rushed me to St. Paul's Hospital, where doctors thoroughly examined me, suspecting a detached retina. The diagnosis was an aural migraine, probably brought on by stress and irregular sleep patterns. We'd worked four night shifts before turning around to day shift, and I hadn't been up all night in years. I put the episode aside, hoping I could ride it out and succeed in my bid for promotion.

23

The Missing Women
Commission of Inquiry

• • •

"Do not wait for the last judgment. It comes every day."
ALBERT CAMUS, THE FALL

I FEEL SO ALONE on my first day of testimony, January 30, 2012. The preparation throughout the weeks leading up to it winds me tighter and tighter as I relive so much of the work I'd done on the file with the commission, Vancouver Police Union (VPU), and City of Vancouver counsel, reviewing documents and memos I'd written begging my supervisors for more resources. Reliving the ineffectual nature of our work, the helplessness in imploring the RCMP to investigate the Ellingsen tip—all of this is like going back to a crime scene for me. The lawyers I work with treat me so well, and I feel grateful for their professionalism and interest.

In the first weeks of the inquiry, witnesses such as VPD Deputy Chief Constable Doug LePard, Peel Regional Police Deputy Chief Constable Jennifer Evans, various experts from the criminology and sociology worlds, and family members of the victims testify for days on end, time a seemingly endless commodity. I become increasingly anxious, fearing I will be on the stand for weeks if people with far less to answer for are taking several days to testify.

I follow the testimony from the commission's start in October 2011, and even listening to that evidence proves difficult for me emotionally. As I listen one day, lawyers for the Vancouver police begin talking about Cara Ellis, a woman who'd gone missing in 1997. Her sister-in-law, Lori-Ann Ellis, first reported Cara missing to the Vancouver police in 1998, when the Calgary woman's own search of the Downtown Eastside turned up nothing. Cara's DNA was found on the Pickton farm in 2004, her blood on a prayer card featuring the words of the 23rd Psalm, "The Lord is my shepherd; I shall not want," located in Pickton's slaughterhouse.

I've known about Cara Ellis as a victim of Pickton but not the timeline of her disappearance; I've always assumed she had gone missing after my time working in Project Amelia, because I'd never heard of her until the last few years. Her file was somehow misplaced, abandoned in a drawer in the Missing Persons office, and Cara's information hadn't been entered or retained in a manner that would have enabled her case to be investigated further. Physically sick at the thought that I missed this entire case, I contact Sean Hern, a lawyer representing the City of Vancouver, during a break in the testimony I have been watching from my office.

"Sean, tell me I didn't have anything to do with Cara Ellis," I blurt. I'd seen Lori-Ann in the press and read about Cara for years since Pickton's arrest, but I'd never had any dealings with the file. Suddenly, I find myself questioning my memory and sanity. Sean, a quiet sea of calm in a noisy, stormy legal world, has become used to my excitability throughout the Missing Women Commission of Inquiry.

"No, her file was lost in a drawer somewhere in the Missing Persons office. You never would have seen it," he reassures me, his voice filled with regret. "It's a mess, but you had nothing to do with it."

"Thank God," I say. "I mean, I wish I'd seen it, but I knew I hadn't. Oh my God, this is awful." Sean agrees.

The days of my preparation are long, and the constant immersion in those events of 1998 to 2002 shakes me deeply, as though I am experiencing all that grief and loss freshly a second time. In small part, I feel excited and energized that finally, after more than twelve years, this inquiry is happening. I feel hopeful that when this is done, I can move on and take all I've learned and use it for good. Working with the commission lawyers and my own counsel encourages me. It is refreshing to be among people who agree that the events of 1999 regarding Pickton and Ellingsen are murky at best and need to be better known and understood.

Each day before my testimony at the inquiry, I walk to a 6:00 AM yoga class to calm myself and physically prepare for long days of sitting. Strict personal routines have been my friend and lifeline as well as my prison since 2002, and this week of testimony further intensifies my need for a regular, predictable daily regimen. I've been practicing yoga since 2005, when I sought it out in desperation, unable to cope with my PTSD. Historically, I've dealt with stress through running and other exercise, but I've reached a point where I ache all the time and my old strategies aren't working. Now, I cling to my yoga like a life preserver.

My class ends at 7:30 AM, after which I walk down the street, drop into a juice bar, and buy a double shot of wheatgrass with an OJ chaser. I am terrified of illness and worried that touching the handholds on the Canada Line trains might cause me to contract the flu or something worse, and I hope that wheatgrass will boost my immunity. I have become a compulsive hand washer and obsessively use hand sanitizer. Wheatgrass is the strongest thing that passes my lips these days.

The juice bar guy recognizes me from the news, and I feel grateful to have him to chat with over these four days. I continue to the grocery store for a couple of bananas and an energy bar, but I stop going there when I see with shock my own image staring out at me from the cover of the *National Post* in the check-out line. When I feel ready to enter the VPD building—an act I've found more and more difficult to perform since 2002—I shower and dress for court.

I brought my court clothes for the week down early on the preceding Saturday morning, hoping not to run into anyone. Since 2002, I've had a great deal of difficulty being in and around the VPD offices and officers, and straying from my normal worksite and routine causes me a lot of anxiety. My isolation is self-imposed, and I push people away and distance myself more and more from the police world over time. I mistrust the police in general and the entire institution's ability to protect or save anyone in need. Berating myself for having these limitations makes me feel even worse. *Suck it up. Go into the office, for God's sake. It's just a workplace. It isn't the damn farm. It isn't your old project room.*

This first morning, I step onto the elevator and run into an inspector I know who says, "So, all ready for your big day?" I nod. There are a couple of other policemen in the elevator I have never met, and one speaks up.

"Why? What's she doing?" asks the young policeman.

"She's testifying at the missing women inquiry," the inspector answers.

"Oh, jeez, is that thing still dragging on? What more do those people want?" the young cop says, rolling his eyes. I just raise my eyebrows at the inspector and step out of the elevator, thankful we are at the bottom. *Welcome to my world.*

"Good luck," the inspector calls. "Is anyone driving you?"

"Nope." I say, walking out of the building toward the Canada Line station.

When I arrive at the federal court building, I ride the elevator to the eighth floor, grateful to be the only person inside. As the doors open, I scan left and right—another habit I've developed since 2002. Never do I enter a room or location without checking left and right. I have no idea why.

The hallway is empty, except for the commissionaire sitting at the entry desk. I ask her where the hearing room is, and she directs me down the hall and to the right. *Maybe this won't be so bad,* I think as I near the end of the hallway. As I turn right, digital cameras whirr and click, and I have no idea where to look or walk. Determined to not appear rattled, I walk up to the hearing room doors and, discovering they are locked, turn around and enter a small meeting room that I will later learn is specifically for witnesses like me when we aren't in court.

I arrive early, as instructed by my lawyers, so I leave the door slightly ajar and stand in the room waiting. I perform a self-check, asking myself, *Am I okay? Do I feel anything? Do I feel weird? Strange? Anxious?* I felt nothing but numbness. I expect to be hyper-aroused for these proceedings, heart pounding through my chest, as often happens now whenever I felt anxious, but I feel pretty good. I hope this is a positive sign. Sean Hern joins me, and his calm, quiet, assured demeanor comforts me, though I can't recall much of what we say or do. The hard work and preparation are done. My Vancouver Police Union lawyer, David Crossin, joins us. I've lobbied hard to have him represent me separately from Fisk and Myers, because I know our interests are in direct opposition. Fortunately, the VPU agrees, and Dave acts for Geramy Field and me, whereas Kevin Woodall's office represents Fisk and Myers.

We enter the hearing room, and Sean instructs me to sit in the gallery until called. He sits with me, and I look past him and see Lori-Ann Ellis, Lillianne Beaudoin, George Lane, and Michele Pineault seated on the other side of the gallery. I know George and Michele but have only seen Lori-Ann and Lillianne in the media, and I want to greet them all. I lean over to Sean.

"Can I go talk to the families? Is that allowed?"

"Of course," he says. I rise and make my way over to them, a little apprehensive, not knowing whether they will welcome me. I greet Michele first.

"Hi, Michele. How're you doing?" I extend my hand, and she takes it. We speak for a couple of minutes. I turn to George and shake his hand. They greet me with warmth, and I feel immediately at ease. I extend my condolences for their daughter Stephanie's death, allegedly at the hands of Pickton. I hadn't been able to reach them the night of the arrest. Like so many people touched by this case, they have struggled over the years with how to manage such an awful tragedy. Michele and I run into each other later that morning in the washroom, and we talk more about our journeys. We share a lot in those few minutes, and I have so much respect for Michele and how she has survived so much heartache and continues to advocate for missing and murdered women.

"I only know you two from the news," I say as I shake Lillianne's and Lori-Ann's hands. "It's really good to meet you both. I am so sorry." They smile, and I like them both instantly.

The entire day is a blur. Commission counsel Karey Brooks leads me through my evidence in chief, which consists of my explanation of my actions working on the file. She listens to my evidence and directs me to documents I want entered into the record. At lunch, I ride the elevator down with Sean, and we step out onto the street together, walking and talking as he approaches his office and I near the Pacific Centre mall entrance. He touches my elbow, steering me away from something, and I turn to see a huge television camera inches from my face as we stand on the corner. I feel completely unnerved, not because it is there, but because I had no idea the cameraman was following us. We part, and I walk into the mall to grab some lunch.

Television screens hang from the ceiling of the food court, and it shakes me further to see Missing Women Commission of Inquiry footage of myself on each of them as the noon news plays. I realize people are staring at me, so I turn and leave without food, too self-conscious to stay and eat. I walk out onto Hornby Street and grab a Subway sandwich, which I eat alone back in the witness room.

I note with some surprise that the intense anxiety in the middle of my chest is absent and has been since I began preparing for my testimony. In its place is hardness, a numbed-out solid mass I envision as the clay from my junior high school art class, gray and dense. I realize then that I have felt no nervousness, no butterflies in these long days leading up to my appearance at the inquiry. Although I feel surprisingly *normal* and very much not how I had felt for the ten years since the search, I don't feel particularly good. I don't *feel* anything. I *hate this.*

Karey continues leading me through my evidence the rest of that afternoon and Tuesday morning. During our preparation the week before, she asks me if I'd be comfortable telling the commission how the investigation has affected me, personally and professionally. I feel no hesitation in answering yes, but immediately after she asks me in our preparation session, I feel fear and uncertainty. *Can I keep my emotions in check?* What will it mean to my testimony, my credibility, if I break down and expose myself for the raw mess of grief that is my mind these past ten years? *Does any of it matter? Is my suffering even relevant? You're the cop, not the victim here. Keep your shit to yourself.* Still, I cannot discount the impact the case has had on me, and I want the commission to know. I want the RCMP to know what their inaction has done to me. I want the VPD to know what their lack of investigative support has left me with.

Karey asks me the question just before the lunch break.

"So, I understand that this investigation has affected you in both a personal and professional way. So, if you could tell us about that."

I start hesitantly. "Well, before I begin, I want to, I just want to be clear that whatever impact this has had on me I think is very minor compared, in comparison to what the families and friends of the missing and murdered women have gone through, and I'm very cognizant of that."

What the transcript doesn't show is how I break down in gulping, wracking sobs as I croak out the rest of what I have to say, all broadcast via the Canadian Broadcast Corporation live feed of the proceedings. I divide my comments into how I was coping at work before the search of the Pickton farm and after.

I mention how VPD Chief Constable Jamie Graham's assignment (I mistakenly say Chief Chambers on the stand) of Doug LePard to chronicle the VPD side of the investigation is the first—and only—acknowledgment of the seriousness of the file I ever saw from the VPD. I speak haltingly and far less articulately than I would like to, but I am desperately trying to hold myself together to speak the words I need to say.

I conclude by saying, "I don't want anyone to go through what these families have gone through, you know, or what I have gone through professionally. So, that's really all I have to say, and I thank you all for your indulgence. Thank you, Mr. Commissioner." I sit there, head hanging, wiping at my tears with the tissue I am thankful someone has passed me at some point.

Commissioner Oppal responds. "I want to thank you, Detective Shenher, for sharing those thoughts with us. You have given us an indication of how much of an impact, on a personal level, this tragedy, this horrific tragedy, has had on you, and I think it helps us understand what happened. And your comments—I am sure by everybody in the room—are very much appreciated. I want to thank you for doing that." He pauses and then reminds us we are to return for 1:30 PM to resume my testimony.

I don't want to move. I don't want to stay there, but I can't imagine going anywhere for lunch, not that I have any appetite. As I sit, head down, in the witness box working hard to collect myself, a line silently forms in front of me. Wrapped up in my own misery and shame for breaking down when I'd hoped I wouldn't, I don't see it.

When I finally look up, there they are. Karey is first to approach and hug me. After her comes an Indigenous woman I first met that day named Marie, then family members Lori-Ann Ellis, Lillianne Beaudoin, Michele Pineault, and a couple of people whose names I don't even know—friends and strangers who feel compelled to share comfort with me, even when I am complicit in their own incomprehensibly painful loss.

Two court-appointed social workers sit with me in the witness room over lunch, and Karey generously brings me a sandwich. Normally, I would chat with the social workers—they are so kind—but I have little to say. I feel laid bare, exhausted, and unable to even feel embarrassed at everyone's obvious reluctance to leave me alone, but the social workers are lovely and don't feel the need to fill the room with chatter. I am completely spent. I can barely think about the challenge that still lies ahead of me that afternoon: cross-examination by less friendly counsel than the commission lawyers. I don't care; I feel the worst is already behind me.

The week continues with each lawyer taking turns cross-examining me on my evidence. I find the majority of the lawyers respectful and professional; indeed, I have pleasant conversations with many of them during the breaks when it is appropriate, careful not to discuss any details of my evidence.

I lose my patience and objectivity responding to the questioning by Darrell Roberts, an experienced lawyer representing Marion Bryce, the mother of alleged Pickton victim Patricia Johnson, touting his theory that the murdered women were victims of "kidnapping by fraud." His position is that we should have been pursuing a kidnapper in our investigation. He argues that this would have somehow changed the manner in which we approached the investigation and given us grounds for a warrant to search Pickton's farm far sooner.

Although I admire his creativity, I fail to understand how you could kidnap someone who willingly entered your vehicle. His "Kidnapping by Fraud" theory extends to me insofar as he feels I had grounds to apply for a warrant to search Pickton's property as far back as 1998, when Bill Hiscox first came to me with his thirdhand information about women's clothing and purses seen in Pickton's trailer.

Roberts applies this theory to his questioning of every police witness in the inquiry, bent on proving we somehow ignored the possibility that the women were kidnapped. Obviously, if Pickton's intent was to murder the women at some point in the interaction, that interaction was fraudulent in that it was not the simple sex-for-money transaction he led the victims to believe, but how would that change how we investigated him? How could you prove there was fraud in the transaction without the statements of the victims? I simply cannot understand how we could be expected to get inside Pickton's head to know his intentions.

Roberts seems to not understand how police officers speak or work, continually asking me what criminal charge I was pursuing at any given time in the investigation. It is far more intuitive work than that; I *knew* there was a serious crime committed, probably murder. I expected to uncover the physical or witness evidence to prove it. I can grasp his reasoning in some ways, but it just doesn't come from a place of reality, in my view. He asks me several questions about my knowledge of kidnapping, and my answers are frustratingly inadequate, and I know it. Of course, I know what the crime of kidnapping is, but in trying to keep my annoyance in check and my answers brief, I realize I am not fully explaining myself or my experience with kidnapping, and that is a mistake. It is not my finest hour.

My anger rises to the surface during my cross-examination by Kevin Woodall's second chair, Claire Hatcher, who is acting for vpd constables Fisk and Myers. She attempts to defend them as hardworking and earnest investigators, unfairly ostracized from Project Amelia and single-minded in their desire to catch a killer. Each time she tries to steer me toward agreeing that they had been merely misunderstood and their efforts had been laudable, I remind her and the commission of the manner in which they withheld vital information from me and the rest of Project Amelia by failing to report that women on the Downtown Eastside had picked Pickton's photo from their "lineup."

Hatcher attempts to have me say that I documented no tangible evidence that Fisk and Myers kept secrets from Project Amelia. I feel this is a critical issue for the investigation, and I refuse to be caught in her web. It is difficult for me, however. I fear testifying against colleagues, no matter how badly I feel they might have performed. Every evening for months after giving this testimony, I look over my shoulder in the darkness as I walk my dog around my neighborhood for fear—albeit irrational and unsubstantiated—that one of them will confront me. To be clear, neither of them ever threatens me, nor do I believe them to be bad people, but I know a small percentage of VPD members condemn me for speaking out against Fisk and Myers.

"You haven't ever documented a secret that you've discovered they've kept from you?" Hatcher asks.

"Yes. The fact that they didn't acknowledge to me that three women, three sex trade workers, had identified Pickton from the photographs that they showed around the Downtown Eastside," I reply.

"Regardless of how you feel that came to be or regardless of your beliefs about that, there's no evidence that they deliberately kept that from you?"

"All I can tell you is I never saw any notes and they never had any conversation with me coming back to the office saying, 'Hey, guess what, we think Pickton is in the Downtown Eastside. We found three sex trade workers that know him.' That was never communicated to me. That's my evidence."

"That's clear. But as far as, aside from that issue, you haven't been able to find in all your interviews with LePard and Evans, you haven't identified any tangible example of a secret that they kept from the team?"

"I think I've testified to what I believe is the secret they kept from the team."

I look at her hard, thinking, *How many more times do you want me to say it? Is prompting me to repeat this really helping your clients? "Aside from that issue"? That issue is* THE *issue.* No matter how hard Fisk and Myers might have worked or how misunderstood they might have been, I feel they committed an egregious error by keeping this information from the team. I understand that she doesn't have much to work with, but I just will not agree to something that isn't the truth.

Commissioner Oppal would determine the following after hearing all testimony and document it in his report: "In April, several women in the DTES (Downtown Eastside) identify Pickton from a group of photographs shown to them by Det. Cst. Fisk and Det. Cst. Myers. Other members of the MWRT (Project Amelia) are not advised of this information. Shortly after, the two constables go to Lethbridge to arrest the suspect they had been investigating."

ON FEBRUARY 2, 2012, a familiar bittersweet sensation comes over me at the completion of my first week of testimony. My friend Tim Timberg, himself a lawyer, waits for me in the gallery as Commissioner Oppal tells me I am free to go. Tim sweeps me up in a big hug, and, as usual, I choke up. He returns with me to the witness room and we close the door and talk for a long while. Once he leaves, I begin collecting my various binders and notes. As I do, there is a knock at the door. I open it, and there stands Commissioner Oppal, no jacket, shirtsleeves rolled up.

"Can I come in?"

"Of course." I motion him in and close the door behind him. "How are you doing?"

"Okay." He smiles. "I'm doing okay. How are you?"

"Pretty glad this week is over," I say. We both laugh.

"I wanted to thank you again for your testimony." He looks at me fixedly. "You brought a high level of integrity to your testimony and your contributions have been very important to this inquiry." I see his eyes tear up. "I know you've had a really tough time of it all these years."

I swallow hard. "Thanks, Wally. You're going to get me crying again."

I never seem to know when I might break into tears. He gives me a hug, and I remember that despite all my criticisms of the Missing Women Commission of Inquiry and the choice of him as commissioner, I've always felt that he cared about the women. I feel he is a good person, trying to do his best, like all of us. He steps out and leaves me alone.

So many times over these nearly fourteen years I have hoped the case might finally be over, but I fear and sense another step remains for me. The topic of my manuscript arises several times in my first week of testimony, and Dave Crossin advises me to prepare so that I can return to testify to its contents. Once again, I am done *but not finished*. From 1998 until mid-2012, this case continues to hold me in its grasp.

I sleep almost the entire next day, my younger son's ninth birthday. Never have I felt such complete and total exhaustion, not even after running marathons and triathlons. I want to take the following week off and recharge, but I don't want to hide from my workplace. In some way, I feel if I don't go back on Monday, I will never go back. I can't let this case and this career beat me. I reason I can take some time off in the next few weeks, once I have shown my face around the office enough for everyone to know that testifying against colleagues and sharing my innermost emotions about the last fourteen years is not going to force me into a closet. I've been hiding for so long, and I've had enough. I return to work February 6.

But, still, I do hide. I hole up in my secure office for a few hours that first Monday back, catching up on email and taking care of what I can manage. I fight to drag myself out of bed at 5:00 AM, still exhausted. I leave later in the morning, driving my work van around the city aimlessly, BlackBerry by my side in case the office needs me. I hope if I push myself through the extreme dread and anxiety I feel at work, it will make things easier for me in time. I receive a text from my sister, Jocelyn, in Calgary and pull over to read it. She asks whether I am free for a phone call. I text back, "Who died? I'm just out driving around." She replies, "Melanie*."

I call Jocelyn, who has been closer to Melanie throughout the years than I have, though Melanie had been my very first friend. Our years growing up together flash through my mind.

She lived two doors down, and we had been in the same kindergarten class. After that, she attended French immersion while I went to Catholic school, so summers were the only time we could do much together. One day, her head popped up from behind our back fence, which was slightly unusual because we rarely used the alley to get around.

"Wanna see some clowns?" she asked, breathless, eyes alight with excitement.

"Not really," I said, displeasure etched across my face. I hated clowns and was one of the few kids in elementary school who gave away their free Shrine Circus tickets every year. "Where are they?"

"Down there." She pointed down the alley away from the more familiar homes and people we knew. "That house on the bend," she clarified.

My frown deepened. I suspected which house she meant and felt immediately sceptical. "The Parkers*?" I asked.

She nodded. "Let's go. It'll be neat." Her eyes pleaded with me. "They invited me."

"I dunno." I paused, worried that she would go alone but not wanting to go with her.

"I'm going either way," she announced with a touch of false bravado, as though sensing my indecision. "I love clowns!"

"You know I hate them," I reminded her. "Didja ask your mom?"

"Of course not. She'd say no," she said.

"Maybe she'd be right to."

"Aw, come on. Don't be such a goody-goody. How bad could it be?" Ironically, I would turn out to be the rebellious teen and Melanie the model student and daughter, but when we were preteens, she was the wild one.

I shook my head at her in silent defeat and slunk toward the back gate into the alley after a quick glance toward our kitchen window; my mom wasn't standing over the sink, and I hurriedly left the yard.

The Parkers' two daughters were mean. The younger one, Sally*, played on my hockey team, and I steered clear of her. She and the other mean girl on the team were always teasing the weaker players and playing pranks that revolved around leaving various disgusting items in their gear while they were changing. They'd never bothered me, but they were bullies. Sally's older sister, Mia*, was cut from the same cloth and ran with a tough bunch in the neighborhood. I couldn't remember ever seeing either of them with a parent.

We reached the small garage at the rear of the Parker property. The big back door was shut. I turned to Melanie, hoping she'd be satisfied.

"See? It's a hoax. They aren't even here." I turned to walk back up the lane.

Melanie would not give up so easily. "Don't be silly," she said. "They're probably in there." Powered by the heady fuel of clown-love, she marched up alongside the garage toward the small door, which was also closed. I reluctantly followed her, hoping the closed door would satisfy her no one was offering clown entertainment.

I jumped a little when Mia opened the small door and stepped out, holding the handle close to her so that we couldn't see inside. "Glad you came, kids," she said with a sickly sweet, superior air I found annoying given she was only two years older than us. Both she and Sally always pretended not to know me and forgot my name, and today was no different. "Come inside." Before I could say anything to Melanie, she stepped in with enthusiasm and I resignedly followed her, cursing under my breath.

The garage was dark. The windows were blacked out with blankets or towels, and for a few seconds, I couldn't see at all. As my eyes adjusted, I made out a large clown. It made no attempt to act like a clown, and its painted-on mouth looked sinister and angry, like a psychotic Ronald McDonald. I felt Melanie press against my side, and I knew she was now as scared as I was. I searched for the door and saw Sally and Mia standing in front of it, arms folded like bouncers. As I was trying to determine how many other kids were in there, the clown began lunging at all of us, swinging something and entreating the kids to run in a circle.

"Run! Run! I AM the dark clown and you WILL do as I say!" I felt something strike me hard across the legs like a whip. I grabbed Melanie's hand and began to run to keep the maniacal clown at bay. I realized he was swinging a hard rubber skipping rope, the pastel type with those dense rubber ends. As I tugged Melanie around in a serpentine direction to avoid another whipping, I heard screams as the rope struck the others. I couldn't tell how many there were. I just knew I didn't want to be hit with that hard rubber again.

Everything in my brain screamed *Escape!* I dragged Melanie, aiming us in the general direction of the door. Hurling myself at them, I body checked the startled Sally and Mia aside with a power I didn't know my skinny seventy-pound frame possessed. I grabbed the doorknob, turned, and pushed hard. We tumbled out and ran without looking back.

We sprinted about sixty yards, slowing down only when we reached my back fence. As we bent over, hands on knees, panting, it seemed hard to imagine we had only been here a few short minutes earlier. The lane was empty. They obviously hadn't chased us. When I caught my breath, I glanced down at Melanie.

"Still like clowns?" I asked.

She smiled sheepishly. "I still like *some* clowns," she allowed. "You?"

"I still hate them." She watched me to see whether I was angry. I smiled a little and bent to examine the large throbbing welt on my left calf.

"Oh, they *hurt* you." She peered closely at the raised red bruise. "Thanks for coming with me," she said quietly. "I don't know what would've happened, you know, if you weren't there."

"Are you gonna tell your mom?" I asked her. She shook her head hard.

"No way. She'd just worry. Are you?"

"Uh-uh. She'd just tell me how dumb it was to go there, especially without asking."

"Yeah."

Somehow, we'd managed to avoid being seriously hurt in our youth.

Jocelyn tells me how on the Saturday after I completed my first four days of testimony at the Missing Women Commission of Inquiry, Melanie took her own life at the age of forty-seven. She remained on life support until she died, just before Jocelyn calls me. That same exuberant girl who wanted to see clowns had been unable to cope with an emotional pain I'm ashamed to admit I have no idea she suffered from for much of her adult life. Her family and mine lived as neighbors and friends for forty-eight years, but Melanie and I drifted apart after junior high school.

She left behind an exceptionally close and loving family. Her inability to escape her pain presents yet another reminder of how fortunate I am. I wish she could've seen herself the way all of us who loved her saw her.

Her tragic death leaves me numb and hollow, as though I have absolutely nothing left to feel anymore. Suicide has played a large role in my adult life. Melanie is the fifth close friend I've lost since the early '90s, and I will lose yet another in the fall of 2013. Back in patrol, nothing bothered me more than the suicides I had investigated, and there were many. The sadness, the waste, the blood, the violence against the self, the utter senselessness of the act. The helplessness I feel seems unbearable.

I want so desperately to go back to Calgary for her funeral—I know her entire family and her elderly mother so well—but I just can't do it. I want to be a support to them, but I can't even support myself emotionally. Images of going there and breaking down the way I had on the witness stand during the inquiry are enough for me to know I just can't go. Instead, I write her mother and brothers long notes explaining how sorry I am that I can't be there for them, hoping they'll understand. It is all I am capable of, but still, I feel guilty and angry for everything this file has taken from me.

I saved her once, but that was from an angry clown. I am not a superhero; I am barely even a cop anymore. All I see around me are people dying, and I can't save any of them.

24

Defending My Writing

●　●　●

*"As Hemingway is reported to have said, 'It is easy
to write. Just sit in front of your typewriter and bleed.'"*
WILLIAM C. KNOTT, THE CRAFT OF FICTION

IT IS APRIL 4, 2012. I am once again sitting in the witness box
of the Missing Women Commission of Inquiry.

I have returned to the federal court to testify today and
tomorrow, answering lawyers' questions about the contents of
the first draft of a book manuscript I wrote after the search of
the Pickton farm began in 2002. A manifesto of bitterness and
regret, a venting of the spleen that never would have seen the
light of day had my fear, anxiety, and compulsion not spurred
me to try to publish it. *I feel sick.* How many times have I written these three words?

Sick that I have somehow become the focus of this
inquiry, which has morphed into a parody of itself. Sick that
this nightmare is never really over. Sick that my manuscript
joins the many other red herrings, which, like the investigation itself, have distracted attention from finding these women

and learning why we didn't find them sooner. Sick that my attempts to survive this tragedy have now taken valuable time and attention away from the real issues that few other than the lawyers for the families seem interested in exploring. Sick of the ass-covering, including my own. Sick that my candid comments about some of my coworkers now form the basis for cross-examination. Sick that my analysis of the events that led to this tragedy remain much the same today. Sick of reliving this entire tragedy over and over for years and years.

Shortly after the Pickton farm search began in February 2002, I sat down at my computer when I awoke from nightmares and couldn't get back to sleep and began maniacally hammering out the details of the investigation. The shock of the investigation shook me to the core. I felt no confidence in the police investigation that was taking place as I furiously typed out my part from the early days. I was seized by the terror that somehow Pickton would walk free and I would be made a scapegoat for this epic failure, and I feverishly tried to explain all I had done and all I had yet to learn and understand. I worried that the failure to pursue Pickton in 1999 would be covered up, and I refused to let that to happen.

In some ways, writing my story felt therapeutic, but it also reinforced how messed up the entire debacle was. Mercifully, my manuscript was not mentioned during Pickton's criminal trial, and I escaped having to testify there because my work as a detective on the missing persons cases was admitted into evidence in his trial.

However, the lawyers at the inquiry were aware of the manuscript and pressed Commissioner Oppal to include it as an exhibit. In legal terms, the manuscript constituted just another form of my notes on the case. Many of my writer friends were shocked to learn that had I written about the case in a private journal, they would be considered my notes and part of my documents from the case. A police officer's written thoughts about the details of a case are not private. Eventually, the commissioner agreed to a compromise and allowed the lawyers and their clients to read a redacted version of the manuscript and then question me on the contents. I was permitted to redact my "private thoughts," which I found quite funny, given that the entire thing contained my private thoughts. I blacked out very little; my lawyers went through it and removed a little more. Commissioner Oppal continued to appear disinclined to admit the document into evidence for anyone to read, despite pressure from the lawyers. Ultimately, he did not allow the manuscript entered as an exhibit.

Q: *Did you write this?*

A: *Yes.*

Q: *Did you mean it?*

A: *For the most part, yes.*

Occasionally, I am able to testify that I have since learned information that has changed my views from those in the manuscript or that it was in no way ready for publication in the state of that initial draft. These opportunities help, but they are few and far between. I admit to the areas where I was harsh or unfair to people, and I am able to assert that it hadn't been assessed by a lawyer for errors or omissions or for libel, for my protection. Over and over, I explain that this was a first draft, that these were *my impressions* of what went on, formed in the absence of anyone's presenting me with evidence of their side.

Very little in this process contains a shred of concern for my protection, including my own actions. My lawyer, Dave Crossin, tries to look out for me but sees me for the difficult client and loose cannon I've become. I stick my jaw out like a drunk mouthing off at the biggest guy in the bar, poking my finger in any chest and hoping to be punched, to take the punishment

I know I deserve. My boundaries desert me and I lay myself bare, in some misguided hope that if they see how open and honest I am about my own experience, they will think, *Ah, there's a police officer who is decent and thoughtful, different.* Most of the other cops have clammed up and hunkered down; I have placed my heart on Commissioner Wally Oppal's desk and don't understand that this simple act is killing me. I don't know now that I won't see that result for a couple of years. Remnants of my boundaries were still with me the first week I testified, January 30 to February 2, 2012, but sitting here a few weeks later, they've vanished.

Much has changed. I'm now seated to the left of Commissioner Oppal; two months ago, I was in a witness box to his right, before the inquiry shifted from a one-witness procedure to the more expedient and less truth-enabling multiple-witness panels, designed to move the hearings along more quickly so that the inquiry will conclude before the funding runs out. A recent B.C. provincial commission of inquiry into the salmon fishery ran well beyond its terms of reference in this same courtroom; fish warrant deadline extensions, but human beings apparently do not.

Shortly after my first stint, the inquiry's pace began to speed up and limit opportunity for the lawyers' questioning. Now, police officers in decision-making positions sit on panels with two and three cohorts, their time for giving evidence short and the lawyers' opportunity for cross-examination even shorter. Police managers and decision-makers with far more to explain than me are able to hide on three- and four-person panel discussions, the ever-ticking clock their friend, whereas I'm returned here without any cover, willing the days to end. In some ways, I prefer this, because I have nothing to hide, but I have lost sight of what's best for me as a person, not as a witness.

More and more frequently, I hear lawyers express their inability to exercise their mandate on behalf of their clients because of the ridiculous time constraints imposed on their cross-examinations. Names arise of numerous police officers inexplicably not called to testify about their roles in the file. I am baffled, but lately, that is not new for me.

My mind keeps wandering as I sit here; last time, I was sharp, focused, and listened intently to every word said to and about me, not wanting to miss a thing or give anyone an opportunity to unfairly judge or assess my job performance. I felt clear about what my responsibilities were and where my own many culpabilities lay, as well as what was not my fault and what I wanted answers for. Now, I'm all about survival, but I know I'm not doing a very good job of it.

AS MY APRIL 4, 2012, testimony continues, Cameron Ward, the lawyer for the missing and murdered women's families, is reading long passages of text aloud so that they will form part of the record, because the commissioner has refused to have the "document"—my manuscript—entered as an exhibit. I suppose I should be grateful, for this will allow me theoretically to publish one day and not have any supposed thunder stolen, but this process makes me cringe. I wonder how many other writers have had to defend their work in a similarly inquisitorial forum. I tune out, because listening is excruciating.

"That damned book," as my partner has occasionally referred to it, has caused me nothing but grief. How can I explain that I see it as both my undoing and my salvation? From those dark days in the autumn of 1999, I knew I had to write it. The circumstances of the case compelled me to write it. I began composing it in my head whenever the investigation became too bizarre to make sense of. My identity as a writer provided safe harbor when the rough waves of policing showed no sign of subsiding. Writing was home to me; policing an on-location acting job.

Throughout my policing career, I felt like an imposter—as a queer person, as a female, as left of center, as a writer, as someone who questioned the police culture and the system. I was different, and never before had I felt that as intensely as when the Pickton case broke. Far stronger than my sense of being a cop and detective was my need to be a truth teller—a need that simmered just below the surface throughout Project Amelia but that could not be expressed for so many reasons, most relating to job security and the culture I toiled within.

Now that need was replaced by a loud screaming voice inside my head that told me I had to tell this story, my story, *their story*. It was not a desire; it was a compulsion, and I briefly tried to fight it, knowing there was nothing I wanted more than to just forget this whole damn thing. But as a writer, I saw no choice. As a human being, I bore a responsibility. As a police officer, I felt a duty. Sitting here in the Missing Women Commission of Inquiry hearing room, I think of the media accounts I've read of my pending testimony, of those reporters wondering how I could possibly cite burnout and breakdown and at the same time have the energy and ability to write a book. Some of the lawyers in the inquiry pursue this line of questioning, asking me how I could possibly write a book if I was so shattered by my work on this file. I struggle to articulate that writing the manuscript both tortured and soothed me. Writing was never an effort for me, but reliving the investigation was another matter.

Am I obligated to share the details of the horrific nightmares that woke me every morning at 4:00 AM in those first months after the Pickton farm search, plus several sleepless years before and after? That I'd sit in front of my computer obsessively pounding out the details of the investigation until I went to work at 6:00 every morning? That overwhelming anxiety is a powerful motor driving you forward, unlike depression, which presses down on your head and pulls at your heels like a ball and chain? Anxiety made me very productive, but its effects don't last forever, as I would discover. I wrote like a person possessed because I felt my life depended on it.

They wonder how I could quit the investigation and then write and consult for *Da Vinci's Inquest*. How has this commission of inquiry become about me? Why are the brightest lights of scrutiny glaring into my eyes when so many others are much more deserving of audit? Because I had dared to put myself out there. Why should I have to publicly point out that my trauma has never been about the actual events on that farm, tragic and deplorable as they were, but is rooted in the lack of support for our investigation from the VPD and the RCMP? Why do I feel the need to explain myself and be known?

My trauma was about knowing horrible things were happening out there on that farm and not being able to convince the right people to act on it. My trauma was about lack of operational and investigative support. My trauma was about failing my oath and knowing I could never again trust that our policing institutions had the best interests and safety of the public at heart. I knew when I signed up for the VPD and set my sights on a career as a homicide detective that I would see terrible, terrible things. I felt prepared for that as well as anyone could be. I wasn't prepared for spin and deflection of our responsibilities.

My trauma was about taking an oath to do a dirty job and finding the tools to do that job were withheld from me. Indeed, the very obligation to do that job was questioned by the people in place to provide those tools. How could I continue when I had no confidence the same thing wouldn't happen again on other cases where other people would die from our inaction? Why did I work at the VPD and do the job I was paid for when that job wasn't supported? When my findings weren't listened to? What was the point of even being here if our inaction was allowing people to die?

I exhale loudly as Commissioner Oppal calls it a day and asks that I return again tomorrow. My mind has wandered throughout the day's proceedings, and I fear I've missed questions or sat there mute while lawyers and participants awaited answers from me. I scan the room and feel calmer when no one eyes me strangely. Apparently, I've performed adequately. As I gather my materials, commission counsel Art Vertlieb approaches me.

"All of these lawyers are watching us," he says quietly, a benign expression on his face, "so I know you'll understand— because you are a very sharp person—I can't be seen to be too friendly with you." His eyes bore into mine. He begins to wax eloquent, making various observations about my keen mind, and I feel the color rising in my cheeks.

I'm used to Art by now and I like him; his exclamation of "You are a most fascinating person!" and other over-the-top praise took me by surprise the first time we met in the commission office as I prepared my evidence. Usually, I laugh and say something along the lines of "Thanks, Art, you're killing me," but today I stare at him, mouth agape, a little unsure of how to play my part in this pantomime he is initiating.

I'm not sure if I should nod or try to look as though we aren't speaking and he isn't heaping superfluous compliments on me for my work as a witness. I do my best to look unaffected by his words or the feeling we are doing something wrong, and eventually, he bids me good-bye. I am overcome with sadness that the legal system makes Art feel he has to mask his desire to say something kind to me from his colleagues.

I stand there for a few seconds, feeling a little bit stunned. I am acutely aware—as I have been throughout the almost fourteen years since I began this file—that I belong nowhere. I am a person without portfolio, an orphan of the justice system, an outsider within. Among the police, I feel like a giraffe grazing with zebras; I am mistrusted by the families and the activists advocating for them, separate and distinct from the lawyers, and unable to trust the media, of which I used to be a part.

Elizabeth Hunt, one of two new lawyers assigned to represent Indigenous interests, asks to speak with me. This is the first week back after the commissioner suspended testimony for three weeks to give Elizabeth and her co-counsel, Suzette Narbonne, time to get up to speed with the file after Robyn Gervais resigned in protest of what she believed was a lack of inclusion of Indigenous interests throughout the proceedings.

I'd felt a powerful connection to Robyn's mandate, and I'd emailed her when she left the Missing Women Commission of Inquiry to tell her so. Her experience advocating and probing the reasons for the deaths and disappearances of so many women—many of them Indigenous—and feeling like a useless token resonated strongly with me, as did her sense that the only way to bring attention to that problem was to resign in protest. She responded to my email, even though both of us acknowledged that we shouldn't be communicating during a legal proceeding. We agreed that this wasn't much of a legal proceeding, however, as no one else seemed to be following any rules or legal decorum, and if there weren't enough police to assign to find missing human beings, there sure as hell weren't police to investigate our innocuous breach.

Elizabeth asks me if I'm comfortable speaking on the stand tomorrow about my experience as a lesbian and a minority in the VPD. *Sure, no problem.* We speak for a few minutes. Dave Crossin approaches me as she walks away.

"You okay?" he asks.

"Yeah."

"What did she want?" I tell him what she asked of me for the next day. He frowns. "Are you sure you want to do that?"

"I'm okay with it," I answer, thinking it's a good thing to be forthcoming about my experiences, to shed some light on the VPD and what it's like as an insider, as if I am one. "I'm happy to do it."

"You don't have to do this. I would advise against it as your counsel," Dave continues.

"I know," I reply. "Thanks." I know he's just doing his job, just looking out for me, but after today's testimony in which we have strayed into all sorts of questions about my personal thoughts and perceptions of the investigation, I have completely lost sight of my purpose here. If today was a distraction and red herring, I worry I have unwittingly ensured tomorrow will wander completely from any relevance.

25

Testifying for the Last Time

• • •

"Justice is itself the great standing policy of civil society;
and any eminent departure from it, under any circumstances,
lies under the suspicion of being no policy at all."
EDMUND BURKE

THE DAY BEGINS with lawyer for Indigenous interests
Suzette Narbonne cross-examining me. Tomorrow is Good
Friday, and today is my last day of testimony no matter
what, because the inquiry has to move on. I *hate* that I am taking up time that could be used to question other police officers.

Listening to Narbonne, I realize how important it has been
to me that the unique needs of the Indigenous community—
and the extent to which the First Nations, Métis, and Inuit
peoples have been wronged historically and currently—be
properly acknowledged by this inquiry, by the police, and by
Canadian society. Sitting here, I wonder how I have come to
this position, but I can't help thinking back to my time growing up in Calgary, hearing and even telling "Indian" jokes,
accepting this racism and colonialism as "the way it is."

I remember working in rural Alberta as a reporter and suddenly understanding with a jolt how manifestly wrong our treatment of Indigenous people has been. Not all the missing women were Indigenous, but as I look out into the courtroom, I see so many Indigenous people who are not blood relatives of a missing woman but are here simply to be here, *to bear witness. To bear witness to colonization and genocide.* I decide I will no longer participate in anything that supports this dismissal of human beings.

I feel my throat choking at the realization that I am injured from bearing witness to human suffering for a living. I am damaged, yet still occupy a place of entitlement. I feel my weakness, comparing myself and the other police and lawyers paid to be here with these warriors who observe us day after day from beyond the inner circle of the court. Who among us would be here on their own time? I feel ashamed to realize that my fight—while brutal and exhausting—spans so little time and struggle in comparison with the battles of First Nations, Métis, and Inuit peoples in our country. I've always thought of myself as a fighter, but am I? My privilege burns like a scarlet letter.

This entire experience has eroded my strength. How will I ever regain it? Is that what the psychologists were talking about when they told me I had PTSD? I had dismissed those observations then because I couldn't connect it to my life, but suddenly, sitting here, I can. The nightmares, the panic attacks, the anxiety, the headaches, the obsessive-compulsive behaviors, the twisted visions—*this* is what they were talking about. As Elizabeth Hunt begins her cross-examination, I realize that I haven't been listening. I give myself a stern talking to. I will not let this file break me again. *I fought back once. I can do it again. I will do it again.*

And so it goes. Several lawyers question me briefly, and I appreciate their seeming lack of desire to take me to task about the manuscript. Ravi Hira, counsel for retired Coquitlam RCMP inspector Earl Moulton, takes me through an interesting cross-examination in which he asks me if I am aware of a second meeting between the police and then–attorney general Ujjal Dosanjh—a meeting I did not attend and not the same meeting where I gave a presentation about the missing women investigation to elected officials, as I described in the manuscript.

I am gobsmacked and testify that I have absolutely no knowledge of this second meeting. This information floats out into the inquiry waters, but nothing seems to come of it, and I am unable to ascertain any more information about what went down. To this day, I am not privy to the details of the meeting or to who else was in attendance. Another behind-the-scenes mystery I can't solve. Another secret in my own investigation.

The day ends for me, and I walk away from Courtroom 801 for the last time.

26

Losing My Grip, Again

• • •

"When you get to the end of your rope, tie a knot and hang on."
FRANKLIN D. ROOSEVELT

ON APRIL 12, 2012, disgusted with what I am witnessing, I tell myself I am watching the Missing Women Commission of Inquiry live feed in my office for the last time. But in the following weeks, I find I can't tear myself away. Before giving my own testimony, I found it easy to look away and do some work rather than remain glued to the desktop, but since the end of January, as I watch the testimony spin more and more out of control and into farce, I can't stop.

The week of April 9 was to be devoted to the 1998 decision of the Criminal Justice Branch to stay the attempted murder and forcible confinement charges against Pickton for his alleged attack on Vancouver sex worker Anderson. Anderson was scheduled to testify at the inquiry on Monday, April 9, 2012, with assurances that there were strict measures in place to ensure her privacy. She was living clean and sober with her family and remained terrified of Robert Pickton and traumatized by the events of March 1997 that had left her nearly dead.

On that morning, commission counsel Art Vertlieb announced to Commissioner Oppal that Anderson had reconsidered and would not be testifying out of concern for her privacy and that of her family. I could only assume Anderson had concluded that she didn't want to speak publicly about her reasons for fighting back in self-defense, for being a poor, drug-addicted sex worker, for needing the drugs she used to self-medicate to survive the ensuing weeks and months after the attack, and for using the drugs that fateful night, a decision that supposedly made her such a poor witness that the charges could not proceed to court. When I heard of her decision not to testify, I felt secretly elated for her, thinking, *Good for you. Why should you have to defend yourself and become a spectacle in front of a system that completely failed you?*

The remainder of the week brought Coquitlam regional Crown prosecutor Randi Connor to the stand to discuss her decision to stay the charges against Pickton in the Anderson attack and the fact that the Crown prosecution's entire file on the incident had been lost. Her testimony and the special protections afforded every Crown prosecutor involved in the decision pushed me into a deep depression I wouldn't shake for several weeks. It didn't seem right, but all of the lawyers seemed to accept this obvious double standard in place to protect Crown lawyers.

Commissioner Wally Oppal summarized the challenges in investigating the Criminal Justice Branch in his report *Forsaken: The Report of the Missing Women Commission of Inquiry*:

"Due to the protections afforded to prosecutorial independence, both Commission Counsel and Participants' Counsel were not permitted to put questions to Ms. Randi Connor that asked her to second-guess her decision to stay the proceedings or to consider different evidence in reflecting on the reasonableness of her decision. Similarly, I cannot second-guess Ms. Randi Connor's decision. Different decisions can be considered reasonable, and in these circumstances two reasonable people could make different decisions based on the same facts.

"In the absence of the Crown file, I have been unable to fully assess the work Ms. Randi Connor conducted on the file."

Commissioner Oppal goes on to state his conclusions: "With respect to her circumstances as a prosecutor, Ms. Randi Connor had 16 witnesses left to prepare one week before a five-day trial. The evidence shows that Law Enforcement Notifications (LENS) were issued to the police witnesses as a routine matter. There is no evidence that Ms. Randi Connor contacted the other witnesses for the trial, therefore I find as fact that she had not contacted them."

I found it intensely frustrating to watch and couldn't help yelling "Oh my God!" and "Are you kidding me?" at the computer screen while my work partner, Rowan, sat toiling away in the background, empathizing with the lawyers in the hearing room who were obviously as incensed as we were. Much of Randi Connor's testimony consisted of vague references to what she "would" do as normal practice on similar files, but very little if any clear recollection or statements of what she actually did on the Anderson file, which the Crown no longer possessed.

Had Anderson died, all sixteen witnesses would have been called to testify. They would have been there if it had been a murder trial. As I had said in my own testimony, as morbid a thought as it is, had Anderson died, this would have been a slam-dunk murder conviction.

EVER SINCE THE provincial government had grudgingly announced the creation of the Missing Women Commission of Inquiry, I had openly criticized it as unwanted, imperfect, and underfunded. As the hearings progressed, I found much of the testimony and the lawyers' inability to fully cross-examine police witnesses disappointing. I was most disappointed that my questions about the inaction of the RCMP in late 1999 and early 2000 surrounding Ellingsen's information were not answered. The Missing Women Commission of Inquiry did little for me other than make me feel even worse and more in the dark about the mysteries of the investigation.

As for the manuscript, it continued to sit in my computer. Every time I'd tried to look at it over the years, the frustration and horror of the investigation and the pain of the past years rose up like a summer thunderstorm, and lightning struck down on me, plunging me into an even darker mood and worsening my anger, agitation, and depression. I suppose on some level, rereading the manuscript provided me with some kind of psychological payoff, as though I could punish myself for all the mistakes I had made on the case by taking myself back there over and over again. Maybe I hoped that if I went back there often enough, I might get it right. But I never could get it right. All it did was keep me stuck.

The Missing Women Commission of Inquiry finally rested on June 6, 2012. I was invited to a gathering at Crab Park late that afternoon and decided I had to attend. The intent was for healing; and everyone associated with the inquiry—police, lawyers, media, Indigenous people, and families—was invited. Police were asked not to wear uniforms, which wasn't a problem for me, since I never wore mine anymore.

I hung out most with Tim Dickson, counsel for the City of Vancouver, and Damon Vignale, producer of the award-winning documentary film *The Exhibition*, which chronicled Vancouver artist Pamela Masik's struggle to bring her large striking portraits of the missing women—many of them depicting the same photographs I had used to create the reward poster—to exhibition at the B.C. Museum of Anthropology. There is no doubt the families would have found the exhibition difficult to view; I know I found it hard to see the paintings in the film. There was immense opposition to the exhibition from the women's families and other Downtown Eastside activists, which created negative publicity and pressured the museum into canceling it. Damon interviewed me for the film, and despite the difficult questions it raises, it is a project with which I have been proud to be associated.

I felt the cancelation of Pamela's exhibition was a missed opportunity for the story of the missing women—and the larger issues of poverty, colonialism, and racism—to play out on a larger stage. I interpreted Pamela's use of bold, slashing markings of dark paint across the faces in the paintings as indicative of societal violence against and suppression of women, not as any disrespect toward the victims. Although I tried to understand the concerns that the exhibition might be seen as exploitive, I felt this was yet another example of how the activists and advocates for the missing women perpetuated the very climate they railed against by suppressing their own story and not granting the issue of violence against women a wider audience.

I left Crab Park after an hour or so, hoping Commissioner Oppal's report—set for an October 2012 release—would mark an end to the investigation and represent the start of healing for all associated. As October approached, word got out there would be yet another delay and the report would not be released until December 2012. I felt confident the report would not be inordinately critical of my efforts as an individual, but that didn't matter much to me, and the delay did little to alleviate my anxiety and inability to function.

FINALLY, DECEMBER 17 arrived. So many times throughout those years, I'd longed to join the crowd protesting, marching, and bearing further witness to this tragedy, but I was afraid of the very real possibility that I would break down in public again. So I stayed in my office and watched the live feed of Commissioner Oppal's press conference on my desktop. Snippets of the report were leaked via Twitter throughout the morning by media members frantically scouring the report's hundreds of pages in lockdown, so I knew most of the highlights before Commissioner Oppal spoke.

As I watched, I felt a familiar anger coupled with a sense of activism rise in me. The press conference was staged in a hotel meeting room and it was packed with advocates for the missing and murdered women and their family members. As Commissioner Oppal tried to speak, the crowd booed and catcalled for several minutes and he could not be heard above them, so he waited. I understood their frustrations, but I felt anger that he wasn't given the courtesy to speak without ridicule and interruption. Conversely, I felt pride in those present singing loud and proud, not allowing themselves to be silenced. Finally, the crowd allowed him to speak and present the report. Again, I understood both sides, but I longed for those present to hear Wally, to give him—*to give all of us in the criminal justice system*—the chance to say and do the right things after so many years of getting it wrong. We all got it wrong.

I desperately hoped I would feel better now that it was truly over. I left work, drove home, and went out for a run, one of many activities I used to love whose joy continued to elude me these last several years. I ran with my iPod on, letting the music move me and touch me, and soon tears came. I found myself on my favorite hill in Queen Elizabeth Park, a quiet wood-chip trail beneath tall evergreens, and I ran up and down over and over. I let the grief and frustration and pain flow out of me, and I just ran, hoping the dam had burst. I arrived home wiped out after an hour or so, feeling somehow cleansed and deeply exhausted.

Over the following week, the exhaustion remained. On the morning of December 24, I sat alone in my office, expecting to work until noon. No one else was there, and I didn't need to be there either, but I felt too low to be around my family and bring them down. I continued to feel like I wasn't so much interacting with other people as inflicting myself on them. I felt it was best for everyone if they left me alone. At times over the years, I'd felt it would be better for my family if I just lived alone in a basement beneath them rather than impose this unpredictable, agitated, angry parent and partner on them. It seemed a perfectly reasonable way to live to me then.

I opened the locker in my office and gathered up all of my gear: uniform, hat, toque, gloves, socks, bulletproof vest, assorted jackets and fleece tops, handcuffs, radio pouch, earpiece, belts—everything I needed to be a uniformed police officer other than my boots. I placed it all in a huge duffel bag. Then I opened my locked desk drawer where I kept my sidearm, a Sig Sauer P226 .40 caliber, along with my ammunition, magazines, and cleaning kit. My gun hadn't been out of my desk since November 2012, when I'd passed my yearly qualification at the range.

That day, as I had prepared to take my place on the line at the indoor range, Gary Fisk—my Project Amelia teammate whom I had testified against in the inquiry—walked in and took a position several places to my right. Without warning, I began hyperventilating, and I knew I was going into a full-blown panic attack. The range officer noticed my condition and helped me gain control of my breathing. I'd been beset by bizarre fears at the range ever since working on the Pickton file, fear that I'd be accidentally shot or injured, but never anything like this, and I wasn't about to share my true fears with him. This time, there was someone on the firing line *who might actually feel justified in shooting me,* but I told the range officer I was just worried about qualifying.

In a workplace of more than thirteen hundred sworn officers who each had the entire year to qualify, what were the odds Fisk and I would select the same range time and day? I wondered if he'd sought me out or asked to see the schedule, though I knew this thinking was totally irrational. I became angry and determined to not let this person and my PTSD stop me from completing my annual pistol qualification. I didn't want to come back, knowing what it had taken to get myself there this time. I'd rescheduled twice already because of my anxiety.

Luckily, I had a few minutes to get it together during the routine safety briefing, and by the time we'd loaded our pistols, I'd situated myself as far from Fisk as possible and felt ready to go. I qualified easily, with one of my better scores, and looked far down the line with relief to see that Fisk hadn't qualified and would have to shoot another course of fire. I rushed into the cleaning room, cleaned my equipment, and hustled out, hoping I wouldn't have to see him again that day.

As I thought back to that day in November, I imagined the furor I would spark if I handed in my pistol to Stores on Christmas Eve without documenting it or advising my sergeant. I locked it back in my drawer and made an entry in my calendar to ask him to keep it for me when we got back after Christmas holidays. He was a good guy, and I knew he would safeguard it for me without raising any unnecessary procedural alarms about my ability to work. I didn't need a gun in my current position.

Knowing that the building would be deserted on Christmas Eve, I lugged the heavy bag over to the adjoining police station and saw with relief that the Stores window was open for business. I hefted the duffel bag up onto the counter and waited.

A young clerk eventually came to the desk and apologized to me for having to wait.

"No problem," I said. "I just want to drop this stuff off." He looked at me quizzically.

"Okay." He paused and stared at my pile of gear. "That's a lot of stuff. Are you retiring?"

"No, I'm just not going to be needing it anymore." He looked into my eyes and I immediately realized his concern.

"Are you *okay?*" I felt like a jerk for causing him any worry, not wanting this kid to be afraid some twisted cop was going to do something to ruin his Christmas Eve forever.

"Oh my gosh." I laughed uneasily. "No, I'm *fine.* I'm just done with this stuff. I'll be plainclothes from now on." I wasn't "fine," but I wasn't suicidal.

"Okay." He smiled with relief and started emptying my duffel bag. "Merry Christmas!"

"Thanks. You have a Merry Christmas, too." He finished and handed me my bag.

I walked back to my office, gathered up my things, and went home, hoping 2013 would not be a worse year than 2012.

27

Shaking Hands
with My Own Devil

❦ ❦ ❦

"I became insane, with long intervals of horrible sanity."
EDGAR ALLAN POE

RETURNING TO WORK after Christmas 2012 left me feeling no better. For years, I had relied on my early-morning wake-ups and high anxiety to power me through my life. I had begun to believe this state of hyper-arousal was normal. I had no idea workaholism was a secondary flight response PTSD sufferers sometimes employ to avoid their real problems. I pushed aside everything I'd experienced intensely since February 2002: poor sleep marred by nightmares, a stressful job, and a very sick child and the strain that accompanies that. In 2004, our three-year-old son was diagnosed with acute lymphoblastic leukemia, and we battled for three-and-a-half years to save his precious life. My partner quit her job to be with him through his torturous chemotherapy treatments, and we took care of our other two children while I worked to support us financially. I was determined to be strong and handle it all.

And I did. For more than ten years. Suddenly, over only a few months, I found that energy waning fast, and more and more, I struggled to get myself out of bed for work.

I had submitted a Workers Compensation Board (WCB) claim for PTSD in 2002, shortly after the Pickton search began, and my mental and physical health had declined even further since then. My file was stamped with a short and sweet "Denied" after a cursory investigation into my claim, as was common practice, because mental health claims were not in the legislation at that time. An adjustor phoned me and asked questions around the theme of "Were you *actually involved* in the search of the farm?" I knew my experience was so much more complex than that, but WCB only had the ability to see things through the lens of physical injury. *Can you still use your arm? You lost your leg in a saw?*

I think I'm losing my mind from pursuing a serial killer and receiving no support to catch him. It isn't like you see it on TV, where a detective goes rogue and sorts it all out solo in an hour. There are procedures to follow. Jurisdictions to respect. You need help. Is there a box on your form I can tick for that?

Although I had been on the farm in the early stages of the search in February 2002, I couldn't even begin to try to explain how much more loaded my involvement and failure was. I felt as though I had no right to feel as I did, even after Geramy and I stood in the Pickton slaughterhouse and trailer, looking at bloody mattresses, freezers, and buckets and seeing things no one should ever have to see, seeing evidence of the victims and knowing they had died there. I had no ability to explain that it was not only the avoidable human suffering but also the massive systemic failure and my part in it that haunted me. It didn't make sense even to me.

Rennie Hoffman, my good friend and supervisor at the time, encouraged me to appeal, but I couldn't bring myself to ask him for help and reveal that I was incapable of even writing the appeal myself. Talking about the events and my experiences on the investigation and their impact on my own life was too painful. I remember a vague awareness that I *should* appeal the claim, that my suffering was real and I may very well have needed the benefits a successful claim would entitle me to, but I possessed zero ability to process what happened or articulate the depths of my grief. I didn't even know it was grief back then. All I knew was that this experience had damaged me, and I had no idea how to survive it, let alone ask for help. On another level, I felt ashamed seeking out benefits for this tragedy when I wasn't a victim. There were people far more deserving of help than me.

I sought out a trauma counselor yet again in April 2012, just days after my last day of testimony at the inquiry. I knew then I was in trouble: I felt hopeless and unable to imagine my future, and although I didn't have any plans of suicide, I thought of it in vague terms. I was profoundly depressed, but knowing firsthand the suffering of those left behind by suicide, I couldn't imagine doing that to the people I loved and who loved me, no matter how much pain I felt. I felt far more inclined to isolate myself, perhaps say good-bye and go live in the woods somewhere or in a basement suite all by myself where no one would have to put up with me.

I knew for certain I wanted to live. I would later learn that having a partner, a close family, and children and quitting drinking were "protective factors," and I now see that they saved my life. I had sunk very low, but as Detective Rust Cohle said on the TV show *True Detective*, "I lack the constitution for suicide." I didn't know where there was left for me to go professionally or personally, but I knew enough to hope this couldn't last forever.

Little had changed with the VPD-recommended psychologists in the ten years since I'd first sought treatment.

None of the people on their very short list had formal training in trauma, which astounded me given the nature of police work. I searched online for someone specifically trained in trauma and located an office I could easily access so that I wouldn't quit prematurely, as I'd done with other therapists since 2002. I found Dr. Joanne MacKinnon, called her up, and began my journey.

We began working together weekly to slowly untangle the last twelve years of my life. I explained that I'd tried neurofeedback, EMDR (Eye Movement Desensitization and Reprocessing), art therapy, meditation, yoga, cognitive behavioral therapy (CBT), and a multitude of other treatments with varying degrees of mild success, but I continued to feel broken. I'd never stuck with anything for long, other than yoga. I told her I'd done EMDR with Margo Weston in 2002, but her number was no longer in service, and I had no energy to track her down. She had helped me, and I thought I should do more EMDR. I also returned briefly to my neurofeedback therapist, the wonderfully caring and generous Barb Macnaughton, and found relief from some of my agitation through that and the cranial-sacral massage she also practiced.

Dr. MacKinnon and I began my treatment while I continued working as an intelligence officer with the VPD, analyzing and assessing threats in the public domain of the City of Vancouver. She helped me manage my ongoing frustration and anxiety as the final months of the Missing Commission of Inquiry degenerated into farce and spectacle, complete with internal accusations of sexual harassment in the commission's own office, cries of conspiracy from the lawyers for the victims' families and Downtown Eastside interests, resignations, and the provincial government's choking off of hearing time and public funds to properly conduct the inquiry. Using EMDR, she helped me to loosen the grip these old and newly inflicted traumas held on my body and mind. In those months, Dr. MacKinnon kept me from slipping deeper into the pit. It was no mean feat.

Each appointment stirred up old skeletons, not buried, merely discarded in the ditches along the road of my consciousness. For the rest of the day after each appointment, I felt crankier and more agitated and was short with my kids and partner. It seemed like I was getting nowhere, but I felt a need to keep going, to have some faith in the process. Dr. MacKinnon assured me this was common with EMDR treatment and told me that some people were so stirred up after a session that they were advised not to drive. I trusted her; there was nowhere else to turn, and I couldn't remain the way I was.

With her support, I submitted a new claim to the renamed WorkSafeBC in the summer of 2012, hoping my case would be accepted under the new provincial legislation recognizing operational stress injuries such as PTSD in the workplace. My claim was once again denied, in the space of a few weeks. No one from WorkSafeBC interviewed or questioned me. This time, I sought union assistance to submit an appeal.

In May 2012, I advised the VPD Human Resources Section I would no longer be competing for promotion, despite my favorable chances. I copied the email to Deputy Chief Constable Doug LePard; a sergeant in HR responsible for the competition; my inspector; and my supervisor, Sergeant Mike Purdy. Only Mike responded or talked to me about how I was doing and helped me through that year before I finally booked off, because he was my boss and that was his job.

In early 2013, my physical body began failing me further. Digestive problems, aching muscles, and severe allergies had plagued me since 1999, but I'd written them off to normal stress and tried not to worry. Worry was the one thing I could count on, however. I worried incessantly about everything from my own physical health and that of my kids and partner to the world at large. I began to follow politics obsessively. I carried hand sanitizer everywhere, terrified I would contract bird or swine flu and bring it home to my family. I lugged our one-year-old king-sized IKEA mattress back to the store and left it there on the floor, convinced it was causing my pain and nightmares each night, leaving the staff there shaking their heads at the crazy person. I started having visual migraines and eye infections.

I began to avoid driving alone, because whenever I did, I became enraged at everyday traffic and careless drivers. I could keep it in check with my family on board, and I knew enough not to put myself in danger by confronting other drivers when I drove alone, but I railed, hollered, and seethed in the driver's seat and carried the anger with me for hours. I'd cycled to work for most of my career, but I found myself terrified of being hit by vehicles or crashing my bike, and my commute became more and more unbearable. I wrote nasty emails to colleagues who parked in my assigned parking stall. I ranted at office social functions when I found the conversation ridiculous or lacking in appropriateness or sensitivity—I, who used to enjoy a good dirty joke as much as anyone, began to hate and judge everyone and everything.

On January 10, 2013, a WorkSafeBC review officer drafted an eight-page decision on my appeal, varying the earlier 2012 decision that did not allow my claim of PTSD brought on by my participation in the Missing Women Commission of Inquiry. A couple of days later, I came home from work and found the decision in my mail. I opened it and read, throat choked, eyes welling with tears, which prompted my partner to ask, "Did they deny it?"

"No," I croaked. "*They accepted it.*"

I read the review officer's critique of what I'll politely call the "lacking" investigation she found WorkSafeBC to have done into my original claim. She dismissed my union representative's request that my claim be reopened and reinvestigated; instead, she accepted the claim outright based on the information provided. She got it. She accepted Dr. MacKinnon's diagnosis of PTSD.

I felt like a grossly overfilled balloon someone had finally mercifully popped. I immediately booked off from work, even after learning that WorkSafeBC benefits would not be available to me until a forty-day appeal period passed. It made me think of Lent and my Catholic upbringing. I felt quite certain the VPD and WorkSafeBC wouldn't appeal the decision, and I didn't care if either of them did.

The next day I slept in and took in a matinee at my local movie theater, where *Zero Dark Thirty* was playing. The film is loosely based on the true story of a CIA agent's attempts to locate Osama bin Laden and have him brought to justice. I enjoyed the film but was left obsessing about what the story might have looked like had no one listened to the agent's theories or provided her the resource support to catch bin Laden. What if she had merely languished in her knowledge of where he was and agonized that no one helped her make a plan or go out to catch him?

I stayed off work for three weeks before succumbing to various pressures—many of my own creation—to return. When I had first booked off, I acted with no plan other than to try to feel better, and although I felt more rested, I remained highly anxious and agitated and was drawn back into my routine of workaholism. Dr. MacKinnon said she would support whatever I decided, but I know she feared that returning to work would not be helpful to me. The work itself was fine, but I hid in my office as I had for eleven years, interacting with others as little as possible. Each morning, I awoke to my 5:00 AM alarm depressed and exhausted from my nightmares. It felt as though I had a ten-ton anvil strapped to my waist. I panicked at the change in myself from the highly anxious, hyper-productive workaholic to someone drowning in depression. I shared this with no one and tried to act as though everything was normal.

Over the spring of 2013, I continued to spiral downhill mentally and physically. I felt agitated, trapped, and hopeless about my future. In April, a friend of mine who was a sergeant in the VPD contacted me to talk about a PTSD treatment program one of her employees had taken and benefited from greatly. I was open to anything. She connected me with her employee, and we met for a coffee and talked about our experiences. At one point, I nervously said to him, "I don't know. I don't know if I really need something like that."

He smiled and laughed, not unkindly. "I said the same thing. Trust me. You need it."

I knew he was right. I did need it. I needed something.

28

Doing the Hard Work

• • •

*"All art is a kind of confession, more or less oblique.
All artists, if they are to survive, are forced, at last, to tell
the whole story; to vomit the anguish up."*
JAMES BALDWIN

THE VETERANS TRANSITION Program (VTP) is a ten-day residential PTSD treatment program developed by Dr. Marv
Westwood of the University of British Columbia (UBC)
Psychology Department. It's split into two four-day weekends and one two-day weekend, and no drinking or drugs are
allowed. The program is based on creating a sense of safety and
trust in the group, which allows participants to take part in a
therapeutic enactment of a past trauma they feel is keeping
them emotionally stuck.

The therapeutic enactments are well planned in consul-
tation with the participant and the clinicians. Most group
members are given a role to play in each other's enactments,
including someone who acts as the double for the person
whose enactment it is so that they never have to "stand" in

their traumatic event the way they did in the past. They watch their double go through the incident and often will step in and say things they may not have been able to say in the actual moment. They are frequently asked what they are feeling physically and where in their bodies they feel it. This is designed to guide the trauma out of the body and allow the mind to reprocess it, effectively leading the person to become "unstuck."

It's an incredibly powerful and cathartic tool designed to take the experience through both the mind and the body to process it effectively. It gives the person a different perspective and a voice, which they may not have had during the traumatic event. I am in no way an expert on group therapy or therapeutic enactments, but participating in my own therapeutic enactment and witnessing and taking part in those of others has been and continues to be a very large part of my recovery. The clinicians like to use a logjam analogy, guiding participants to loosen that one log, which will often loosen the rest to start the flow of mental health again. It certainly achieved that for me.

At the end of May 2013, I found myself sitting in the cafeteria of a Roman Catholic retreat center eating breakfast with several men with military and first responder backgrounds, waiting for our VTP to begin. We chatted easily, but our nervousness wasn't far from the surface. We all knew why we were there, and this was far more terrifying than arresting bad people, driving an ambulance, or deploying to a war zone. Our enemies were within us, and we all later confessed we'd been more scared to be there than of anything else we'd faced in our lives. We worked in a group therapy setting, guided by two psychologists and two paraprofessional graduates of the program. We started telling our stories.

Respecting the confidentiality of the program and its participants is of paramount importance to the success of any group therapy. We came from diverse backgrounds, and our traumas were varied, ranging from experiencing terrible sights and smells, suffering traumatic events at early developmental stages, and lacking support from our institutions and communities domestically or upon return home from combat missions. Often, we suffered from a combination of experiences, but all were horrifying on one level or another.

Drs. Matt Graham and Mike Dadson, two UBC PhD graduates with vast experience in leading group therapy and treating trauma, led us through an introduction to the program. Assisting them were two paraprofessionals, both Canadian Armed Forces leaders, both due to retire on medical release for PTSD, and themselves graduates of the VTP. Immediately, I felt we were in safe hands. *I may as well give this all I have, because I've tried everything else.* Later, as I came to know the other participants, I learned we all felt the same way: each of us was desperate for a last chance at recovery.

It's difficult to describe the changes I saw in the men I worked alongside in the VTP and felt in myself over the ten days of the program and the following year. I watched the light return to eyes that on the first day or two had been glassy, distant, and devoid of feeling. It was as though our bodies had been freed—even if only temporarily at first—from the ghosts haunting them. We've gone our separate ways, but I know I could call any one of them and they'd be there for me in a heartbeat, and we do keep in casual contact.

We all placed our trust in the clinicians and each other and shared our deepest terrors and experiences, trusting that this was a safe place to do so. The energy in our circle was palpable; at one point, I asked Matt Graham if it was unusual to feel this so tangibly, and he told me that it was what they strive for, but our group was extraordinary. The care the clinicians took to create that circle and foster that trust seemed effortless, but I knew it was born of a great deal of skill and planning on their part. I am truly indebted to all the men in my group and especially to Matt and Mike.

After the first four-day VTP weekend, I knew I couldn't go back to work. Sharing some of my experiences and attempts at coping with the others, I understood that I'd pushed myself far beyond a healthy place. Did I believe I could learn to manage my PTSD? Absolutely. However, I also learned that suffering with it for more than ten years meant my case bore many elements of complex PTSD, and I would need to take better care with myself and practice self-care to a much greater degree than I had to that point.

When I completed my VTP, I was only the second female among more than two hundred men to take part. Women were not excluded, but the VTP had been tested and developed using men, and women weren't aware of the program or didn't express interest in it. I am thrilled to say I was able to complete my first paraprofessional VTP assignment on the pilot all-female VTP in the spring of 2014, and I hope to work with men's and women's groups in this capacity in the future. The skill and compassion of the clinicians is impressive, and the results they achieve are miraculous. To work alongside them to help people who are suffering is truly a privilege for me.

In October 2013, the VTP held a medal ceremony, and Senator Roméo Dallaire—a retired Canadian Forces general who suffered from PTSD as a result of his peacekeeping work during the Rwandan genocide in the early '90s—presented medals to program graduates. More than two hundred men and two women had completed the VTP by then, and the program had not lost a single one to suicide. Many of the graduates did not attend; it is hard to stage an event and bring together people who still suffer from varying degrees of social anxiety or agoraphobia, but many, including me, managed to make it to the UBC Armoury for the event.

I felt good. I dressed in business clothes—which I hadn't done in more than a year—and drove to UBC in a thick, chilly fog, determined to get my medal and see "my guys" with whom I'd completed the program. Lt. Col. (Ret) Chris Linford, one of the paraprofessionals on my program, as well as Dr. Mike Dadson, Dr. Matt Graham, and Stan*, another participant from our group, were there, and it was fantastic to catch up during the cocktail portion of the evening.

That was another test for me. In the past, I would invariably drink far too much at "work" (VPD) functions, and after I stopped drinking, in December 2006, I avoided such functions and socializing with police people. The only exception was the annual Canadian Security Intelligence Service (CSIS) contact party every January. My relationships with CSIS people were by far the most satisfying and enjoyable of my career, and with them I felt minimal temptation to drink and was able to manage socializing at their parties.

As I mingled at the VTP medal ceremony, I saw Senator Dallaire across the room. I'd brought my well-thumbed copy of his book *Shake Hands with the Devil: The Failure of Humanity in Rwanda*, hoping he would sign it. I had devoured the book back in 2003, sensing that we shared the similarly faith-shattering experience of doing our jobs and reporting our shocking findings, only to have them ignored or minimized by the people to whom we reported. I knew our situations were much different, but they shared enough common elements that I felt a kinship with the senator. I made my way over to him in a moment when he was alone.

"Senator, I'm Lori Shenher," I said, extending my hand. I felt a flush of embarrassment, recalling that I'd emailed him years back in frustration with my own PTSD and isolation, asking if he had any advice or treatment information that might help me. His assistant had kindly replied with some suggestions of potential resources, but I knew they saw me for what I was back then: an unstable, desperate, suffering person emailing a stranger as though I knew him.

"Ah, yes, how are you?" He shook my hand and looked me squarely in the eye. I felt fairly sure he wouldn't know of or remember me. We made some chitchat about his busy travel schedule and Vancouver weather. Eventually, I held up my book.

"I'd be honored if you'd sign this for me," I said. "I read it during a particularly tough time, and your experiences really resonated with me. I'm planning on writing my own book." He nodded, listening intently. He took the book from me and began looking for a place to sign. I'd known that he continued to suffer greatly from his PTSD and that he was an ardent supporter of the VTP, despite not having participated himself.

"You should try the VTP, Senator," I ventured, immediately regretting my suggestion and hoping it didn't seem intrusive. Suggesting that someone undergo a ten-day residential group therapy program is probably best saved for good friends and family interventions, but I wished that something would help his suffering. He looked up, still holding my book.

"Well, you know, Chris has been after me to try it, but it's very hard for me to find the time." He passed me my book.

"Thank you," I said. "I hope you didn't find my suggestion impertinent." I remembered I was speaking to a Canadian senator and retired general. Respect for rank was a habit that didn't die easily.

"No, not at all." He smiled. "Maybe one day I will find the time." We stood and talked a little longer, until he was called away by an assistant to prepare for the medal presentation. He shook my hand again, we exchanged pleasantries, and he was off.

After the senator left me, I found myself near the bar talking to the guys from my program. I felt a tap on my elbow and was surprised to see a retired VPD inspector beside me.

"Lori!" He wrapped me in a hug, then released me to shake my hand. "It's so good to see you."

This was a man I had worked near for years but didn't know well. He had been good to me in our interactions, and he was now working outside of policing. I know he meant well, but he launched into a monologue of how badly he felt for me during the inquiry, what a raw deal I got from the VPD, how it was garbage that my investigation hadn't been supported, and so on. It was clear to me he had no idea or hadn't considered why I was there or in what capacity.

I froze. In all my years of PTSD and policing, I had never frozen in place, unable to move or react. My feet stayed rooted to the floor, even as my head was screaming *Run!* My chest was tightening like a fist. I'd been doing so much work on myself, but I hadn't yet figured out how to talk about it. I felt desperate to escape, but I could not move. I just nodded and uttered the occasional "Thanks for saying that" or "I really appreciate that" as I struggled for a proper breath. A part of me wondered how he couldn't see or notice I was having a meltdown right in front of him.

As he spoke to me, another VPD inspector joined us, someone I'd worked more closely with but did not know very well either. He'd been in Afghanistan recently, a secondment the VPD allowed its members to voluntarily participate in whenever Canada had peacekeepers or active soldiers deployed anywhere in the world. He was a harmless guy, but I knew I didn't have the energy for him that evening.

"Lori!" He clapped me on the back.

The first inspector welcomed this second one into our conversation. "I was just telling Lori what a shitty deal she got on the missing women thing," he said. And the two of them began to talk about me as though I weren't there, which wasn't all that far from the truth, because I couldn't even talk at this point. They channeled all their own anti-VPD bitterness through the vent of my failed investigation.

Stan, the one other participant from our VTP program, saw me and came to my rescue. People with PTSD seem to recognize each other, and, certainly, when we already know each other, it's easy to see when someone's in trouble. Stan and I were pretty good pals, and I felt a flood of relief when I saw him coming. He came to my side and whispered in my ear, "You okay?"

"No, I can't move," I whispered back. Stan steered me by the elbow with a casual wave back at the other two.

"Sorry, guys, she's all mine, now!" I managed a wave that they probably thought was intended to be faux tragic and helpless, but I was not acting. Stan had to pull me a little to unstick my feet from that spot, and we moved far away from the noise. A few minutes later, we were asked to line up to go out into the auditorium to receive our medals. I thanked Stan, and we silently walked to our seats as the formal speeches and presentation began. Senator Dallaire spoke and then gave each of us our medal—a challenge coin bearing the VTP insignia. Challenge coins have a long history in the military, dating back to the Roman Empire. Members of individual units or divisions can challenge their comrades to present their coins, often in the form of a drinking game. Military units also present them to outsiders for outstanding service or performance of duty in aid of the unit. When the Senator presented me with mine, he leaned over and whispered in my ear, "I hope you publish your book."

The event exhausted me. I resisted the urge to run out to my car without saying any good-byes, but it was very difficult. My conversation—if you could call it that—with the two VPD inspectors left me anxious and overwhelmed. I felt I had somehow failed by not handling myself with more grace

and aplomb. *Was I ever going to get better?* It felt like a significant setback. As I made my way out, the first VPD inspector
I'd encountered earlier caught up with me and invited me out
for drinks with the others. I thanked him, told him I needed to
get home, and wished him well. I walked through the dense
fog back to my car, my heart racing with pent-up anxiety. Once
inside, a feeling of safety slowly returned, and I drove home.

The incident bothered me for several days. My anxiety
increased, my nightmares worsened, and I felt agitated. All my
hard work seemed for naught. Freezing in place was new to
me, and I was afraid that I wouldn't react appropriately in similar stressful situations in the future, which could place me in
danger. I had always been able to react effectively in the past.

My partner, Dr. MacKinnon, and my WorkSafeBC-assigned
occupational therapist, Natasha Coulter, all told me the same
thing: this had been a significant trigger, but I'd survived, managed it, and learned from it. Such triggers would be become
easier to manage over time. Reluctantly, I decided not to beat
myself up about it any further. Dr. MacKinnon helped role-play
similar conversations with me for the future, which helped a
great deal. In time, the anxiety slowly abated.

Dr. MacKinnon and I began to use EMDR to unravel the
events of the investigation that bothered me most: the women
who went missing after we'd the received the Ellingsen tip, the
POI 390 investigation, my testimony at the inquiry, my grief
over the murdered and missing women, the loss of my good
health, and the stalling of my career in law enforcement. Slowly,
as we worked through each event step by step, I became able
to write about them, bit by bit, an hour or two a week. I could
do it without sinking into a pit of depression or yelling at
everyone around me. I began to believe I might publish this
book.

Epilogue

* * *

"It is not the strongest or the most intelligent
who will survive but those who can best manage change."
HERBERT SPENCER, SURVIVAL OF THE FITTEST

F OR SO MANY years, I focused on what I'd lost working
on the failed missing women investigation. My belief in
myself, my faith in humanity, my trust in law enforcement,
my career potential, my health, my optimism, my enjoyment of
my work—all had been shaken. I couldn't think of anything I'd
gained from the previous fourteen years other than bitterness.
I couldn't even identify or isolate what was the *worst part,* aside
from the obvious loss of so many lives. It wasn't enough to
know there was a lot wrong; identifying *the worst* seemed
important.

Heading into my final two days of the Veterans Transition
Program in July 2013, it hit me like a bolt of lightning as we
were working on defining our goals: *I have lost my life's purpose.*
Not only had I lost it, I wondered if I ever knew what it had
been in the first place. Did I *have* one? "Sobering" didn't begin

to describe this realization. In my VTP and subsequent therapy with Dr. MacKinnon, we did a lot of work on grief, but it wasn't until then that I saw I needed to accept and grieve my loss of purpose. I could no longer pretend my job as a police officer gave me sense of purpose. It used to, early in my career, when I felt that I actually helped people, made a difference in some small way when tough things happened to them. But now I was battered and bone weary from trying to prove I was one of the good ones.

One day in 2013, my partner made an observation that resonated with me.

"You know," she said. "I think if we can encourage the kids to pursue jobs where people are actually happy to see them, they'll be on the right track." Armed with degrees in social work and law and several years of experience working in child protection, she knew as well as I did how it felt to show up on someone's doorstep knowing they hated you, everything you represented, and what you were there to do. When she first said this, I thought, *I don't need for people to like me.* But just as quickly, I thought, *Actually, I really do need to be liked sometimes. Or at least respected for what I try to do.*

Not since I had sold running shoes had I felt that I made a positive difference in someone's day. Not since I had coached high school basketball had I seen the work I did bring about direct improvement in the performance of the people around me, making them better and me better. Not since I'd written a *Calgary Herald* feature piece on suicide prevention had I believed I might save even one life. Right then, I resolved to redefine my life's purpose.

My PTSD treatment continued, and I held onto the goal of returning to the VPD in some capacity, but it felt unattainable because of my panic attacks, angry outbursts, and anxiety. There are many, many police officers out there who do fantastic work in the community and as investigators, but I accept that my time is done and my faith in the criminal justice system too shaken for me to be an active participant. There is some damage that can't be undone. I pass the torch.

When I took my oath with the VPD, I imagined I would work there for thirty years before retiring. Never did I expect to be so deeply affected by my work as an investigator that my career would be cut short.

As I write this, in 2015, in my twenty-fifth year with the VPD, I am on medical leave, hoping to find a way to work in some field outside policing. I hope to be able to one day pursue an advanced degree. I've never wanted to merely coast, pension intact, into my retirement years and do nothing. I hope to find fulfillment by contributing, doing something I love for as long as I love it.

I continue to receive treatment for PTSD from my team, knowing I will have to take extra care of my mental health for the rest of my life. I'm finally at a place where I'm grateful for the things this experience has taught me about myself and about the world. Everything happens for a reason. Still, it's damn hard work.

Resolving to be a more present partner, a more patient parent, a more compassionate friend, and a more aware human being are enough of a life purpose for me right now as I continue to work on healing from this experience. I'm so deeply, deeply sorry the missing and murdered women and their loved ones had to endure this nightmare, but I'm no longer sorry I lived a small part of it with them. I'm glad they had me, as imperfect as I know my contributions have been. I know this will inform everything I do from now on, and I can finally accept that experience as much more than a dark curse.

A Letter to All the Women

• • •

Why?

I look at all of you staring back at me from posters, websites, newscasts and ask myself over and over again.

Why?

I hoped to have answers by now, but all I have are more questions, and I'm learning to accept I will always have more questions than answers. I could ask you what really went on out there and get all the sordid details people seem to have to know, but those things don't interest me. I've seen enough of people like Pickton to form my own picture of what he did to you, and that is more than enough. I'm sure the truth is worse than any of us can imagine, and I don't need that truth to see this as the complete tragedy it is.

If I could talk to you, I'd want to tell you that you didn't die in vain, that through your suffering—before and after you ever went to the damned farm—you raised awareness of what it means to live in poverty and addiction and urban squalor. Maybe I'd be able to tell you things had changed— the way police deal with missing persons, missing sex workers, and drug addicts had changed. I'd like to tell you people finally see you as valid, as people who matter.

If I could talk to you, I'd ask you to sit down with me and tell me what your lives were like—*really* like—and what you would do to help people in the same situations you found yourselves in. Who let you down? In what ways—beyond those that seem obvious to someone like me who has never been assaulted, spat on, never wanted for a meal, a kind word, or a safe place to sleep?

I could fantasize about you telling me not to worry about the risks I didn't take, the times I didn't stand up in a meeting and scream "Bullshit!" when I wanted to so badly. You would tell me I did my best and did all I could considering even you didn't want me to find out about that place, that none of the women wanted to blow the whistle. You would tell me none of you made it very easy. What a fantasy, what a lot to ask of any of you to absolve me, to absolve *us*. I know to you I still represent The Man—the scales of justice, the voice of authority and of the establishment—all the institutions responsible for you meeting the kind of violent, degrading, frightening ends I know you met. Maybe you stare out from those photos and say, "Take your conscience and your left-wing, Monday-morning-quarterback analysis and go to hell." Some of you know me—would you tell the others I was all right? That I wasn't a power-hungry jerk on the street? That I listened, even back then?

Maybe you'd all just say "Fuck you. Fuck you and your after-the-fact apologies and need for absolution." Maybe I would explain to you how it is, that what I need is only for you to know that I thought about things, I asked questions beyond what you had done to get yourselves into a mess like that. I found it very hard to blame you for your situations, but a lot of police officers did just that. I tried and, in their own ways, everyone who worked on the investigation tried to some degree—to do the right thing, to figure out what that was. All I'm questioning is how much trying is enough. You guys tried—to leave the street, to get your shit together— and you know it can be hard. I don't need your blessings, but if we could talk, I would hope we would find some common ground about where the other was coming from.

Maybe I'd just tell each of you about all the people you had in your lives who really loved and cared for you. I don't know if some of you knew that or felt it, especially in your darkest times. People searched for you, advocated for you, loved you. Some did more than others, but all did the best they could. Maybe we'd just talk about that.

Lori

Acknowledgments

* * *

THE PUBLICATION OF a book such as this requires the support and encouragement of many people. I fear that no matter the pains I take, I will almost certainly forget someone who made a big difference to me along this long road. Please accept my apologies.

Deep love and gratitude to Dr. Joanne MacKinnon, Dr. Mike Dadson, Dr. Matt Graham, Barb Macnaughton, Natasha Coulter, Margo Weston, Dr. Art Lopes, and Tanya Chernov, members of what I like to call my "Fixing Broken People Team." You don't all know each other, but together, over time, you all gave me a life back. Thank you to the staff at WorkSafeBC for trying to understand what people with PTSD need.

To all the folks at the Royal Canadian Legion, the Veterans Transition Network and all my Canadian Forces and first responder brothers and sisters who journeyed through the Veterans Transition Program with me: I wish you all continued peace and healing and thank you for sharing your experiences and letting me share mine. I couldn't have written this without you all. To those of you I haven't met who are struggling, please reach out for help. You are worth it.

To my parents, Joseph and Suzanne; my brother, Paul; my sister, Jocelyn; my brother-in-law, Ken; my sister-in-law, Maureen; their families; and the rest of my Alberta crew, thank you all for standing by me. To my late grandfather Terence William Harding Thompson for teaching me to type and to write. To my Vancouver family of Audrey, Charlie, Norma, David, Catherine, Glenda, Doreen, Tim, John, Janet, Doug, Christine, and Tyler, your support, dinners, and acceptance meant the world to my family and me during very hard times. So many of these people heard my story over and over again, because I couldn't stop telling it. For all of your patience, generosity, and grace, thank you.

To my soul brother, Darren Lamb, thanks for putting up with my mania and being there for me all these long years. To my personal training clients from the old 'hood: Jasmine, Lauren, Louise, and Darcy, you guys get me out of bed in the morning, even though you think it's the other way around. Thank you for all your continued hard work and the gift of your enduring friendship. You have helped me redefine my purpose and envision a future for myself.

To Sandra Gagnon, Michele Pineault, and Cameron Ward, who have never let me forget for whom the police work. You each have my enduring respect. To each and every family member and friend of the missing and murdered women, I offer my deepest condolences for your losses and my sincere apologies for my failings.

To everyone on Vancouver's Downtown Eastside who selflessly works with and advocates for our city's less fortunate inhabitants. Many of you have provided them with family and love when they so sorely needed it. You make a difference to many.

To my dear friends and trusted writing pals Denise Kask, Maggie de Vries, and Rachel Rose, who have seen this manuscript through several different drafts. Your skill as writers is only exceeded by your capacity for friendship, and your critical eyes and writers' sensibilities kept me on track through the years of planning, writing, and rewriting. Thank you Jan Derbyshire for your acceptance and encouragement over so many years of friendship.

To Martin, Jill, Paul, Donal, Matt, and Melissa, who were the best sleuths, colleagues, and friends in my professional detective, secret spy world. You guys are true pros and made my last ten years bearable. To Steven Epperson and my many dear friends at the Unitarian Church of Vancouver, thank you for your support, notes, cards, gift baskets, casseroles, hugs, and love before, during, and after my inquiry testimony. You have no idea how much your kindness means to me.

My VPD years post–Project Amelia were very difficult for me, and I was not an easy employee or coworker. Thanks and love to Rennie Hoffman, Rowan Pitt-Payne, Rick Smitas, Malcolm McNeight, Steve Sweeney, Max Chalmers, Rick McKenna, Adua Porteous, Doug LePard, and Mike Purdy for valuing the skills I brought and accepting they came with idiosyncrasies and outbursts sometimes found in PTSD sufferers. You all made my contributions feel considerable, even when I felt the organization had forgotten me. Thank you, Rowan and Jess Ram, for your calls to chat and for staying in touch. Thanks to Mike Porteous for calling me a good cop; it means a lot coming from you.

To Lindsay Kines for your discretion, your friendship, and your standing offer of partnering with me in our two-man private detective agency. I might just be ready.

To Leanne Dospital, Lynn Barr and Catriona Strang for never forgetting. To Tom Stamatakis and Barry Shaw for taking on the fight for my full pension.

To Douglas Gibson, Doug Pepper, Michael Levine, Damon Vignale, Miho Yamamoto, and Chris Haddock for affirming that I did, indeed, have a story to tell. To so many writers over these years for teaching me the art of the memoir and the value in sharing pain. I dove into this genre to learn and surfaced thirsting for more.

Much gratitude to my Greystone publisher, Rob Sanders, and to Colleen MacMillan of Annick Press for your support and kindness through the tough years and for leading me to Greystone. Thanks to everyone on the fantastic Greystone team for your patience and generosity in bringing this book to press and preparing me to face the music.

And finally, to my brilliant editor, Nancy Flight. Your guidance, patience, and kindness have made this process far less painful than I feared. Thank you for your gentle yet persistent nudges toward making this book far better than I might have been content to let it be.

LS